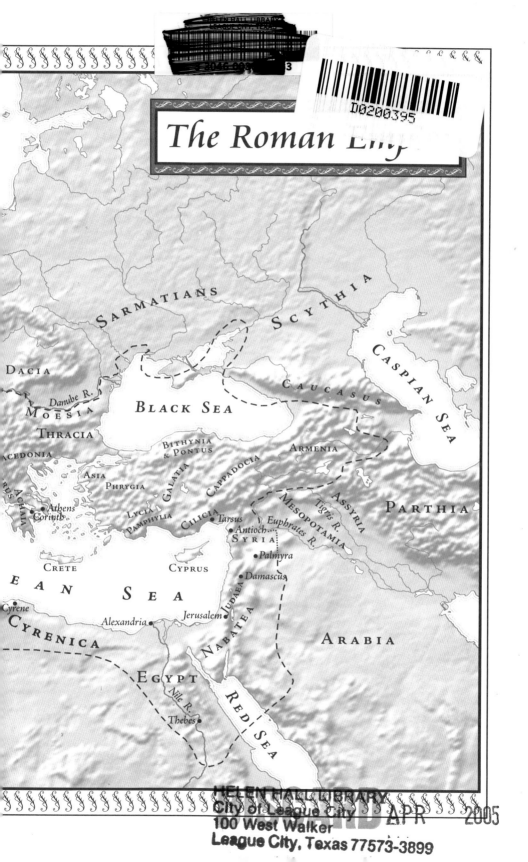

The Roman Emp[ire]

Jesus

Jesus

An Intimate Portrait of the Man, His Land, and His People

LEITH ANDERSON

BETHANYHOUSE
MINNEAPOLIS, MINNESOTA

Consulting Editors:

Dr. William W. Klein
(Ph.D. in New Testament Exegesis from
University of Aberdeen, Scotland)
Denver Seminary
Denver, Colo.

Dr. Scot McKnight
(Ph.D. in Theology from Nottingham
University, Nottingham, England)
North Park University
Chicago, Ill.

Dr. Jeannine Brown
(Ph.D. in New Testament from Luther
Seminary, St. Paul, Minn.)
Bethel Seminary
St. Paul, Minn.

Dr. Gary Meadors
(Th.D. in New Testament from
Grace Theological Seminary,
Winona Lake, Ind.)
Grand Rapids Theological Seminary
Grand Rapids, Mich.

Jesus
Copyright © 2005
Leith Anderson

Cover design by *studiogearbox.com*
Interior design by Sheryl Thornberg

Scripture quotations identified NIV are from the HOLY BIBLE, NEW INTERNATIONAL
VERSION®. Copyright © 1973, 1978, 1984 by International Bible Society. Used by permission of
Zondervan Publishing House. All rights reserved.

Bethany House Publishers is a division of
Baker Publishing Group, Grand Rapids, Michigan.

Printed in the United States of America

Library of Congress Cataloging-in-Publication Data

Anderson, Leith
    Jesus : an intimate portrait of the man, his land, and his people / by Leith Anderson.
      p. cm.
    Summary: "An expanded retelling of the life of Jesus, including all the details from the Gospels
in chronological order, the geopolitical scene, the historical and cultural setting, and the likely emotions and motives of those who interacted with Him. Conversational storytelling style suitable for
a wide range of audiences and ages"—Provided by publisher.
    ISBN 0-7642-2479-4 (alk. paper)
    1. Jesus Christ—Biography. I. Title.

BT301.3.A53   2005
232.9´01—dc22

2004024407

The Life of Jesus

Books by
Leith Anderson

Dying for Change
Jesus
Leadership That Works

A Note to the Reader

What is this book? At its most basic, it is a biography of Jesus, harmonizing and integrating the four Gospels from the Bible in a reasonable chronological order. Beyond that, with contemporary readability it weaves in his story's first-century historical setting, along with the cultural and political perspectives of the time.

The Gospels, the first four books of the Bible's New Testament, were written by four disciples of Jesus: Matthew, Mark, Luke, and John. These original biographers drew from personal experience, eyewitness interviews, and historical resources.

They sometimes arranged their material chronologically and other times topically. When they quoted Jesus, some included more of what he said than others. In this biography, multiple accounts of teaching and miracles are merged into single reports. Quotes are paraphrased and blended, sometimes taking part of a quote from one Gospel account of an event and the rest of the quote from the other places where it is reported.

The intention here is not to replace the original biographers' accounts but to present the story in a fresh, readable and reliable style that is both comprehensive and consistent. The serious student will want to compare to the Bible in order to read complete quotes and reports of the events of Jesus' life in their original wording and context.

Jesus uses a literary device currently popular in the writing of historical biography, adding descriptive language to conversations, emotions, and thought processes to facilitate the telling of the story. While they may not be historically documented, these embellishments are likely, based on historical or archaeological evidence of the times.

If I have done my job well, whether Jesus' story is new to you or very familiar, reading this book will send you to those four original biographers.

Leith Anderson

January 2005

CHAPTER ONE

Circa 6 BC §

§ Calendar calculations based on solar or lunar years (365 days vs. 360 days per year) make some variables on the year of Jesus' birth. The Gregorian calendar of 1582 put that year at AD 1, but since Jesus was born during the reign of King Herod, who died in March or April of 4 BC, his birth was most likely between 6 BC and 4 BC.

There was no good way to hurry the pregnant young bride as she traveled the caravan route from Nazareth to Bethlehem. Her husband, Joseph, may have wanted to encourage her to greater speed, but she already was doing her best.

They needed to make it to Bethlehem before the baby arrived or their tax would increase by fifty percent. The Roman government required all Jewish citizens to register in the town of their family of origin, and Joseph already could ill afford this head tax. It was difficult enough to pay for the two of them, but three would stretch him to the limit. It certainly would help if they could reach the village and register with the Romans before the baby was born. And every day on the road was a day away from his carpenter shop. No work meant no income. If all went well, they could travel to Bethlehem, register with the Romans, and soon return to Nazareth. Maybe the baby would wait until they got home to make an appearance.

Nazareth was not a particularly important place. A frontier town, it was located in northern Palestine and set in a high valley not far from major caravan trade routes. Because the government didn't always have political control over the area, an independence of style of life and perspective marked many of its citizens. The mainstream

of Jewish culture tended to look on those from Nazareth with disrespect and contempt because it was in Galilee and not Judea, but
this probably suited Joseph just fine. It was a good place to live, far
from the larger cities with their inherent problems.

As the couple traveled southward, Mary must have thought about
her cousin Elizabeth. She was married to a priest named Zechariah,
and they were exempt from the travel part of this oppressive census.
The priests' heritage didn't include "ancestral homes" like everyone
else. So Mary was struggling to make this journey, difficult in the best
of times but many times worse at nine months pregnant. She needed
to rest, her feet were swollen, and where could she relieve herself?
All this while Elizabeth was no doubt sitting comfortably at home
nursing her new baby.

But Elizabeth had lived with many years of infertility. There
wasn't a greater burden any woman could bear than never to have
children. Once Elizabeth had passed menopause, she and Zechariah
had given up and accepted their destiny as from God.

Zechariah, a direct descendant from the first high priest of Israel,
Aaron, was part of an honorable but crowded profession. There were
so many priests that they were separated into divisions and assigned
to duty in the Jerusalem temple on a rotating schedule.

The honor of a lifetime came to old Zechariah while his division
was serving at the temple. As part of the liturgy, he was selected for
the sacred assignment of burning incense to God. Filled with awe
and nervous beyond description, Zechariah carefully lit and burned
the incense at the altar while thousands of Jews worshipped in the
outer courts of the temple.

And then, multiplying Zechariah's already heightened anxiety, an
angel appeared at the right of the altar. The angel told him, "Don't
be afraid, Zechariah. God has heard your prayer. Your wife, Elizabeth,
is going to have a son, and you are to name him John. He will be a
joy and delight to you as well as many others. He will be great in
God's opinion. Your son will be filled with the Holy Spirit from the

day he is born. He is never to drink wine or other alcohol. He will restore many of the people of Israel to the Lord their God. Your son will walk before God in the spirit and power of the prophet Elijah, turning the hearts of fathers and children back to each other and leading people who are disobedient back to right living. He will prepare his people for the coming of the Lord."

Genuinely wanting proof of this incredible announcement, Zechariah recovered from his fright enough to ask, "How can I be sure this is really going to happen? I'm an old man, and my wife is past her child-bearing years."

The angel's answer surprised Zechariah again. "I am Gabriel. I am the angel who stands in the presence of God waiting for his instructions. God himself sent me to tell you this good news. Let me give you some proof—you are going to lose your ability to talk so you won't be able to speak until the day John is born. Every silent day you will remember that you didn't believe my words, right up until the day you see them come true." Meanwhile, those thousands of worshippers waiting outside wondered about the priest's delay. When Zechariah came out, he indeed was unable to speak and tried to communicate with a quickly improvised sign language. The audience sensed that something supernatural had happened, but they didn't know they were eyewitnesses to the beginnings of a miracle with implications far beyond a priest who had suddenly become mute.

As for Zechariah, he did his best without speaking during the rest of his priestly tour of duty. When he returned home to the hill country of Judea, sexual intimacy with his wife, Elizabeth, resulted at long last in conception. While the angelic encounter was the significant event for Zechariah, the pregnancy itself was the dream come true for his wife.

Elizabeth didn't leave her house for the first five months of her pregnancy. Expecting a child was difficult to explain at her age, but she was not ungrateful. Her constant thoughts and words were that "the Lord has done a miracle for me. He has blessed me and removed the disgrace of my life that everyone knew about."

What a memorable day it must have been when Mary's family first heard of Elizabeth's pregnancy. We can almost see Mary's smile behind her hand and her mother's reproving look at her. Who could remember anyone that old having a baby?

Elizabeth's extended family eventually learned that this late-in-life pregnancy culminated in the normal birth of a son. The neighbors and relatives shared in the excitement and celebrated the birth with joy while Zechariah celebrated in silence, still unable to speak. When their boy was eight days old, his parents took him to the synagogue for his circumcision and naming in accordance with ancient Jewish traditions.

The custom was to name a son after his father, and the expectation was that he would be named Zechariah. Elizabeth surprised everyone and announced that his name would be John. Objections were voiced because there was no one else by that name in the family, and mothers didn't normally name their sons. Everyone turned to Zechariah to overrule his wife's choice of a name. Zechariah wrote, "His name is John."

Breaking traditions was fodder for gossip in rural villages, and the story of this unorthodox naming spread around the countryside. Not that the people of the hill country were critical. On the contrary, it was the beginning of a growing sense that something unusual was happening and that the baby John was destined for greatness. They of course could not have known the boy would grow to enormous fame and influence that would someday impact their nation and history.

As Mary thought about all that had happened to her cousin, she must have wondered what her own labor and delivery would be like. At least Elizabeth was at home with family and a midwife to help. What was she going to do if her water broke and the baby started to come here during the trip? What could she expect from Joseph? After all, it wasn't his baby.

She thought back to how she had become pregnant thirty-six weeks earlier. It certainly hadn't been something she, who had never been intimate with a man, had anticipated. She had fully intended to come to her wedding night as a virgin—the alternative was unthinkable and the stigma would have been unbearable.

Almost two years earlier, Mary had been engaged to marry Joseph. In their culture it was common for parents to make the arrangements. When the engagement moved toward the formal betrothal, a girl might consider backing out, but that was unlikely because it would bring shame to her family.

If theirs was a typical engagement, Mary may have met Joseph only a few times and never had been alone with him. §

§ There is a tradition saying that Joseph was older than Mary and that he may have lost a first wife through death, though there is no historical evidence for such a theory.

If her parents believed he was the right man for her to marry, it wasn't a young woman's place to ask questions about her future husband's personal history. Truth be told, a girl in Mary's situation may have worried about his sexual experience in contrast to her innocence, but that wasn't the kind of thing she could talk about to anyone else. Mary certainly knew of married couples who loved each other, and that's what every bride wanted and prayed for.

Betrothal was serious—equivalent to marriage without living together. The day they were betrothed, she was referred to as Joseph's wife and he as her husband, and it would take a legal divorce to end their relationship. A year would pass before they would actually marry and she would move in with Joseph and his family. Brides in every century and culture have dreams about their weddings, and Mary would have known what to expect. The wedding, which would include the whole community, would last for a week, and the celebration would be a joyful time of eating and dancing around the "king and queen."

A smile curved Mary's lips as she remembered the wedding, but she quickly sobered as she acknowledged there had been no wedding-night intimacy with Joseph. Her thoughts went back even further to the most defining moment of her young life. As had happened to Zechariah, an angel had appeared to her and identified himself as Gabriel. "Greetings, favored one!" he said. "The Lord is with you."

Gabriel's greeting began in the typical manner, but the rest of his declaration was upsetting and troubling to the teenager. Recognizing her fear, Gabriel added, "Don't be afraid, Mary. God has specially favored you. You're going to become pregnant, give birth to a son, and name him Jesus. He will grow up to be famous and will be called the Son of the Most High. The Lord will give him the throne of his forefather David, and he will reign over the house of Jacob forever. His kingdom will never end." In less than a minute, she was told of an imminent pregnancy that would produce a son of divine origin, and he would have a royal position and power that would last forever.

Mary probably blushed every time she relived the angelic encounter, remembering how she had immediately cut to the most practical part of the prediction. She had asked, "How is this going to happen, since I'm a virgin?" The obvious and expected answer: that she would marry Joseph and immediately become pregnant. But that was not the explanation Gabriel gave. He said, "The Holy Spirit of God is going to make this happen. In the shadows of the supernatural, you will experience the power of the Most High God. You are going to give birth to a holy child who will be called the Son of God. And this isn't all. Your relative Elizabeth, the wife of Zechariah, is six months pregnant even though everyone thought she would never have a baby. You see, nothing is impossible with God."

Mary had been taught from childhood that nothing was impossible with God, but all this went far beyond her understanding. The angel had said that the Holy Spirit was going to do this. But how?

Anticipating Mary's need for some accreditation of this extraordinary prediction, Gabriel had included Elizabeth's miraculous pregnancy in the announcement. Since conception was unlikely for a woman past menopause and impossible for a teenage virgin, if the first proved true then Mary could expect that the second was the "divine impossibility" the angel had revealed to her.

Now walking down the caravan road with the full-term baby inside her, there must have been a thousand questions swirling through her mind. As she struggled to make sense of all that was happening, she held on to the words she had told Gabriel: "I am the Lord's servant. May everything happen to me just as you said."

Many events had occurred during the year since the angelic visitation. She had hastily announced a trip to see Elizabeth, who lived south of Nazareth. Whatever explanation she had given to her parents, they must have accepted it and let her go. Mary wanted to verify the first half of the prediction. If her relative Elizabeth was indeed pregnant, then Mary could know what to expect.

When Mary arrived unannounced at Elizabeth's house and greeted her, Elizabeth had a supernatural experience of her own. She felt her baby suddenly move inside of her and at the same time had a sense that her whole body was filled with the Holy Spirit of God. She was so thrilled that she called to Mary, "Blessed are you among women, and blessed is the child you will bear! But why am I so special, that the mother of my Lord should come to visit me? The moment you said hello, my baby jumped for joy inside of me. God bless you, Mary, for believing that God is going to do what he said!"

Mary responded in poetry, words very much in the style of the Old Testament prophets she heard quoted each Sabbath in the synagogue:

> "My soul glorifies the Lord!
> My spirit rejoices in God my Savior, who has
>   paid attention to the simple life of his
>   servant—me!
> Every generation from now on will know my
>   name and call me blessed, because the
>   Mighty God has done great things in my life.
> Holy is his name!
> God is merciful to every generation of those
>   who fear him.

Look at the miracles he has done.
He has scattered those with
  proud hearts; he has even
  crumbled the thrones of
  monarchs.
At the same time God has
  honored the humble.
He has filled the stomachs of
starving people and sent the rich away
hungry.
God has specially blessed his servant Israel,
  keeping his promises of mercy to Abraham
  and his descendants forever." §

§ Mary's native language was Aramaic. When her poetry was later translated into Latin, this poem was titled "The Magnificat," the Latin word for *glorifies* in the first line.

Certainly this expressed her own heart as she reflected on the greatness of God to her Jewish people and particularly to her. Mary was deeply humbled by the honor of bearing a supernatural child, and her words were reminiscent of the famous Jewish mother Hannah, who rejoiced over the birth of her son Samuel, one of Israel's greatest spiritual and political leaders. But more than Mary's feelings and her familiarity with Hannah's words, God had divinely inspired Mary. Here was far deeper meaning and greater significance than she could have realized at the time.

It was not a brief visit to the home of Elizabeth and Zechariah. Mary stayed there for three months, the remainder of Elizabeth's pregnancy. She may have been there to hold Baby John when he was only a few hours old.

There was no way Mary could have known then that John would turn out to be such an unusual man. He left home at adulthood and lived in the desert, part of his personal journey to especially connect with God and prepare him to become one of Israel's greatest prophets.

As the couple from Nazareth was nearing their destination, Bethlehem, just a few miles south of Jerusalem, Mary had to know that the baby would be born very soon. Calculating from when her periods stopped, Mary would figure it was around the time she returned home from visiting Elizabeth that she became pregnant.

The facts had been clear: she was pregnant and she was still a virgin. Her emotions ranged from awe to embarrassment. How had God done what had never been done before? How did she explain this to her family and friends—and to Joseph? The obvious assumption by everyone would be that she'd been unfaithful to him and had had an affair with some man during her three-month journey to visit Elizabeth. The only explanation she could give was what Gabriel had told her—that the Holy Spirit of God performed some inexplicable miracle inside her uterus, producing an unprecedented and clearly supernatural pregnancy.

Pregnancies are hard to keep secret for very long. When Joseph found out, he faced an agonizing moral choice. That probably was the worst part so far for Mary. She had seen the hurt in his eyes and heard the anger in his voice. He justly had felt betrayed, and she no doubt felt guilty for his anger and sorrow even though she had done nothing wrong.

Under Jewish law he could accuse her of adultery, which was a capital offense, since engaged couples were considered legally married even though they had not yet had their wedding or sexually consummated their relationship. §

But Joseph cared for Mary. He was a good man. He decided that a quiet divorce was best—least humiliating for her and least awkward for everyone.

Mary would never forget the day Joseph changed his mind. In the midst of his agonizing and wrestling with what he should do, he

§ In practice, few if any women were actually stoned to death for sexual immorality. There were too many legal hurdles to overcome, and who would want to kill a pregnant woman anyway? Yet it wouldn't be an easy life for a single mother or for her child. In their male-dominated society, she was disgraced, had few prospects for marriage, and could even be forced into prostitution in order to survive.

had a dream. An angel told him, "Joseph, son of David, don't be afraid to marry Mary. The baby she is carrying was conceived in her by the Holy Spirit. She will give birth to a son and you are to name him. Call him Jesus, because he will save his people from their sins."

Like most of his generation, Joseph believed in dreams and heeded them, since dreams were one of the ways God communicated with humans. Not that it was an easy dream to obey—he was being asked to believe that Mary was still a virgin, that God had initiated the pregnancy, and that her child was to be the savior of Israel. Joseph was told to wed Mary and raise the boy, to be named Jesus, as if he were his own. Only an angel could ask this much of someone.

Since that never-to-be-forgotten night, Joseph may have done some research of his own and learned that his dream was consistent with an old prophecy from Isaiah, who had predicted: "The virgin will be with child and will give birth to a son, and they will call him Immanuel, which means 'God with us.' " However, it's one thing to hear ancient words read from a scroll in the synagogue and quite another to discover that these words from God apply specifically to you and to your family.

§ Officially, the order came from Caesar Augustus in Rome. Locally it was under the authority of Quirinius, the Roman consul since 12 BC (he later became governor of Syria in AD 6). Lacking other historical references to this particular census, it may be that it was actually conducted by King Herod with Roman approval. Such a census was not unusual in the Roman Empire, for purposes of taxation, military recruitment, or political districting. The Romans used census and taxes as tools for controlling conquered nations.

When he awakened the next morning, Joseph made a life-changing decision to obey the dream. Soon after this he moved the wedding date forward and married Mary in accordance with the angel's instructions. The pregnant young girl he married remained a virgin throughout her nine months of pregnancy. How unusual was that? Married for almost nine months without consummating their marriage?

Then late in Mary's pregnancy, it turned out that the Roman government ordered a census of the area that included Nazareth. §

This particular census required that people return to their communities of family origin. Because Joseph was a descendant of the famous king David, he and his immediate family were required to register for the census in David's hometown of Bethlehem. There were no hardship exemptions for pregnancy. Joseph had no choice but to transport his nine-months-pregnant wife more than sixty miles from the lowlands of Nazareth in the north to the higher elevation of Bethlehem in the Judean hills to the south. Inns were few and crowded, although they couldn't have afforded to stay in one even if rooms had been available. Roads always had bandits. Bethlehem was an out-of-the-way obscure village. §

§ Its claim to fame was that King David was born and raised near Bethlehem. He left as an adult and eventually established the capital in the nearby city of Jerusalem.

So why Bethlehem?

§ "Ephrathah" was an additional point of reference because this was not the only Bethlehem (which means "House of Bread" in Hebrew); it had always been and still was "small among the clans of Judah," the tribal district in which both Jerusalem and Bethlehem were located.

Centuries earlier the prophet Micah had predicted that Bethlehem would be the birthplace of the Messiah. "But you, Bethlehem Ephrathah,§ though you are small among the clans of Judah, out of you will come for me one who will be ruler over Israel, whose origins are from of old, from ancient times."

Since he was a distant descendant of David and technically had royal blood, Joseph and his family must have often talked about their ancestral hometown. Travel to Bethlehem normally would have been too far and too expensive, but now they had to go under orders from their Roman masters. As they neared the village, they would have known there were many other pilgrims coming for the same reason and housing would be a problem. They found temporary lodging in the animal quarters of one of the Bethlehem homes. Not long after their arrival, Mary went into labor and soon delivered a baby boy, whom they immediately named Jesus. For a typical delivery of the times, only women were present. Far from her Nazareth home, Mary did not have the support and presence of her mother and other familiar women kinfolk, and maybe the woman of the house delivered the baby. The infant was wrapped in long strips of cloth resembling the Egyptian mummies of that neighbor nation. One of the animal feeding troughs, a manger, was used as a makeshift crib for the bundled newborn baby.

Bethlehem was sheep country. The hills served as pastureland where sheep were raised for wool, for food, and for sacrifice at the not-too-distant Jerusalem temple. Shepherds tended community flocks. In the social order of the culture, they held a low status. §

§ So many shepherds were considered untrustworthy that many courts would not permit their testimony in civil or criminal cases.

So it was a huge surprise when an angel appeared to a group of shepherds in the hills outside of Bethlehem. A brilliant heavenly light illumined him while he told the terrified shepherds, "Don't be afraid. I have great, joyful good news for everyone. Today in the town of David a Savior has been born to you; he is Christ the Lord. This will be the sign for you: you will find this baby wrapped in cloths and lying down in a manger." Then a large number of angels joined the first angel and spoke to the shepherds in unison: "Glory to God in the highest heaven. Peace to everyone on earth who pleases him."

It would have been the angels' appearance out of nowhere more than the instructions they gave that most stunned the shepherds. After all, even though it was somewhat unusual that a baby would be cradled in a manger, it was common for a baby to be wrapped in cloths.

Recognizing they were in the middle of a supernatural event, they consulted with each other in great excitement and agreed, "Let's go into Bethlehem and see what the Lord has told us about." In town they found Mary, Joseph, and the baby exactly as had been described to them. When they left the manger, they told of their experience throughout the village, though many found shepherd stories far-fetched. But the shepherds knew what they had witnessed and accepted it as being from God. They worshipped and praised him for including them in the events surrounding the birth of Jesus.

———— ❉ ————

Mary and Joseph without doubt were trying to understand it all. It would be years before they began to truly grasp the implications and meaning of the extraordinary events surrounding the birth of Jesus.

A baby born to a virgin is truly an amazing occurrence, but there was even more going on behind the story in Bethlehem. Though Jesus was not biologically related to Joseph, he was Joseph's legal son through adoption. Because Joseph was a descendant of King David, Jesus was lawfully in the line of royal succession. Although he had a supernatural birth, his family tree documents the humanity of Jesus. §

§ Two different family trees are given by Matthew and Luke in the New Testament. Scholars have long debated the significant differences. Some think that Matthew traces Joseph's lineage and Luke traces Mary's lineage. Others say that Matthew gives Jesus' legal line of descent from King David while Luke gives Jesus' physical line of descent from Adam. (The two genealogies of Jesus are found in Matthew chapter 1 and Luke chapter 3.)

Jesus was born into a community with important religious and cultural traditions. As had happened to his relative John, the first significant ceremony after Jesus' birth was his circumcision when eight days old. This marked him as a Jew in the tradition of Abraham. §

§ Circumcision literally cut to the essence of life and reproduction but also was the physical symbol of God's covenant with Israel as his specially chosen people.

It was at the circumcision ceremony that he was formally given the name assigned by the angel before he was conceived—*Jesus.*

The next milestone required a journey to the temple in Jerusalem for a ceremony where the firstborn male of every family was consecrated to God. Jewish law required the presentation of a sacrificial lamb as part of the ceremony, although the poorest families were allowed to substitute two young pigeons. Away from home and probably low on money, Joseph and Mary presented pigeons for sacrifice when Jesus was consecrated. God had supernaturally and dramatically intervened in their lives. They held a baby they loved with the same passion as parents all through history. For them, one of the highlights of their lives was their baby's dedication at the temple, but they couldn't afford the normal sacrifice. While others brought expensive lambs, they held a pair of pigeons. It was at least humbling—possibly embarrassing.

Such consecrations were everyday occurrences at the temple. There were many parents and babies, and the liturgy was predictable and routine. Joseph and Mary would have been simply part of the crowd. But they were surprised by the words and actions of two elderly people who spent every day at the temple. The first was Simeon, a devout and righteous man whose life focused on expectation of the Messiah. §

§ Messiah is the term used to identify the person Jews have looked for to free their land from bondage and lead them to political power.

Few parents welcome the touch of a complete stranger on their baby, but Simeon took Jesus in his arms and spoke a prayer of gratitude: "Great God, you have fulfilled your promise to me, your servant. Now you can let me depart in peace because I've seen your gift of salvation with my own eyes. I've seen the Savior for all people, both Gentiles and Jews."

Simeon's lifetime dream was now fulfilled. He looked at Mary and spoke a prophecy that was at the same time wonderful and troubling: "This child's destiny is to bring failure and success to many people in Israel. Many will criticize him, and the inner thoughts of many people will be revealed by him. And—" Simeon paused to search Mary's eyes—"someday he will pierce your own soul too." §

§ Sons can indeed bring pain to their mothers' hearts, but none quite like the pain that would pierce Mary's heart when Jesus died.

Then came an eighty-four-year-old named Anna. She was an acknowledged prophetess who virtually lived at the temple. When she approached Jesus and his parents, she publicly declared that Jesus was the one whom everybody was expecting to bring redemption to Jerusalem.

All of this was strange and unfamiliar to two rural visitors from Nazareth. They were seeing further confirmation from a wide assortment of people and circumstances—confirmation that this was no ordinary child; confirmation that he was the long-predicted and expected Messiah.

The trip to Bethlehem and Jerusalem was supposed to be brief—just long enough to register, pay the tax, and return to Nazareth. But Joseph and Mary decided to make their home in Bethlehem, possibly because of the ancient prophecy from Micah. Before settling in, they returned to Nazareth to show off their new baby to family and friends and to pack up their belongings.

So Bethlehem became their new home. Joseph was a carpenter. Mary nursed and raised her son. New friends surrounded them. But just when those first years seemed as if they would become the peaceful norm, another unexpected encounter forced them to flee the country as refugees.

Around the time of Jesus' birth, there were Magi a thousand miles east in the land of Persia (modern Iran) who diligently studied the stars. They belonged to a caste of priests who specialized in interpreting life and predicting the future through astrology. While modern scientists would classify them as superstitious, those same scientists would have to acknowledge that the ancient celestial studies and records of these men were disciplined and detailed.

The Magi were drawn to a star in the western sky that beckoned them toward Jerusalem. Combining the star with the cultural expectation of a coming king of the Jews, they decided to form a caravan and make the long journey to see for themselves. Upon arrival in Jerusalem, they explained to all who would listen that they were seeking the king of the Jews in order to worship him. Word of the search of the Magi soon reached King Herod at his family palace just inside the western wall of the city. Herod was threatened by any hint of competition for his throne and its power, and when Herod was upset, everyone was upset. §

§ Herod was part Jew and part Idumean—which was a source of consternation to Jews, who wanted a fully Jewish king. Further, Herod was really a vassal king of the Romans and therefore an agent of Roman authority among a people who yearned to be independent.

Herod ordered a gathering of religious scholars and asked them where the Messiah was to be born. They quoted the prophet Micah and pointed the way to Bethlehem. In his paranoia, Herod secretly met with the Magi in order to manipulate them into helping him find the baby who was prophesied to be king. He asked when they first saw the star, calculating the baby's age at two years or less. Then he asked the Magi to report back to him when they found the child so he "could join them in worship," he told them.

With the beckoning of the star and the directions given by Herod and his scholars, they headed out and found the house of Joseph, Mary, and Jesus. Delighted to reach their goal, they worshipped Jesus, presenting him with expensive gifts of gold, incense, and myrrh. Joseph and Mary were encountering new wonders: visitors from a distant empire and gifts worth a small fortune for their family. What they didn't realize then was that they and their son were in mortal danger from their own king.

The Magi often dreamed and interpreted the dreams of others, a standard medium for hearing from their gods. So they weren't surprised by the dream that followed their encounter with Jesus. It instructed them not to report back to Herod and to find a different route back to Persia instead of returning through Jerusalem.

An angel again visited Joseph. The angel warned him to "get up, take the child and his mother, and escape to Egypt. Stay there until you hear from me, because Herod is going to search for the child to kill him." The threat was imminent and they responded immediately. The small family made the very long trip to northeast Africa, where they remained as foreigners until King Herod died. Such an expensive journey would not have been possible without the resources from the Magi's gifts.

As soon as Herod realized that the Magi had deceived him, he ordered a massacre of all baby boys aged two and younger in the town of Bethlehem, his way of making sure he killed any boy who might someday seek his throne. What he did was an atrocity that took innocent lives, bereaved loving parents, and impacted Bethlehem for an entire generation.

Herod died in 4 BC. Since his death wouldn't have been common news in distant Egypt, an angel informed Joseph in another dream, "It's time for you to take Mary and Jesus back to Israel, because those who were trying to kill him are dead." Joseph planned to return to Bethlehem but then evaluated the possible locations for residence upon return and decided that their old hometown of Nazareth in the Galilee area was safest. Thus Nazareth became their long-term home, where Jesus grew up and where Joseph made his living in carpentry until his death.

Little is known about the rest of Jesus' early childhood. Unconfirmed legends report childhood miracles and supernatural powers, but these stories appeared long after Jesus' death and are historically unsubstantiated. What we do know is that his childhood was positive: he grew strong, became wise, and evidenced the grace of God on his life.

The Feast of the Passover that commemorated the escape of the Hebrew people from Egyptian slavery nearly fifteen hundred years earlier was an annual event. Jews gathered in Jerusalem for the Passover from around the Mediterranean world, and the city's population swelled by hundreds of thousands. It was the dream of every Jew to go to Jerusalem for Passover at least once in a lifetime. Although the distance from Nazareth was a not-so-easy sixty miles, Mary and Joseph made the annual pilgrimage with Jesus. The year when Jesus was twelve, they made the journey as they had in previous years. Because of bandits and other dangers, it was normal for them to travel in a caravan for protection. When they began their trip to return home, they didn't know they had left Jesus behind in Jerusalem. Assuming him to be with other traveling families and friends, they didn't realize he was missing until they had traveled a day's journey toward home. They faced the same worries and panic shared by all parents of missing children. Perhaps their fear was greater because they understood he was a special child who had been entrusted by God to their care.

It took them three days after returning and searching the streets of Jerusalem before they finally found him. Jesus was sitting in the temple courts asking questions and listening to the answers of the religious leaders and teachers of Judaism.

It takes great knowledge, experience, and wisdom to ask a profound question. Besides that, the young Jesus was giving answers to his own questions, often providing insights that were beyond the ability of the professional scholars. A crowd gathered. Everyone was amazed at his level of understanding, his questions and his answers.

When his parents finally found him and saw what he was doing, they were astonished. They lived with him every day but did not realize he was capable of such interaction and dialogue with the spiritual leaders of the country.

But in typical parental reproach, Mary recovered from her amazement and said, "Son, why have you treated us this way? Your father and I have been worried sick looking for you." But this wasn't about them. This whole episode was another step toward Jesus' destiny and another step away from being an ordinary young man growing up in Nazareth.

Jesus answered his mother, "Why were you looking for me? Didn't you know I would be in my Father's house?" Jesus was saying to his adoptive father that his true father was God and that the temple in Jerusalem was God's house and therefore a very natural place for Jesus to be. This idea went right over the heads of Mary and Joseph. They didn't understand what he was talking about. They just wanted to get him back home to Nazareth.

Jesus did return home with them. It wasn't time yet for him to go public. Eighteen more years of ordinary human life in the obscurity of the province of Galilee lay before him. At home, Jesus filled the role of an obedient son, working with his carpenter father, while Mary kept pondering all these things in her heart.

CHAPTER TWO

Though popular, John was a scary-looking fellow. But some of his fans thought he was the Messiah. §

Compared to rich and powerful people like Tiberius Caesar in Rome or Herod Antipas in Galilee, John wasn't famous—yet. He lived in the Judean desert, wore rough camel's hair clothes with a leather belt around his waist, and survived on a diet of locusts and wild honey—

§ This was not unusual, however. There was always some self-appointed prophet with at least a few followers who thought their man was the promised Messiah. None of them lasted long or amounted to much. Over the years, Messianic figures quickly came and went.

a lot like the ninth-century BC prophet Elijah. Though not compelling in terms of appearance or political office, John had the power of God and was a popular preacher. Even though his message called people sinners, named their specific sins, and told them to repent, thousands flocked to hear him out in the desert. He offered them public baptism in the Jordan River as an evidence of their sorrow for sin and a new life of obedience to God.

Because so many people came to hear him teach and to be baptized, he was nicknamed John the Baptizer. §

§ Also called John the Baptist, his title had nothing to do with any later Christian denomination. John was not a Christian in the modern sense of the religion.

John was a Jew, very much in the tradition of the fiery prophets of previous generations, shouting warnings about the judgment of God and the urgent need to forsake sin and do what God says. But he was more than the prophets of the past. John was a bridge to the future. His call from God was to connect yesterday with tomorrow, the old with the new, and to prepare the way for Jesus. His loyal followers saw him as a fulfillment of a prediction from the prophet Isaiah in the eighth century BC:

> A voice will shout in the desert,
> "Prepare the road for the Lord,
> straighten things out for him.
> Fill in the low valleys,
> lower the mountains and hills.
> The winding roads will be straightened out,
> the rough roads will be smooth.
> The entire human race will see God's
> salvation."

John was a populist, and crowds gathered around him out of spiritual need, fascination, and curiosity. He had no official credentials. Unlike his father, he was not part of the religious establishment as a practicing priest. He was one of those unusual personalities accredited and acclaimed because of his persona and message.

The man had many distinctive characteristics. Unlike leaders who win favor with pleasing words, continuous compliments, and optimistic promises, John was critical, condemning, and often caustic in what he had to say. Yet people loved him and gravitated to him. His personality, his own integrity of godliness and lifestyle, and the truth of what he said underscored the obvious power of God in John's life. Additionally, he attracted people who would normally avoid one another.

Observing the crowd that followed John, one could identify people from just about every group of Jewish society. Having both Pharisees and Sadducees coming to see and hear John was unusual, but there were also Roman soldiers in the crowds to whom he preached. § And almost everyone had a different opinion of who John was and what he was doing.

§ Most Romans were pagans—they didn't believe in the God of the Jews but adhered to the Greek and Roman pantheon of gods like Zeus, Jupiter, Venus, Mars, and others. Many looked down on the Jews and in a sense considered their religion inferior, even atheistic, because there were no images or idols to worship.

PHARISEES & SADDUCEES

Two primary religious groups of first-century Judaism were the Pharisees and the Sadducees.

The Pharisees were a devout religious party committed to keeping every detail of the Old Testament Law of Moses as they interpreted it. The word *Pharisee* means "separated one," although others claim it means "careful interpretation." Both are descriptive of many Pharisees. Four hundred years earlier religious Jews had returned to Palestine from humiliating captivity by the eastern empires. They acknowledged that the glory days of the nation were past and concluded that God was punishing Israel for disobedience. Their response was admirable: they focused on protecting and keeping God's laws.

Pharisees heartily believed in the supernatural—God, angels, demons, resurrection from the dead, and future rewards and punishments. Although some may consider them religiously conservative, their goal was relevance. They sought to apply the Old Testament laws to changing situations with practical applications.

It's certainly not fair to classify all Pharisees with one label. Many were devout, pious, and God-fearing. Others became legalistic, and in their zeal to please God they developed hundreds of regulations. For example, going beyond the principles of the Ten Commandments, they wanted to know exactly what they could and couldn't do on the Sabbath day of rest. So they established how much you could pick up on a Saturday without breaking the law of God, including how much food you could lift up to your mouth without calling it work.

Because they had such a clear vision of the right way for everyone to live, they were evangelistic in recruiting others to their sect and became a popular and powerful political presence in Israel. Their beliefs, practices, and politics turned the Romans into natural and immediate enemies. Their political activities alienated them from King Herod to the point that he had many Pharisees killed. The Jewish historian Josephus reported six thousand Pharisees in Israel during the first century. Their influence far exceeded their comparatively small number.

The Sadducees were even fewer in number and less popular among the Jews. They insisted that the only binding religious laws were those written by Moses and that all other additions, interpretations, and regulations were unnecessary. Because the historian Josephus contrasted them with the Pharisees, we tend to know more about what they denied than what they affirmed. Sadducees didn't believe in life after death, heaven and hell, angels, or divine predestination. They strongly believed in human freedom of choice. While fewer in number, the Sadducees had political power because their ranks were filled with priests and the members of the wealthy upper class. The Sadducees shared a more friendly relationship with the Romans and were therefore considered to be collaborators by the anti-Roman Pharisees. In everyday life, the Sadducees often had to accommodate the Pharisees just because they were more numerous.

If John was asked what he was trying to accomplish, he answered, "Think of me as the advance man setting up for the Messiah." He saw himself in the tradition of messengers sent to announce the arrival of Oriental kings. Preparations for a royal visit usually included cleaning up the city, whitewashing buildings, rounding up beggars, guaranteeing security, rehearsing musicians, preparing food, and recruiting a crowd. But John had a very different agenda than those other advance men. He called his audiences back to God and the Old Covenant faithfulness so many had abandoned. He wanted to clean up the moral lives of the people in preparation for the Messiah. His method was preaching and baptism. His message was educational, inspirational, and confrontational, expecting that the listeners would acknowledge their sins, confess their wrong, and determine to live righteous lives.

Ordinary folk liked what he had to say. His message was simple and practical. The citizens of Israel knew there was no realistic way for them to ever measure up to the rules of the Pharisees. But when they were baptized in the Jordan River, it was a specific act at a specific point in time. Also, John's message gave hope for the future because it anticipated the arrival of the Messiah, the promised leader from God.

One day word spread through nearby towns that John was preaching out in the desert. Crowds of working-class people left their jobs and fields to come out to see and hear him. John was again preaching against sin and calling for repentance and baptism. His booming voice bounced between the rocks as the people listened intently to every word.

Then the elite Pharisees and Sadducees showed up on the periphery of the crowd. John stopped his sermon and spoke directly to the new arrivals: "Hey, you! Yes, I'm talking to you religious leaders. You know what you are? You're a pack of poisonous snakes and vipers! You should feel right at home with the rest of the snakes out here under the rocks! Who warned you to get out of town and run away from the coming judgment of God?"

Nobody—absolutely nobody—ever spoke to these Pharisees and Sadducees like this. "You snakes need to start producing some signs of repentance for your sins," John reiterated. When their mouths started to open in self-defense, John anticipated what they were going to say and answered, "Don't tell yourselves, 'We have Abraham as our father.' That's not the big deal you think it is. Let me tell you, if God wanted to, he could take these desert stones here and use them to give birth to children for Abraham. He doesn't need you! So don't count on your family tree to save you." Then he threw in a common expression about useless trees: "The ax is already at the root of the trees, and every tree that doesn't produce good fruit is going to be cut down and burned in the fire."

John was telling the truth about the sins of the religious establishment. But others in the crowd were not satisfied with John's confrontation of the Sadducees and Pharisees. They went on to ask, "What should *we* do then?"

John was very specific: "If you have two coats, give one of them to someone who doesn't have any coat. If you have food, share it with someone who is starving."

The crowd stirred and looked around at the momentum that was growing. Next on the docket were the tax collectors, often an extremely unpopular group. Some of them made a lucrative living collecting taxes on behalf of the Roman government to underwrite the Roman occupation of Israel, making their profit by overcollecting and keeping the difference. When some brave souls among this group asked what repentance meant for them, John said, "Don't collect any more than the legal amount."

Even more resented were the Roman soldiers who had come to the desert to see what was going on. When they asked what God expected of them, John replied, "Don't threaten false charges against people so that you can extort money out of them. Be content with your regular soldier's pay."

These weren't easy instructions to hear, but they hit the mark. There were religious leaders, tax collectors, and soldiers who became rich by oppressing the poor. John made it clear that God is on the side of the poor and these injustices must stop. People lined up to be baptized by John. §

§ Baptism by placing the entire body under water was familiar to the Jews in the crowd because their religion required it for certain purification rituals. However, it was most humbling for someone born and raised a Jew to be baptized as if he were an outsider seeking admission to the people of God.

The excitement was high, and a rumor rolled through the crowd that John was actually the Messiah himself. Why not? He looked and sounded and acted the part. When John heard what was being said, he called the crowd to silence and made clear his role: "I'm definitely not the Messiah, so you can stop saying that I am. You haven't seen anything yet! This is nothing compared to what you will see and experience when the Messiah comes. He will immerse you in the Holy Spirit of God. He will sort out the good guys from the bad guys. You think I'm great? Well, I'm not even worthy to untie his shoes for him."

This raised the excitement of the crowd to greater heights. Their hope soared as they tried to imagine someone immeasurably better than John the Baptizer.

Then came Jesus into the desert crowd. Unknown and unrecognized, he was merely another face in a long line of those waiting to be baptized.

It had been a long day, and the strain was enough to make even the energetic John weary. Preaching, confronting, and baptizing were what he was called to do, but intense focus no doubt made the faces merge into one as the hours passed. Then John, standing in the Jordan River near where it empties into the Dead Sea, lifted his head to see who was next to be baptized. It was Jesus.

The prophet suddenly was subdued, and the fire in his voice quickly cooled. He had no idea what to do. He was reluctant to baptize Jesus. "I'm the one who needs to be baptized by you in this river! Are you seriously asking me to baptize you?" John asked.

Jesus responded, "Exactly! I want you to baptize me right now. It's the right thing to do!"

John was the authoritative preacher taking on religious leaders with a boldness that bordered on brashness. Now it was Jesus talking, and John had trouble figuring out what he meant and why he wanted to be baptized. After all, Jesus wasn't among those who needed to repent. He hadn't been greedy with his clothing, embezzled tax money, extorted from the poor, or complained about low wages. Why on earth would Jesus want to be baptized?

Jesus was a master of symbolism. By their baptisms, the masses were demonstrating their moral preparation for the coming of the Messiah. When Jesus was baptized it wasn't to repent or to prepare. It was to identify with the people. His baptism was a symbol of solidarity with all of them.

While the two men stood side-by-side in the river, Jesus prayed. Already a memorable scene, both of them sensed the historic significance. But the mingling crowd didn't recognize that anything unusual was going on. It was one more baptism in a day that had grown tired with so many in and out of the water.

Bright light suddenly poured out of the sky. The Holy Spirit of God came out of the light in a form that looked like a dove fluttering down on Jesus. A voice spoke through the bright light and announced, "I love you, my son, and I am totally pleased with you and all you are doing!" Those words launched Jesus onto the center stage of fame and recognition. John had prepared the way. Now it was Jesus' turn. John would soon be gone and all the attention of the crowds would focus on the carpenter's son from Nazareth.

Much of the rest of Jesus' life bordered the Jordan, making this a fitting place for him to launch his public career as a teacher, prophet, and miracle worker.

JORDAN RIVER

The Jordan River valley is the deepest depression on earth. The river begins at Mount Hermon and meanders south 223 miles to the Dead Sea. The headwaters start at 230 feet above sea level, and the river descends down through Galilee Lake, is joined by various tributaries, and ends at the Dead Sea, 1,312 feet below sea level. Sometimes nicknamed "the muddy Jordan," the water often appears brown and dense. Although it waters much of the region, it is not an appealing river for swimming, bathing, or baptizing.

§ The Judean desert is one of the bleakest places on earth. An area of 425 square miles between the city of Jerusalem and the Dead Sea, it was and still is largely uninhabited. There are large hills, deep ravines, dry crusty soil, minimal vegetation, and dangers galore.

The emotional and supernatural high of Jesus' baptism in the river was immediately followed by forty of the most difficult days in his life. The same Spirit who celebrated and affirmed him in the Jordan now led him further into the desert. §

Everything we know about what happened during the next forty days is from Jesus himself because there were no other human witnesses. He told his friends and they passed the story along.

From the start of his six-week ordeal, the purpose was clear—Jesus would be tested by the devil. The meaning of the desert tests would have been obvious to the broader Jewish community if someone had pointed out the parallels: the devil had confronted Adam and Eve at the beginning of history, and they failed their test; the nation of Israel had spent forty years wandering around the desert after escaping Egyptian slavery, and they behaved badly and suffered the consequences; Jesus was going to face similar tests. If he passed these tests, he would be eligible and prepared for the coming three years of rigorous supernatural encounters. If he failed, he would be disqualified to be the Messiah.

First was the fast. Not that there was food available out there anyway, but Jesus intentionally abstained from eating for forty days. § Since the area was arid, add dehydration to his food deprivation. Jesus was starving.

§ In modern western industrialized countries, an active healthy thirty-year-old male burns up to 4,000 calories per day. Even burning just 2,500 calories per day, 40 days of fasting reduces body weight by 40 pounds.

Discipline and deprivation of his body were preparation for his soul. The focus was on the spiritual rather than the physical, and his dependence was on the supernatural, not the natural. As wonderful and idealistic as this may sound, Jesus was weak, hungry, and thirsty. His physical condition left him emotionally, psychologically, and spiritually vulnerable.

§ His name comes from the Hebrew word for adversary because he is the adversary of God and good. There are many other names by which he is called, including *the devil*, which means "slanderer." As a supernatural creature, he is able to appear in various animal and human forms—whatever works best to accomplish his purpose.

Then came Satan, § the evil archrival of God. Satan's first effort to defeat Jesus was with a simple suggestion for a very practical miracle. "So, Jesus, you're supposed to be the Son of God, right?" Satan mocked. Pointing to some of the limestone rocks, he said, "Okay, then order some of these stones to become loaves of bread." The underlying assumption, even by his enemy Satan, was that Jesus had the supernatural power to perform a miracle.

Jesus refused. "The Scriptures say that people don't live just by eating bread but by all the words that come from the mouth of God." He quoted from the Old Testament Law of Moses. What would be wrong with Jesus making some bread? Wouldn't it be a good thing to do, demonstrating his supernatural power? But there was more behind the test than first appears. Satan was seeking to control Jesus' behavior and exercise of his powers by causing him to place his physical needs above spiritual needs. It didn't work.

Satan's next test took Jesus from the desert to Jerusalem, where the two of them stood at the highest point in the city. Satan said, "If you're really the Son of God, jump off. After all, the Scriptures say that God will command his angels to take care of you, and they will come and hold you up so you have a soft landing—not so much as a stubbed toe when you land." This was a brilliant temptation, going right to the heart of many human instincts: a deep desire to be acknowledged and accepted by others. Popularity is a powerful temptation for all of us, and it would have been for Jesus as well.

Jesus and Satan were standing on the portico of the temple that extended about 450 feet above the Kidron Valley. The idea was for Jesus to stand on the edge until a crowd gathered to see what was going to happen. At just the right moment Jesus could jump from the portico and free fall forty-five stories toward the crowd below. As the people gasped with expectation of his crushing death, angels would come and catch him at the last second. Then Jesus would stand on his feet for everyone to see, and the crowd would be mesmerized by this spectacular display of supernatural power.

Jesus would have been tempted by this invitation. Satan had provided Jesus' first conversation since those long, lonely weeks in the desert. Popularity would feel very good, and it would give an immediate platform for what he had come to accomplish. The offer incorporated promises from God out of a Hebrew song that devout Jews sang in the synagogue. It seemed that saying yes would actually make God look good.

Jesus was tempted, but he said no. Quoting again from the Old Testament book of Deuteronomy, Jesus answered, "It says: 'Don't put the Lord your God to the test.' " The usual reason for a test is doubt. Apparently Jesus here refused to put God to the test to determine if he was capable of saving him or if he would save him when he jumped.

Jesus refused to set up God.

For the third and final test, Satan took Jesus to a high mountain and showed him the kingdoms of the world. "Jesus, here is a deal you won't want to refuse. All the kingdoms of the world are under my authority, but I'm ready to transfer command to you! All you need to do is worship me, and then they will be yours." This offer was by far the most tempting. It was an opportunity to answer the greatest human criticism of God: "If there really is a good God, why is there so much evil and suffering in this world?"

The usual answer is that sin and Satan have brought untold evil and pain to our earth, but this response is often not very satisfying for those who are in misery. Here was Jesus' grand opportunity to make a difference for good. Satan offered Jesus rule over everything. He could shortcut an otherwise long and painful process and go directly to the throne of the world. He could immediately stop all injustice, eliminate all poverty, and outlaw all sin, pain, and suffering. It would be a wonderful and unselfish thing to do. However, such great good came with a very high price. In order to become king of the world, Jesus was first required to worship Satan. In other words, if Jesus acknowledged the absolute superiority of Satan, he could accomplish the greatest good in history—a classic example of the end justifying the means.

"No!" Jesus fired back. "The Scriptures say to worship the Lord your God and serve only him." Jesus insisted that there is only one God, that "God is God. Right is right. We must never compromise with evil. To give worship and allegiance to Satan is a guaranteed path to disaster."

Jesus passed all three tests. Though left exhausted in every way, Jesus had survived a battle of supernatural proportions. Another supernatural intervention came when angels arrived to attend to Jesus as he recovered from his ordeal.

During the six weeks Jesus was in the desert, John continued to ride his wave of popularity. Like many populists, he started to draw attention from powerful establishment leaders. Because there were rumors that he was the Messiah, a delegation of priests and other religious leaders was sent from Jerusalem, east across the Jordan River, to Bethany, where John was currently preaching. They were direct and to the point, asking him if he was the Messiah. With characteristic forthrightness, he told them, "I am not the Messiah." This was a disappointment to those in his crowds who had pinned their future hopes on John; it was a relief to the leaders who feared John's popular following.

As long as they had John's attention and he was answering their questions, the delegation then rolled out every possible explanation of greatness based on expectations and prophecies from their religious writings and beliefs. They asked, "Then who are you? Are you Elijah? Are you some kind of a prophet? Give us an answer to take back to our bosses in Jerusalem. Tell us about yourself." John was simple and humble in his response, saying that he wasn't any of these great men. He said that he was just "the voice of one shouting in the desert, 'Straighten everything out for the Lord.' " §

§ That was actually a quotation from the eighth-century-BC Jewish prophet Isaiah. His answer was that "I'm really nobody— just an announcer telling who is coming next."

The delegation may have been relieved that John didn't claim special prophetic credentials, but if he was indeed a "nobody," who gave him the right to baptize? They asked, "Why are you baptizing all these people if you are not the Messiah, nor Elijah, nor some great prophet?"

His answer, not very satisfying to his interrogators, went right back to his main message. "You're right that I have been baptizing a lot of people, but I have a surprise for you. There is someone you don't yet know who is coming next, and I'm not good enough to untie his sandals."

The next day Jesus showed up at one of John's large public gatherings. John seized the opportunity. He called, "Look, everybody! Over there is the Lamb of God, who takes away the sin of the world! He's the one I was talking about when I told you that someone is coming next who is far better than I am and was already around before I got started."

They looked around to figure out whom he was talking about. While they were searching, John added an explanation most of them didn't understand: "At first I didn't know him myself, but my whole purpose in baptizing everyone is to introduce him to Israel.

"Let me tell you what happened," John went on. "This is total truth. I personally saw the Spirit of God as a dove come down from heaven and settle on him. The same God who sent me out to baptize everyone told me in advance this was going to happen so that I would know exactly who the Son of God is. God told me that he will baptize with the Holy Spirit."

John's announcement triggered different responses. Some were disappointed because they were loyal to John and didn't want him replaced by another leader no matter how great that leader was going to become. Others were stunned that someone as credible as John would identify anyone else as the Son of God, a clearly messianic description. Most didn't get it. A lot more information would be needed to understand how Jesus could be "the Lamb of God" and "baptize with the Holy Spirit." The introduction of Jesus was powerful but not completely clear. Jesus would grow into his description.

STARTING SMALL

As Jesus moved on toward greater public visibility, he revealed his strategy for the concentric circles of relationships that would characterize the rest of his life. Jesus drew from two popular traditions: (1) John had large crowds of loyal followers; and (2) rabbis had small circles of students, called disciples, who lived with their teacher and were shaped and influenced by him around the clock. Jesus launched the public phase of his teaching by recruiting twelve men as his disciples. The first two were followers of John who now switched to Jesus.

The following day John saw Jesus surrounded by a group of fascinated listeners. John turned to his own disciples and said, "Look, the Lamb of God!" Two of John's followers surprised him by leaving John and going to join up with Jesus. He asked them what they wanted, and the two answered his question with another question, "Rabbi, where are you staying?" §

§ This is one of those times when questions make statements. *Rabbi* didn't necessarily refer to formal theological education or some type of clergy status. It was a term of respect for a teacher. Using the title was a first overture toward becoming two of Jesus' students. They were tentatively inviting themselves along with him by asking where he was going.

Jesus responded to their interest by telling them to just come along and see where he was headed. By then it was already four o'clock in the afternoon, but they stayed with him to listen and talk for the rest of that day.

Andrew, a fisherman by trade, quickly made up his mind to sign on as a follower of Jesus. It wasn't so much the attraction of Jesus himself as it was the recommendation of John the Baptizer. Andrew was convinced that John was sent by God and that he spoke God's truth, enough for him to quit with John and start with Jesus. A natural recruiter, Andrew invited his brother Simon, also a fisherman by trade, to sign on with Jesus as well. His persuasive pitch was short and simple: "We've found the Messiah." Andrew had quickly come to believe in Jesus.

When Jesus and Simon first met, there was an instant attraction that began a lasting friendship. Jesus expressed multiple emotions— a mixture of welcome, anticipation, delight, and laughter all rolled together—when he looked at Simon and said, "You are Simon the son of John?! I'm going to call you Peter!" The nickname stuck. Some still called him Simon; others used Simon Peter to avoid confusion. Most echoed Jesus and called him Peter. §

§ Actually, Jesus said "Cephas," which is Aramaic. The Greek word is "Petros." Both words mean "rock." In modern parlance his nickname would be Rocky.

The next day Jesus headed north to the district of Galilee but not before inviting Philip to join their growing team. His invitation was short and simple: "Follow me!" Philip had already heard about Jesus because he, like Andrew and Simon, was from the town of Bethsaida and the word was quickly spreading. Without first consulting Jesus, he recruited his friend Nathanael to come along. Philip told Nathanael, "We've found the one Moses and the Prophets predicted. His name is Jesus of Nazareth, the son of Joseph." The description sounded strange to those who knew the town. Nathanael blurted out, "Nazareth! Can anything good come from there?" Philip told his friend, "Just come and check him out for yourself!"

When Jesus first saw Nathanael, he gave him this ringing endorsement: "Here is a man who is what an Israelite is supposed to be like. There's nothing fake about him!" Nathanael was skeptical of the unexpected praise. "How do you know anything about me?" he asked Jesus. Jesus said, "Nathanael, I saw you while you were stretched out under the fig tree right before Philip called you."

How could Jesus know so much about a man he had never met? Nathanael had to decide if this was strange, deceptive, or supernatural. Nathanael decided that Jesus was supernatural: "Rabbi, you must be the Son of God, the King of Israel."

Now it was time for Jesus to laugh. "You believe and call me these titles just because I told you I saw you stretched out under the fig tree? You're going to see much greater things than that. I'm telling you the truth. You're going to see heaven open and the angels of God traveling up and down on the Son of Man. You just wait!" § § What he said was reminiscent of Jacob's Ladder in the Old Testament, where Jacob saw a vision of a stairway between heaven and earth— only this time it isn't a stairway but the Son of Man who bridges earth and heaven.

Nathanael didn't have to wait long. Three days later Jesus and his new friends went to a wedding in the village of Cana west of the Sea of Galilee. Cana is nine miles north of Jesus' hometown of Nazareth, so the people and territory were familiar to him. His mother, Mary, also attended the community celebration of the couple's marriage.

When Mary found out from the family putting on the wedding

that the wine had run out, she went to Jesus for help. Since this wasn't really his responsibility, he asked her why she was trying to get him involved. Mary already had seen hints of Jesus' extraordinary powers, although he hadn't yet gone public with them. Without answering his question, Mary asked the servers at the wedding reception to do whatever Jesus ordered.

There were six 30-gallon stone water jars standing outside. Their purpose was to provide water for ritual washing, but they were empty at the time. Jesus asked that the jars be filled with water. When they were full to the brim, Jesus ordered, "Take some out and serve it to the emcee of the banquet." It was a strange request—to take water for washing and serve it to the host in a wine goblet—but the servants did what Jesus asked. When the host took a sip, it was full of high-quality wine. He had no idea what had happened, although the servers had it figured out. He congratulated the groom for serving such excellent wine: "Everyone usually serves the best wine first and saves the cheap wine for later when the guests have had too much to drink and can't tell the difference. You saved the best wine until now."

Most of the wedding guests didn't realize what had happened, but Jesus' new followers had seen it all. They had seen him change plain water into excellent wine, and they became true believers. In their perception, Jesus had changed from a young local rabbi with an endorsement from John the Baptizer into a supernatural miracle worker from God. It was an impressive experience for the newest recruit, Nathanael!

Jesus kept moving, walking great distances and teaching his disciples and other followers as they traveled. His larger entourage gained and lost numbers as Jesus went from place to place. After the wedding, he walked down to Capernaum on the northwest shore of Galilee Lake. § Capernaum would serve as his home base during much of Jesus' travels and teach-

§ Although usually called a sea, it is really a freshwater lake thirteen miles long and seven miles wide. The lake is known by numerous names, including Tiberius and Gennesaret. With a surface 700 feet below sea level and a maximum depth of 160 feet, it is surrounded by high hills and is famous for sudden storms and bountiful fish.

ing. His mother and brothers walked with him, although they didn't yet have the understanding about him that Simon, Andrew, Philip, and Nathanael had developed. The Capernaum visit was short.

Since the annual spring celebration of the Jewish Passover was approaching, Jesus decided to walk the eighty-five miles south to Jerusalem. His arrival in Jerusalem turned into a confrontation instead of a celebration.

TEMPLE

The first temple was built by Israel's third monarch, King Solomon, and completed in 957 BC. It became one of the wonders of ancient architecture, drawing tourists as well as worshippers to see its grandeur. But the Babylonians destroyed it in 586 BC. When Jewish refugees returned to Jerusalem in 538 BC, they started to rebuild the temple and finally completed it in 515 BC, although not to the grandeur of the original. That temple was desecrated by the Syrians in 167 BC (a pig was sacrificed on the altar to humiliate and enrage the Jews) and plundered by the Roman general Crassus in 54 BC. King Herod the Great embarked on a major rebuilding and expansion that lasted most of his reign and beyond—forty-six years. The good news was that the temple was in the best condition it had seen in a millennium.

Upon arrival in Jerusalem, Jesus went to the temple, the epicenter of Jewish faith and worship. The temple leaders asked Jesus what authority he had, and then they made him an offer to prove himself: "Show us a miracle!" It is hard to know why they would make this suggestion unless word of the miraculous winemaking in Cana had made it all the way to Jerusalem. Whatever their logic, they were unprepared for Jesus' response. "Here's your miracle: destroy this temple, and I'll raise it up again in three days." They were shocked and outraged. They challenged, "It has taken forty-six years to build this temple, and you are going to rebuild it in *three days*?" §

In this dialogue with the temple leaders, Jesus switched subjects so that he was using the

§ This became a frequent teaching tactic of Jesus. He made shocking statements that some of his listeners couldn't understand. The words seemed like nonsense. Jesus was using a double strategy: (1) Some of his teachings were intentionally cryptic, meant to be understood by only some of his listeners; (2) his teachings were incrementally moving toward full disclosure, starting with partial information that would add up later on.

metaphor of the temple to refer to his body that would be killed and then raised back to life three days later. He was telling them that the center of worship would not be the temple in Jerusalem but Jesus himself. This was apparent to no one except Jesus, although his followers remembered what Jesus said and determined the meaning a few years later.

The small group from Galilee stayed in Jerusalem through the annual Passover festival. Jesus escalated his miracles, although there was a restraint in what he was doing. He knew that word was quickly spreading about him and he was on his way to celebrity status, but he didn't trust what the people were saying. He knew there was a high probability that his message and purpose were garbled in retelling.

Nicodemus was a prominent religious leader who was fascinated by Jesus but couldn't make sense of Jesus' metaphors and teachings. A Pharisee and a member of the Sanhedrin that served as the ruling council and high court of the Jewish religion, he was curious and cautious. Nicodemus chose to visit Jesus at night rather than risk a public encounter during daylight hours.

He approached Jesus with respect and deference. "Rabbi, everyone knows you are a teacher who has come to us from God, because no one could perform your miracles without the power of God." It wasn't a question, although Jesus answered as if it were: "Let me tell you the truth. No one can experience the kingdom of God unless he is born from above." Nicodemus was now even further confused. "How can a grown-up be born when he is my age?" he asked. "It's impossible to go back inside a mother's uterus and be born a second time from above!"

Jesus seized the opportunity to teach Nicodemus some profound concepts about a person's relationship with God and answered, "The truth is that there are two births. The first one is physical and the second one is spiritual. Our mothers give physical birth and the Spirit gives spiritual birth. So don't be surprised when I tell you that you need to be born a second time.

"Think of it this way, Nicodemus," Jesus continued. "It's like the wind that blows wherever it wants to blow. You can hear it but you can't fully understand exactly where it comes from or how it works. This birth from above is like that, coming from the Spirit of God."

"How can this be?" Nicodemus asked. "I'm just not grasping what you are telling me."

"You are a member of the Sanhedrin and a certified teacher of Israel," said Jesus, "and don't understand what I'm saying? I tell you and others the truth of God with authority, and yet so few accept what I say. I'm explaining the comparatively simple truths of earth; if you don't get this how will you ever understand if I explain to you about heaven? The only one on earth who has been to heaven is the Son of Man, who came from heaven to earth. You remember the story of how Moses put a serpent on a pole in the desert so that the people who looked and believed wouldn't die? In the same way, the Son of Man will be lifted up on a cross and everyone who believes in him will get eternal life."

Then Jesus went on to say what would become his most-quoted truth: "For God so loved the world that he gave his one-of-a-kind Son, in order that anyone who believes in him won't perish but will have eternal life. God didn't send his Son into the world to condemn the world, but to save the world through him. Anyone who believes in him isn't going to be condemned, but whoever doesn't believe is already condemned because of not believing in the name of God's Son. Here's the way it is: light has come into the world, but people preferred darkness instead of light because they like to do what is evil. Those who do evil hate the light and won't come into the light because they're afraid that their sin will be exposed. But those who live by God's truth do come into the light, so that it's obvious that they're doing good with God's help."

Nicodemus went home that night with Jesus' words seared into his memory but still trying to figure out what it all meant. He had never heard a rabbi say such things before. Profound but perplexing! Jesus was opening a whole new world of spiritual insight about God and human destiny. Nicodemus would be back.

Jesus left Jerusalem and traveled through the countryside of Judea, the province around Jerusalem. He taught and his disciples baptized. This caused consternation and jealousy among some of John's followers, who felt that Jesus was winning the competition for crowds. John did not bite the bait of rivalry but reiterated his faith in God and his conviction that Jesus was the Messiah. He explained, "A man only gets what God gives to him from heaven. You all remember what I said: 'I'm not the Messiah but I'm the one God sent ahead of him.' The bride belongs to the bridegroom. The groom's friend enjoys helping him and is thrilled when he hears the groom's voice. That's the way it is with me. I'm full of joy right now because I've heard the voice of the promised Messiah. I know that he must increase in popularity and that I must decrease in popularity." John was not just willing but delighted to turn his popularity over to Jesus.

John went on to distinguish between himself (from earth) and Jesus (from heaven). "The one who comes from above is above all; the one who comes from earth belongs to earth and talks like someone from the earth. The one who comes from heaven is above all. He reports what he has seen and heard in heaven, but people don't want to believe what he says. The one who accepts it has certified that God tells the truth. The Son of God speaks the words of God. God has given him an unlimited supply from the Holy Spirit. The Father loves his Son and has placed everything in his hands. Whoever believes in God's Son has eternal life, but anyone who rejects God's Son is going to see God's wrath instead of eternal life."

This teaching was a major escalation in describing who Jesus was. John began with the fact that Jesus was nobler than he himself, and then he announced that Jesus was from heaven, sent by God, and that belief in him is the basis for eternal life—that belief in him is essential to eternal life.

---- ❋ ----

Jesus headed back north to the province of Galilee, and John was arrested and sent to prison under orders from King Herod Antipas. It all went back to John's public condemnation of the incestuous marriage of Herod to Herodias, his brother Philip's wife. In his condemnation of sin and calls for repentance, John had not been afraid to name names. This irritated some people but absolutely enraged King Herod.

Herod wanted to kill John but was afraid of a popular uprising because so many people considered him a prophet. This added a chronic stress to an already unusual marriage. Herodias so resented John that she became obsessed with ending his life. Not that Herod disagreed, but he was politically astute and therefore protected John. It wasn't totally a political decision; Herod knew in his heart that John was a good and godly man. He didn't like John's confrontational message, but he was fascinated by him and enjoyed bringing John into his court to listen to him.

On Herod's birthday he gave a royal banquet for his government's political and military leaders. He summoned Herodias' daughter to dance for the banquet guests. Delighted with her performance, Herod impulsively offered, "Ask me for anything you want, and I'll give it to you—up to half of everything I have."

Young and stunned by the offer, she delayed her answer until she could get her mother's advice. Herodias calmly told her daughter, "Ask for the head of John the Baptizer." The girl rushed back to the king and blurted out, "I want you to give me right now the head of John on a platter."

Herod was stunned and dismayed. The obvious answer was no, but he had sworn an oath in front of the entire leadership of his government. Herod called for an executioner and ordered him to cut off John's head. The head on a platter was delivered to the girl, who carried it to her mother.

THE ROYAL HERODS

To understand the combination of political power, sexual conquest, and moral indignation requires some explanation about the Herodian dynasty:

• The first and most famous Herod was called Herod the Great, with multiple wives and many children—several of whom he murdered or had executed. He divided his kingdom between his sons, who shared the Herod family name.

• Herod the Great married five women who bore sons, including Antipater, Alexander, Aristobulus, Herod-Philip, Archelaus, and Herod Antipas.

• Herod Antipas was also called Herod the Tetrarch. He was the son of Herod the Great by a wife named Malthace.

• Herodias was also from the Herod family. She was a granddaughter of Herod the Great. Her father was Aristobulus, and her mother was Mariamne.

• Another son of Herod the Great was also called Herod and was the son of another wife, whose name was also Mariamne. This Herod lived as a private citizen in Rome. He married Herodias, who was his niece. Many would call this an inappropriate and incestuous marriage because her father and her husband were both sons of Herod the Great (although by different wives).

• Herod the Tetrarch traveled to Rome and visited his brother while there. He lusted for Herodias, who was both his sister-in-law and his niece. He seduced her and took her back to Galilee with him as his wife. To summarize their relationships, she was his niece, his sister-in-law, and his wife.

• John considered their relationship ethically outrageous and contrary to Old Testament law. But Herod was the king. He had the power of life and death over his people. It was a life-threatening risk to criticize him, no matter how outrageous his behavior. He did whatever he pleased.

• John, knowing he risked imprisonment and death, was convinced he should publicly condemn the sexual immorality of the king. Herod the Tetrarch, with enormous political and police power, had dealt harshly with his enemies in the past. This is exactly what happened. Herod had him arrested, imprisoned, and executed.

John's body was released to his disciples, who then buried him in a tomb. As soon as possible they told Jesus what had happened. He was deeply grieved but not surprised.

Jesus' decision to return to Galilee was rooted in the volatile political environment surrounding John's execution and the growing opposition of the Pharisees in Jerusalem. Not that Jesus was unwilling to face danger and opposition. It just wasn't the right time.

Traveling from Jerusalem to Galilee, Jesus took the most direct route through the province of Samaria, stopping in the village of Sychar, near Mount Gerizim. Samaritans and Jews were similar in ethnicity and religion, although they became bitter rivals by the first century—so much so that some wouldn't even speak to one another. Some Jews traveling between Jerusalem and Galilee chose the longer route east of the Jordan River in order not to have any contact with their Samaritan rivals.

About a mile outside of Sychar was the well of Jacob, dug thousands of years earlier by the early Jewish patriarch Jacob and given to his son Joseph. Jesus stopped by the well at noon and started a conversation with a Samaritan woman drawing water. §

§ Conservative Jews would have considered this outrageous on two counts—talking to a Samaritan and talking to a woman. Many rabbis usually didn't talk to women outside of their own immediate families.

SAMARITANS

The history of the Samaritans is uncertain. The Jews and Samaritans tell very different stories of Samaritan origin. The Samaritans claimed to date back to the Old Testament priest Eli and the old place of worship in Shiloh, arguing that they were right and the Jews were wrong for establishing the temple in Jerusalem. By contrast, Jews said that Samaritans were the result of intermarriage between Mesopotamians and Jews, resulting in an ethnic mix. And there are other explanations. But whatever their origin, in the first century the primary difference was over place of worship. Samaritans said the proper place was on Mount Gerizim and the Jews said the proper place was in Jerusalem. Like many rivalries between groups of people, the central point expanded to mutual animosity.

While his disciples were in town buying food, Jesus asked the woman for a drink of water. She responded, "You are a Jew and I am a Samaritan woman. How can you ask *me* for a drink?"

Jesus answered her, "If you knew the gift of God and who is asking you for a drink, you would have requested that I give you living water."

"Sir," the woman said, "you don't have a scoop or bucket or anything else to draw water, and the well is deep. Where are you going to get this living water? Do you think that you are greater than our father Jacob, who used this well and then gave it to us?"

"Everyone who drinks this water will get thirsty again," he answered, "but anyone who drinks the water I give won't ever be thirsty again. In fact, the living water I give him will become an internal spring of water bubbling up to eternal life."

Ready to take him up on his offer, she told him, "Sir, give me this water you're talking about. I'd really like to never get thirsty again and not have to keep coming back here to draw water from this well."

"All right," Jesus told her, "but first, I want you to go and invite your husband to come back here to the well."

"I don't have a husband."

Jesus said to her, "You said that right! The fact is, you've had five husbands, and you're not married to the man you're living with now. So what you have just said is exactly true."

"Sir, it's obvious to me that you are a prophet. Our ancestors worshipped on this mountain, but you Jews insist that the place where we are supposed to worship is in Jerusalem."

Jesus acknowledged the fact that Samaritans had set up their own place of worship on Mount Gerizim instead of in Jerusalem, but then he announced that the *place* one worshipped ultimately didn't matter. Worshipping the right God in the right way is more important than in the right place. He told her, "A time is coming when you won't worship God here on this mountain *or* in Jerusalem. You Samaritans worship what you don't know; we Jews worship what we do know, because the Scriptures teach that salvation is from the Jews. But let me tell you something. Starting now, the true worshippers will worship God the Father in spirit and truth. That's the kind of worshipper the Father is looking for, because God is spirit, and his worshippers must worship him in spirit and in truth."

Like many of Jesus' early listeners, the woman didn't fully understand what he meant. Yet she was receptive. "I know that the Messiah is coming, and when he arrives he will explain everything to us." She was totally unprepared for Jesus' next statement.

"That's who I am! You're talking to the Messiah."

While she stood in shocked silence, his disciples came back from town and were surprised to see Jesus talking to the woman. But they kept quiet and didn't ask him about it.

Flustered by the group of strangers and the claim of Jesus to be the Messiah, the woman forgot her water jar and hurried back to town. She wasn't quiet once she returned home, telling all who would listen, "You've got to see this! Come out to the well with me. I want you to see someone who told me everything I ever did. I think he's the Messiah!" Like the people of many small towns, their curiosity was aroused, and many of the villagers headed out to the well to see this prophet.

The disciples offered Jesus some of the food they had just purchased in town. He declined, telling them, "I have food to eat that you don't know about." Another strange statement from Jesus, and they wondered who had fed him. He told them, "My food is to do the will of God who sent me and to finish his work. You know the way you say, 'In four more months it will be harvest time'? Let me tell you that if you'll take a long hard look, you'll see that the fields are already ripe and ready for harvest. Those who are harvesting are already getting paid, because they are gathering in the crop for eternal life. It's a happy day for both the sower and the harvester. The popular saying that 'One sows and another reaps' is true. I sent you to reap a crop that you didn't sow or prepare. Others have done all the hard work, and you have reaped the benefits of their labor."

His words were logged one more time into their mental journals for future analysis and understanding. They were still trying to figure out Jesus.

The villagers arrived to check out Jesus based on the recommendation of the woman. They met him, listened to him, and decided she was right. They believed that he really was the Messiah sent from God. They were so zealous that they invited Jesus to stay in Sychar. He stayed for two more days, and even more Samaritans believed he was the Messiah. They told the woman that her words got them introduced to him, but actually seeing and hearing Jesus convinced them that he was the Savior of the world.

When the two days in Sychar were up, Jesus took his followers and finished his journey home to Galilee. Stories from Jerusalem had preceded Jesus. Many Galileans had been in Jerusalem for the Passover and saw for themselves his miracles and heard his teaching. His popularity was spreading, and the people of his home district welcomed him back.

"A prophet has no honor in his own country," Jesus said. At first this didn't seem to be true of him. Although born in Bethlehem, Jesus grew up in Nazareth, in the province of Galilee. He spoke with a Galilean accent, and his relatives lived in Galilee. The people of Galilee knew him and should have been proud of their fellow Galilean who had caused such a stir in Jerusalem. But as it turned out, his initial popularity around Galilee didn't last.

Jesus visited area synagogues where Jews gathered for teaching and worship every Sabbath day. He volunteered or was invited to preach, and he always focused on the same theme: "The time has come. The kingdom of God is near. Repent and believe the good news." He sounded like an upbeat John the Baptizer. The people were hearing from "the hometown boy."

While Jesus was making a return visit to Cana, an important government official from Capernaum came looking for him. He was an officer in the service of Herod Antipas who bore the title Tetrarch but was considered by many to be a king. Speaking with passion and urgency, he begged Jesus to come and heal his dying son. There were plenty of witnesses to the request. Although powerful and important, this father was humbled by the looming death of his boy.

Jesus combined his teaching with this man's plea and turned it into an illustration. He told the audience, "You people don't ever want to believe unless you first see a miracle." He didn't say the words directly to the father, but the statement expressed Jesus' frustration: many were reluctant to believe what he taught unless they saw a miracle to accredit his teaching. The official really wasn't focused right then on what Jesus was teaching. Understandably, all he cared about at the moment was his son. He pleaded with Jesus, "Please come before my boy dies." Jesus didn't agree to go but dismissed him, saying, "You go on home. Your son will live." It may have sounded as if Jesus was getting rid of him without providing much help, but the father took Jesus literally, believing that his son wouldn't die because Jesus said so.

On his twenty-mile trip back home to Capernaum, the father was met by some of his household servants, who ran up to him and said that his son was alive and well. He asked the servants what time the boy had started to get better. They told him, "The fever left him yesterday at one o'clock"— exactly the same time Jesus had said the boy would live. Convinced that Jesus had performed a miracle, the official and his entire household believed in Jesus.

The next Sabbath, Jesus visited his home synagogue in Nazareth, where he had grown up and everyone knew him and his family. The synagogue service followed the same liturgy as in every other synagogue: prayer, Scripture reading, and teaching. §

§ Though the Scriptures were read in Hebrew from handwritten scrolls, they were then translated into Aramaic, because most of the people didn't understand Hebrew. Years of Assyrian conquest and occupation meant that Aramaic had become the language of the people of this region (see sidebar on languages in chapter 8). The teaching wasn't always from the local rabbi but could also come from guest speakers or members of the congregation who were called on or welcomed to teach. After each lesson there was always a time for questions and answers.

That weekend the leader of the synagogue invited Jesus to read and teach. They all knew him well, and Jesus was now famous. It's not difficult to picture the crowd and feel the excitement. They handed the Isaiah scroll to Jesus, who stood to read, as was traditional out of respect for the Scriptures. Jesus carefully unrolled the scroll and read:

> "The Spirit of the Lord is on me;
> he chose me to preach good news to the poor.
> He sent me to proclaim freedom for the
>   prisoners and recovery of sight to the blind,

to give liberty to the oppressed,
to announce that this is the year
of the Lord's favor."

Then Jesus rolled up the scroll and handed it back to the synagogue assistant. He sat down to speak with every eye in the congregation fixed on him, waiting to hear what he would say about this passage of Scripture.

He told them, "Today this Scripture prophecy is fulfilled while you are listening."

The audience response was immediate as they sensed what Jesus was saying. He had made a stunning declaration, particularly in light of the fact that they all believed the words of Isaiah were a prophecy predicting the coming of the Messiah. Was Jesus telling them, "I am the Messiah that Isaiah predicted"?

Whispers were everywhere as they traded comments and stories about how they all knew Jesus and how wonderful he was. "Isn't this Joseph's son?" one of them noted. "He grew up right here in Nazareth. His words are so gracious!" Another one said, "Will he do a miracle?"

Jesus spoke above the whispers. "You probably want to quote the proverb to me that says, 'Physician, heal yourself! Do here in your hometown what we have heard you did in Capernaum.'" This was exactly what they were thinking. Jesus had grown up in a working family, as were most of the families in Nazareth. If Jesus was the Messiah who could bring wealth and healing and good times, it would be great if he would get on with it. Do a miracle right here in Nazareth like the miracle in the town of Capernaum.

But the excited audience approval of Jesus didn't last for long. Jesus went on to say, "The truth is that no prophet is accepted in his hometown. There were many widows in Israel back in Elijah's time, when there was a drought that lasted for three and a half years and caused a severe famine everywhere in the land. Yet Elijah wasn't sent to any of the villages of Israel to help them. Instead, God sent the prophet to a widow in Zarephath over in the region of Sidon. The

§ The short sermon referred to two familiar stories from Israel's history during the ninth century BC. The first was about a three-and-a-half-year drought, and the second was about a soldier suffering from the skin disease leprosy. Elijah and Elisha were prophets who miraculously helped a widow survive the drought-caused famine and healed a foreigner named Naaman of his leprosy. Both stories focused on miracles for Gentiles, with famine-struck and leprosy-infected Jews not miraculously helped while non-Jews were fed and healed. The Sabbath Day crowd immediately knew what Jesus was implying—that he would perform miracles for others but not for them.

same sort of thing happened with the many in Israel who had leprosy during the time of Elisha the prophet, but none of them was cleansed—only Naaman, a foreigner from Syria." § The mood immediately changed to consternation and anger, and the audience turned against Jesus.

The people in the synagogue became so furious that they leaped out of their seats, drove Jesus out of the synagogue, chased him out of town, and were about to throw him off the top of the hill on which Nazareth was built. Jesus didn't perform a miracle for them but did something miraculous for himself—he walked through the angry mob and straight out of town without getting hurt. And he kept walking for twenty miles—all the way back to Capernaum on the shore of the Galilee Lake. From then on he made his home and established his headquarters in that town.

------ ❋ ------

Capernaum had grown from a small village into a midsize town by the time Jesus moved there. But the population of several thousand was small enough that everyone knew that the popular young rabbi was in town. The people saw him at the synagogue, but Jesus didn't limit himself to teaching only on weekends. He walked along the lake and talked to those who would listen. People crowded around him as he taught the truths of God and explained the writings of the Jewish Scriptures.

Walking the shoreline, Jesus saw Peter and his brother Andrew casting a large fishing net into the lake. Jesus had already begun recruiting them to be his followers the last time they had met, but now he added a second invitation that played on their profession. Jesus said, "Come, follow me, and I'll turn you two into fishers of people." They loved the analogy, and they dropped their nets and walked right out of the water to Jesus.

Jesus taught some more as the crowd stood around him and listened along the shore. Then he took the same approach with James and John, the two sons of Zebedee who were in their fishing boat just off shore also working on their nets. They responded to Jesus' call with equal enthusiasm, jumping out and wading straight to Jesus. Their father probably had mixed emotions as he sat in the boat and watched his sons following the new young prophet who was causing such a stir.

Next, Jesus walked over to two boats on the water's edge and got into the one that belonged to Peter. Jesus sat in the boat as it bobbed in the water near the shore and started teaching the crowd again. Now it was easier for all the people to see and hear him. When Jesus finished his teaching, he asked Peter to row the boat into deeper water and lower the nets for a catch. Peter was understandably skeptical. He was the experienced fisherman, and Jesus was a dry-land carpenter. Peter certainly wanted to treat Jesus with respect even if he knew little if anything about fishing. He said, "Master, we've worked hard all night and haven't caught one fish. But because you say so, I'll put the nets back in the water."

Soon after, the nets dropped below the water's surface, filling with fish so the nets started to rip. Peter shouted for help from the nearest boat, and they hauled in so many fish that both boats looked like they were going to sink.

Some would say that Jesus was aware of the way fish migrate through the various thermal layers of the deep waters of Galilee and that a zero catch can be turned into a maximum catch at the same surface if the net is lowered to a different level. But Peter, with a lifetime of fishing experience, saw far more than a simple natural explanation. He saw a miracle, and he fell at Jesus' knees saying, "Go away from me, Lord, because I'm a sinner!" Peter wasn't alone in his amazement and fear at Jesus' display of supernatural knowledge. All the veteran fishermen, including James and John, were equally awed.

Using this fishing experience as an object lesson about their future as recruiters, Jesus told them, "Don't be afraid; from now on you're going to catch people!" It worked—the fishermen walked away from their boats to follow Jesus wherever he went.

The next Sabbath day Jesus was invited to teach at the Capernaum synagogue. It was a large and beautiful building, the center of spiritual life in this thriving lakeshore town.

What most impressed the people who listened was the sense of authority that marked Jesus' teaching. He was different from teachers who merely quoted the opinions of others but seemed unsure of their own answers. Not Jesus! He quoted the Scriptures and explained what they meant. He didn't give multiple choices; he gave authoritative answers. The response was positive and enthusiastic.

While Jesus was teaching, a member of the synagogue stood up and disrupted the service, shouting in a loud, anguished voice. He had an evil spirit in him, and the sound that came out of him was blood chilling. He shouted, "What do you want with us, Jesus of Nazareth? Are you here to destroy us? I know who you are. You are the Holy One of God!" While some were still trying to decide if they believed Jesus was the Messiah from God, there was no doubt coming out of this possessed man. He certainly knew who Jesus was, although he didn't like it.

Jesus took immediate control, forcefully ordering him to be quiet. Then Jesus commanded, "Come out of him!" The evil spirit let out a shriek, dumped the poor man on the floor, and exited his body, leaving him uninjured.

It was a synagogue service the attendees would never forget. They buzzed with conversation: "What is he teaching? He talks like he is the person in charge who has the authority and power to give orders to evil spirits. And then they do what he tells them!" They went everywhere in Capernaum and the rest of the area telling what had happened.

After the synagogue service, Jesus went to Peter's house in Capernaum. Peter's wife had urged the invitation because her mother was sick with a high fever and hoped Jesus could help. Jesus went to her bedside, touched her hand, and rebuked the fever. He then helped her to stand up. And she was fine. The fever was gone, and she was strong enough to help serve dinner. In a single day Jesus had demonstrated that God was dramatically intervening in human history—teaching truth, confronting evil, and healing sickness.

Right around sunset a crowd of sick people and their relatives started to gather outside Peter's house. The word was out that Jesus was healing the sick, including Peter's mother-in-law. Families brought relatives suffering from a wide variety of ailments. Some were physical and others were spiritual, including more evil spirits controlling people. Jesus patiently helped them all. With a touch or a word he healed the sick and drove out demons while they shouted, "You are the Son of God!" But Jesus ordered those demons to keep quiet. He was not ready to announce the reason for his supernatural power.

It was late by the time the last sick person had come for healing. Jesus was tired and stayed overnight in the home of Peter and his family. He awakened before dawn and left the house without anyone seeing him, walking to an out-of-the-way place to pray alone. When Peter awoke and couldn't find Jesus, he gathered a small search party. When they found Jesus, Peter was put out that Jesus had ventured out on his own. "Everyone is looking for you!" he told Jesus.

Then another crowd started to gather. It was just what Jesus expected and also what he was trying to avoid. He wanted time alone to pray, and he hadn't been able to find much of that. He decided to leave Capernaum, but the people physically blocked his departure, not wanting to lose access to his supernatural powers.

Certainly anyone with the ability to heal the sick and to walk away from an angry mob in Nazareth didn't need to explain himself. But

Jesus said, "I need to preach the good news of God's kingdom to other towns beside Capernaum, because that's why I was sent."

§ See the map of first-century Palestine inside the back cover of the book. Galilee was a fairly small province 50 miles long from north to south and 25 miles wide from west to east. The name comes from the Hebrew word *Galíl*, meaning "circle," perhaps because the Jewish area was surrounded by non-Jewish nations. Even in earlier history there were many Gentiles surrounding the district.

Jesus kept Capernaum as his headquarters, but he became increasingly itinerant, moving from village to village and town to town around Galilee. §

Each Sabbath he visited and taught in a different synagogue. During the week he told the good news of God's kingdom to individuals and crowds in the marketplaces and countryside. Everywhere he went there were people to be healed, and he cured every disease. Jesus was drawing all kinds of people who were sick with disease, in severe pain, possessed by demons, paralyzed, and having seizures.

As the news of his miracles spread, people came from all over Galilee, Syria, Decapolis (a loose political and economic alliance of ten Greek-culture cities mostly along the east side of the Jordan River), Jerusalem, Judea, and the west side of the Jordan. It was a diverse group of ethnicities, religions, genders, and cultures, although most were Jews.

One man came to Jesus and fell to his knees in front of him. He suffered from the most dreaded disease of his generation—leprosy. The diseased man started on his knees, then fell face down to the ground in front of Jesus, begging, "Lord, if you're willing, you can make me clean." It is amazing the sick man got that far. The crowd likely would threaten him and run from him.

Jesus saw his deformed hands, bleached skin, and open sores, and his heart was touched. With great compassion, Jesus answered, "I'm willing!" as soon as he was asked and reached out to touch him. It was an occasion for those nearby to audibly gasp. No one ever deliberately touched a leper. And then the crowd gasped again as the leper was immediately cured.

Before the healed man was sent away, Jesus looked him in the eye and gave him a strong and specific warning: "I don't want you to tell anyone what happened. What you need to do is go and show yourself to the priest and give the required offering commanded in the Law of Moses." Jesus asked for secrecy since too much attention from the crowds risked involvement by the government authorities before it was the right time. Jesus had many more places to go, more people to heal, more crowds to teach, and his hand-selected group of disciples to train. It wasn't yet the moment for everyone to know about him.

But the healed man couldn't keep his secret. He told everyone who would listen until the crowds seeking Jesus became unmanageably large. Jesus couldn't go anywhere without being recognized and pursued. No house provided privacy. He sought isolated places to sleep in the outdoors, but people found him even when he was in hiding.

LEPROSY

The term has been largely excised from modern medical vocabulary, technically replaced with a more specific name, Hansen's Disease. It is a progressive, debilitating illness that leaves its victims deformed and without feeling, especially in the extremities. The diagnosis of the desperate man who begged Jesus' help is less certain. Leprosy was a general description for almost every skin rash or disease. At a time when contagious illnesses were enormous public health threats, everyone with any dermatological disorder was quarantined. Not only was the patient physically miserable but socially isolated. Often he was either permanently distanced from his family or his family was ostracized along with him. The law was explicit: "The person with such an infectious disease must wear torn clothes, let his hair be unkempt, cover the lower part of his face, and cry out, 'Unclean! Unclean!' As long as he has the infection he remains unclean. He must live alone." While there were provisions for a priest to examine a former leprosy patient and pronounce him clean, that was rare in a society with deep fears of contagion.

A few days later Jesus returned to Capernaum. Instead of dealing with the crowds around the shore, he boarded a boat and sailed to the north side of the lake for some time alone. Word quickly spread that he was back in the area, and hundreds began gathering to see and hear him. Especially interested were some Pharisees and other religious teachers who had come from as far away as Jerusalem. They had assumed he would eventually return to Capernaum, and they awaited his arrival. Between the locals and the visitors, the crowd was large in and around the house where Jesus stayed when he came back into town from his brief time in the north. While the religious leaders were focused on Jesus' teaching, the families of sick relatives were far more interested in his ability to heal.

The extended family of a paralyzed man had brought him to Capernaum, hoping Jesus would come back. When they couldn't get close to him because of the crowds, four of the men put him on a mat and carried him up to the roof of the house. They removed roof tiles to make an opening, then tied ropes around him and the mat and lowered the sick man down in front of Jesus. It was one of those days when the power of God to heal seemed especially generous, and they didn't want to miss the opportunity. Jesus obviously was delighted by their faith and their ingenuity. He stopped his teaching and spoke to the paralyzed man, "My friend, your sins are forgiven."

The man hadn't come seeking forgiveness of sin; he had come to be healed of paralysis. Forgiving sin is a higher category of supernatural power than physical healing, and the crowd had assumed that God was delegating healing powers to Jesus but would keep forgiveness as his exclusive prerogative. The reality was that both require God's action. The Pharisees and rabbis in the audience quickly caught the theological implications and thought, "Why does this fellow talk this way? He's blaspheming! Only God can forgive sins!"

If the theologians were surprised by what Jesus said to the paralyzed man, they were even more surprised by his next comments to them: "Why are you thinking these things? Let me ask you which is easier: to say to this paralyzed man, 'Your sins are forgiven,' or to say, 'Stand up, take your mat, and walk'? All right, so that you may know that the Son of Man has authority on earth to forgive sins..." And then Jesus turned to the paralyzed man and said, "I'll tell you what: get up, take your mat, and go home." The man stood, rolled up his mat, and walked out of the house.

The crowd was awestruck. Most of the people responded with praise to God, but the Pharisees and rabbis were still trying to figure out how Jesus had known what they were thinking—whether he really could forgive sins and where he got the power and authority to heal paralyzed people.

While they were all reacting to the words and miracles, Jesus left the house and headed for the fresh air by the lakeside. As usual, the crowd followed him, especially curious to see what he was going to do next.

Jesus approached a tax collection booth occupied by a collector named Matthew Levi Alphaeus. § There is no evidence that Matthew was a dishonest tax collector, but he was part of a disliked group, which made Jesus' approach to him suspect and questionable. No doubt Matthew had seen and heard Jesus around town (everyone had!), and maybe he had even thought about who he might be. Jesus seized the opportunity with a simple invitation: "Follow me!" Matthew immediately left his tax collection franchise, followed Jesus, and never returned to his old business.

Matthew asked Jesus to come to his home for dinner and invited a broad cross section of his friends to meet the rabbi from Nazareth.

§ The tax collection system varied. One approach granted contracts with the Roman government allowing the collectors to estimate the value of goods in transit between the lake and land and then assess taxes on the basis of established tariffs. If the tariffs were vague, a dishonest tax collector could be oppressive in his collection. Because of the dishonesty of some there was an unpopularity that extended to them all to the point where they were marginalized from community and religious life.

Since they were all classified as "sinners," they figured this was probably their one opportunity to meet Jesus.

Jesus' critics were still reeling from what had happened earlier in the day, but they found enough energy to mount one more criticism against Jesus. They asked him, "Why do you eat and drink with tax collectors and sinners?"

Jesus was waiting for this question and ready with his answer. "Healthy folk aren't the ones who need a doctor, but the sick. I haven't come to call righteous people, but sinners to repentance."

With Jesus' popularity had come criticism, and not just from the religious leaders. Jealous disciples of John the Baptizer joined the Pharisees in their questioning of Jesus. They emphasized fasting and praying, both of which were a valued and important part of Jewish religious life. Some Jews took both to an extreme or fasted and prayed for the wrong reasons. Many Pharisees fasted every Monday and Thursday, abstaining from food from sunrise to sunset. They believed that by fasting they drew God's attention to their piety. Some also sought to draw public attention by wearing makeup to make them look pale and weak. They publicly prayed every morning, afternoon, and evening.

In contrast, Jesus' disciples were seen laughing, eating, and drinking. Their relationship with him seemed to make them happy. This provoked the Pharisees and some of John's disciples, but it also piqued their curiosity. They truly wondered how anyone who was serious about God could disregard fasting. There may have been a measure of envy, resenting the seemingly inappropriate lightheartedness of others when they always had to be so serious. They asked Jesus, "Why do the disciples of the Pharisees and of John often fast and pray, but your disciples are always eating and drinking?"

Jesus responded with a question and then answered it himself: "How can the guests of the bridegroom fast while he is with them? They can't, as long as he's there, because they're enjoying their time together. But later, when their good friend is gone they will miss him and fast." He obviously was referring to himself and saying that his disciples should enjoy Jesus while he was present and that they would have plenty of time to fast later when he was gone. His analogy referred to a newly married couple enjoying a week-long wedding party, when all the guests provided them with one of the very best times of their lives.

Jesus added an illustration to his answer: "No one sews a patch of brand-new cloth on an old piece of clothing. If he does, the new cloth shrinks and comes loose, making the tear worse. In the same way, no one pours new wine into old wineskins. If he does, the wine will burst the skins, spilling the wine and ruining the wineskins. Instead, a person pours new wine into new wineskins." A new era had dawned, he told them, and it was time for something new in their lives. They carried wine in animal skins that shrank with time. It was fine for storing old wine, but new wine expanded as it fermented and ripped the old skins. Patching didn't work because the patches popped off. It was better to just start over with a new skin. God's kingdom was coming, and it was a time for joy.

As soon as Jesus answered one criticism another cropped up. At first the criticisms were spontaneous and unsophisticated, but his growing cadre of critics started to organize and polish their censure of Jesus. They especially focused on issues related to keeping the Sabbath. Working six days and resting on the Sabbath was a central element of Jewish faith and life. As it became clear that criticizing Jesus' miracles of compassionate healing was unpersuasive, they focused more on Jesus' noncompliance with popular practices of Sabbath observance.

PHARISEES

Why was there growing animosity between Jesus and the Pharisees? A simple question, but it defies an easy answer. Certainly Jesus and the Pharisees shared much in common—belief in the Scripture, the supernatural, sin, repentance, personal piety, prayer, and future resurrection from the dead. Jesus had more in common with the Pharisees than with the Sadducees. And all Pharisees were not critics of Jesus— many were his friends and eventual followers. However, some were protective of their way of life, of their power and position, to the point of self-righteousness. They became upset with Jesus because he seemed disrespectful of their piety and practices. They were trying to please God and keep the law, but Jesus pointed in other directions. Of course, Jesus also wanted to please God and came to fulfill the law, but his approach was very different.

Jesus proclaimed a marvelous coming of the kingdom of God to Israel. He welcomed tax collectors, prostitutes, and sinners. This different vision of Israel's future provoked many Pharisees, who were threatened by Jesus' teaching and associations.

When Jesus seemed to dismiss many of their traditions as unnecessary or unimportant—especially regarding the Sabbath—they were angered and resented Jesus' power and popularity with the crowds. In a sense they were good people who went to extremes that hurt themselves and others. What began as irritations became deep resentment toward Jesus and everything he did. The Pharisees' defense of their values and vision caused them to attack Jesus and his message.

Following the busy days of teaching and healing around Galilee, Jesus once again headed south to Jerusalem for one of the annual pilgrimage feasts. A first stop was the Pool of Bethesda near the city's Sheep Gate. Surrounded by five covered colonnades, it was famous for the alleged healing powers of the pool water. An ancient legend said that an angel periodically stirred the pool water and whoever stepped in first was cured of whatever disease the person suffered. §

§ Modern visitors to Jerusalem can visit the excavations of the double pool in the courtyard of St. Anne's Church in the northeast quarter of the city.

The poolside was filled with people who were blind, lame, and paralyzed and hoping to be healed. One of them had been an invalid for thirty-eight years. Touched by his malady and suffering, Jesus asked him a rather obvious question: "Do you want to be healed?" Rather than directly answering, the disabled man explained, "I don't have anyone to help me into the pool when the water is stirred. While I'm trying to get in, someone else always goes in ahead of me."

Jesus told him, "Stand up! Pick up your mat and walk." Immediately he was healed, and he was able to do as Jesus had instructed him.

It was a spectacular miracle. Unfortunately, some of the religious leaders were not positively impressed. They accosted the recently healed man and told him, "Today is the Sabbath. The law forbids you to carry your mat." He defended himself, passing on the responsibility for working on the Sabbath. "The man who healed me told me to pick up my mat and walk," he explained.

Asking the next obvious question, they inquired who had healed him, who had told him what to do. The man didn't know who the healer was. Whoever had helped him was a stranger who disappeared into the crowd as quickly as he had first showed up at the pool.

Later, when the religious leaders weren't around, Jesus found the healed man in the temple and spoke to him. "Well, look at you! You are well again. So listen carefully. Stop sinning or something worse might happen to you the next time." Once he knew it was Jesus who had healed him, the man quickly left the temple and reported this to the religious authorities.

The religious leaders were so incensed over the mat being carried on the Sabbath that they conspired to prosecute Jesus as one who promoted religious lawbreaking. Jesus' defense didn't impress them when he said, "My Father always works on Sabbaths, and I'm working too." God does good work on the Sabbath, and so does Jesus, he was telling them. To the contrary, they turned this into one more reason to censure Jesus. Now they said he was not only a Sabbath lawbreaker but he was one who made himself equal with God by the way he called God his "Father." They became so outraged that they resolved to kill him.

The allegations of blasphemy because Jesus seemed to be claiming equality with God called for a public response from him. What Jesus said to the people in Jerusalem may have sounded like a defense, but it really was a strategic declaration outlining who he was as the Son of God and directly challenging the authority and accusations of his critics. In his speech, Jesus told the people that God is the Father and Jesus is the Son who does what the Father tells him to do. Here is what Jesus said:

"I'm telling you the truth; the Son can't perform miracles on his own. He does what he sees the Father doing—like Father like Son. God the Father loves the Son and shows him everything he is doing. In fact, to your amazement he will show him even greater things than these so far. Just as the Father raises the dead to life, the Son gives life to whomever he wants. What is more, the Father doesn't judge anyone, but has entrusted all judgment to the Son. This way everyone may honor the Son just as they are supposed to honor the Father. Anyone who doesn't honor the Son really doesn't honor the Father, who sent him.

"The truth is, anyone who hears my word and believes God who sent me has eternal life and will not be condemned. That person who hears and believes has crossed over from death to life. And let me tell you another truth: the time has come when the dead hear the voice of the Son of God and those who hear will live forever. You believe that God the Father has life in himself, but you also need to know that the Father has given God the Son to have life in himself. Plus, he has given the Son his authority to judge, because he is the Messiah.

"Don't be amazed by all this, because a time is coming when all the dead people who are in their graves will hear his voice and come out. The good ones will rise to live, and the evil ones will rise to be condemned. I can't do this by myself. I judge fairly on the basis of what I hear, and let me tell you that my judgment is just because I don't do what I do to please myself. I do what I do to please God the Father, who sent me to earth. My judgments are totally in line with the Father.

"Listen, if I testify as my own witness, my testimony isn't accepted as valid. So I want you to listen carefully to someone else who testifies in my favor, and we all know that his testimony about me is valid. I'm talking about John the Baptizer.

"You went to hear John, or at least heard from those who were sent to listen to John, and he has testified to the truth about me. Not that any human testimony decides the truth, but I mention John's testimony because you know about it and so that you may be saved. John was a lamp that burned and gave light, and you chose to listen and to enjoy his light...at least for a little while you did.

"Now let me tell you that I have a testimony better than John's. My teaching and miracles are the work that God the Father assigned for me to do and finish. You listen and watch and experience for yourselves that this proves God the Father sent me to earth. Actually, the Father who sent me has himself testified about me. The trouble is that you've never heard his voice or seen him and his word doesn't live inside of you. Do you know why? It's because you refuse to believe God the Father, who sent me to earth. This is how bad it is: you diligently study the Scriptures because you think that by them you have received eternal life. Yet you've missed the point that these Scriptures testify about me; you adamantly refuse to come to me to have life.

"I'm not looking for human praise from you or anyone else. It's just that I know all about you—you don't have God's love in your hearts. I came in my Father's name and yet you don't accept me; then along comes someone else in his own name and you accept him. This doesn't make any sense. How can you say that you believe when you base your belief on praising one another, yet make no real effort to obtain the praise that only comes from God?

"Don't think that I'm your first and only accuser before God the Father, because I'm not. Your first accuser is Moses, the one you say is the basis for all your beliefs and hope. If you really believed Moses, you would believe me, because he wrote about me. But since you really don't believe what Moses wrote, you're not going to believe anything I have to say, are you?"

It was a powerful speech, but it didn't persuade his critics. To the contrary, it inflamed them all the more. They started looking for additional evidence to accuse Jesus of wrong behavior and beliefs. It didn't take long.

On a following Sabbath, Jesus and his friends walked through grain fields near Jerusalem. Those with Jesus were hungry, so they picked some of the heads of grain. After breaking them open and rubbing them in their hands, they blew away the chaff and ate the grain. It wasn't considered stealing because the Jewish law taught that "if you enter your neighbor's grain field, you may pick kernels with your hands, but you must not put a sickle to his standing grain."

The Pharisees had spies watching Jesus and his friends, especially on Saturdays (the Sabbath was from sundown on Friday to sundown on Saturday). They soon confronted Jesus with another accusation: "Look! Your disciples are breaking the Sabbath rules!"

Jesus' answer confounded them, using their own Scriptures with two examples of similar activity on the Sabbath. Jesus said, "Don't you remember what David did when he and his companions were hungry? They went into the house of God and ate the consecrated bread, which was legal only for the priests to eat. Or don't you remember that it says in your Law that on the Sabbath the temple priests 'desecrate the day' because they are working but they are considered innocent because that's a necessary part of their jobs?"

Of course they had read this, but they had never thought of it in this way before. King David ate bread exclusively reserved for the priests. The priests worked every Sabbath to fulfill their temple responsibilities. In some circumstances it was acceptable to break lesser rules. Actually, it really wasn't breaking the law at all. They were blameless because a greater law ruled. "The Sabbath was made for people, not people for the Sabbath," Jesus concluded, telling them that certain human needs were more important than keeping regulations.

This teaching led to another question. If sometimes it is all right to break the Sabbath law against work, who decides what is acceptable and what is not? Jesus had an answer for this question before they asked it. He announced, "The Son of Man is the Lord of the Sabbath." Since Jesus was referring to himself as the Son of Man, he was saying that he was in charge of the Sabbath and what he said ruled, therefore nothing had been done that was illegal. But the criticisms and attacks did not end. The Sabbath controversies weren't going to go away.

SON OF MAN

Jesus referred to himself as the "Son of Man" more than any other title or description, although others didn't pick up the title to refer to him. Early Christians chose other names and titles like "Christ" and "Son of God" instead. Part of the reason is that "Son of Man" was a thoroughly Jewish title and difficult for Gentiles to understand.

The Old Testament prophet Daniel introduced the title when he recorded a vision of the future: "In my vision one night I saw in front of me one like a son of man, coming with the clouds of heaven." Daniel described this person as humanlike but with clearly supernatural powers given by God. "In the presence of God, the Ancient of Days, he was given authority, glory, and sovereign kingship; all peoples from every nation and language will worship and serve him. His dominion is an everlasting dominion that won't pass away, and his kingship will never be destroyed."

The title "Son of Man" designated a figure from heaven with divine origin and power but humanity as well. It was a clear signal to his Jewish listeners that he claimed to have the authority of God and was a fulfillment of prophecy.

That same Saturday Jesus entered a synagogue. Anticipating that he might heal someone, his critics watched closely so they could accuse him one more time. They asked Jesus straight out, "Do you consider it lawful to heal on the Sabbath?" He shot right back with a question for them: "If one of you has a sheep that falls into a pit on the Sabbath, won't you reach down and pull it out? People are much more valuable than sheep! Of course it is lawful to do good on the Sabbath!"

Jesus asked a man with a misshapen hand to come out of the audience and stand in front of the congregation. The mood must have been tense as both his friends and his enemies watched to see what would happen. Jesus looked right at his critics and asked them, "Which do you say is lawful on the Sabbath: to do good or to do evil? Is it better to save life or to kill life?" The religious leaders were trapped. If they said to heal the man, they were doing exactly what they accused Jesus of doing, condoning work on the Sabbath. If they said not to heal the man, they were lacking compassion and saying that he wasn't worth even as much as one of their sheep. So they sat in silence.

Their silence provoked Jesus because of their verbal games and stubbornness. He turned to the man standing before them all and told him, "Stretch out your hand." He did so, and it was completely normal.

The Pharisees were furious with Jesus for embarrassing them in front of the synagogue congregation and were more determined than ever to kill him. In their anger they arranged a meeting with another political party, the Herodians, to see if they would join in a plan to have Jesus eliminated.

Enough was enough. The Pharisees weren't going to change their minds, so Jesus left Jerusalem and turned back north to Galilee. People followed him all the way from Jerusalem, walking for days. More joined the crowd from every place they passed. Along the way, Jesus healed those who were ill. The more he healed, the more they came. People from Judea, Jerusalem, Idumea, across the Jordan, and from as far away as Tyre and Sidon were there to greet him by the time he arrived home again. They pushed and shoved to come close and touch Jesus. People with evil spirits in them fell on the ground in front of Jesus shouting, "You are the Son of God!" As before, Jesus told them to keep quiet, but they didn't always obey. Fearing that the crowd would push him into the lake, Jesus told his disciples to have a small boat ready for him to escape.

His popularity, compassion for the hurting, and exercise of supernatural power fulfilled a quotation from God that Isaiah had written more than eight hundred years earlier:

> This is my chosen servant;
> I love him and am delighted with him.
> I will put my Spirit on him.
> He will proclaim justice to all nations.
> He won't argue or scream.
> No one will hear him shouting in the streets.
> He won't break off someone who is like a
> bruised reed.
> He won't snuff out anyone who is like a
> smoldering wick.
> Eventually he will make justice victorious.
> In his name the whole world will have hope.

The picture of Jesus was coming into focus. He was much more than a rabbi with a new spin on religion. He was better at healing than any physician though not primarily concerned about physical health. A teacher of truth, he was Messiah—the King announcing the kingdom's arrival. His message was framed to communicate God's expectations of people. His strategy was to influence and shape the lives of a few who would then take the message out to large numbers of people who hadn't yet seen or heard him.

CHAPTER FOUR

H e often slipped away from the crowds that mobbed him all day in order to pray alone—early in the morning, at other times all night. Actually, prayer was central to Jesus' life and relationship to God, and it preceded his most important decisions as he sought the counsel and confirmation of his Father in heaven.

Out of the thousands who thronged around him, listening to his teaching and hoping to see a miracle, Jesus chose and endorsed twelve men as his primary corps of disciples and friends—twelve, parallel to the twelve tribes of the nation of Israel. With no shortage of candidates, he could have chosen a hundred or a thousand.

He had previously extended invitations to Simon, Andrew, James, John, and Matthew, so they were already on the list of candidates. They had accepted the invitation and traveled with him around Galilee and south to Jerusalem and back. Now it was time to add seven more to complete his group. After a full night of prayer alone, he announced the final dozen. Destined to be more than disciples—learners—they were to become apostles, "sent ones" commissioned by Jesus to receive his most intense teaching. They then would go out with authority to preach his message and to exercise his power, including driving out demons from those who were possessed.

Excitement must have run high as Jesus announced their names:
- Simon Peter
- James the son of Zebedee
- John the son of Zebedee
- Andrew

- Philip
- Bartholomew
- Matthew
- Thomas
- James the son of Alphaeus
- Thaddaeus
- Simon the Zealot
- Judas Iscariot

Training the twelve § and teaching the crowd overlapped on the day Jesus preached his most famous sermon. He climbed the mountain outside Capernaum, followed by

§ Ordinary men, eleven of them were natives of Galilee. Judas was from Kerioth in Judea. None was theologically trained or part of the official religious leadership in Israel. Many had nicknames, most of which were given by Jesus: Simon was "Rocky"; James and John were "the sons of thunder"; Thomas was "the twin"; the second Simon was "the zealot" (a political designation). Thaddaeus also went by the name Judas the son of James. Judas from Kerioth was distinguished from Thaddaeus/Judas by the nickname Iscariot, which means "the man from Kerioth." Two were brothers. Four were fishermen, one was a tax collector, one was a political loyalist, and the rest were never known by their occupations.

his chosen dozen along with a large crowd of seekers, many of whom wanted to be healed. When they reached a level place large enough for all to sit on the ground, Jesus stopped and began healing their diseases, casting out evil spirits, and managing those crowding around who simply wanted to touch him. There was enormous supernatural power flowing from Jesus that day. When everyone was satisfied enough to settle down for teaching, Jesus began his Sermon on the Mount, about how to live as a citizen of the kingdom of God.

KINGDOM OF GOD

The nation of Israel had high hopes for the reign of God on earth. The Jews looked back to earlier history when they sought to live as God's people in the land they believed had been promised to them. After generations of wars, captivity, humiliation, and difficulties, they yearned for God to intervene and bring his rule down to earth. In Jesus' words, "May your will be done on earth as it is done in heaven."

The "kingdom of God" or the "kingdom of heaven" became a central theme of Jesus' teaching. He presented God's kingdom in opposition to Satan's kingdom. He taught that God's kingdom was better and stronger, that it was both present and future, confirmed by Jesus' miracles and clearly connected to him as the King. His message invited his listeners to become citizens of God's kingdom through repentance and belief—repentance of sin and belief in the good news about God's sovereignty and salvation.

When he preached his Sermon on the Mount, Jesus summarized his frequent teaching about the ethics of the kingdom of God. It was a lesson on how to live as a loyal subject of God—not primarily by laws but by love.

The more his listeners heard, the more they began to understand that Jesus had a different notion of the kingdom of God than what most of them expected. They were looking for a political government with all the usual trappings of geography, army, and laws. Jesus had a much more significant vision, that of God invading history to bring his final rule. God's reign was embodied in Jesus as King—not of a nation but of individuals.

This is what Jesus taught that day.

BLESSINGS FIRST

Blessed are the poor in spirit, for yours is the kingdom of heaven.

Blessed are you who are poor, for yours is the kingdom of God.

Blessed are those who mourn, for you shall be comforted.

Blessed are you who weep now, for you will laugh.

Blessed are the meek, for you shall inherit the earth.

Blessed are those who hunger and thirst for righteousness, for you
　　shall be filled.

Blessed are you who hunger now, for you will be satisfied.

Blessed are the merciful, for you shall obtain mercy.

Blessed are the pure in heart, for you shall see God.

Blessed are the peacemakers, for you shall be called sons of God.

Blessed are those who are persecuted for righteousness' sake, for
　　yours is the kingdom of heaven.

Blessed are you when people hate you, persecute you,
　　insult you, and reject you as evil because of the Son of Man.

Rejoice and be happy, because you will receive a great reward in heaven. After all, this is exactly the same way that previous generations treated the prophets.

TROUBLES NEXT

But woe to you who are rich, for you have already received your comfort.

Woe to you whose stomachs are full, for you are going to go hungry.

Woe to you who are now laughing, for you will mourn and cry.

Woe to you when everybody speaks well of you, for that is the way earlier generations treated the false prophets.

BLESSING AND RESPONSIBILITY

You are the salt of the earth, but if salt loses its taste, how can it be made salty again? It's good for nothing except to be tossed on the ground and trampled underfoot.

You are the light of the world. Cities built on the side of a hill can't be hidden. Folks don't light an oil lamp and then cover it with a bowl—they put the lamp on a stand so it illumines the whole house. In the same way, shine your light so that everyone can see the good you do and will praise your Father in heaven.

OBEYING THE LAW

Don't get the wrong impression. I am not here to get rid of Scriptures, God's Law, and Prophets. The reason I came is to fulfill them. The truth is that even if the earth below and heaven above disappear, the tiniest part of the Law will not go away until it has accomplished everything it says. Keep the Law, because anyone who doesn't will be least honored and anyone who does will be most honored in the kingdom of heaven. You should do better than the best of the Pharisees and Law teachers; otherwise, you won't make it into God's kingdom.

You know what was taught so many years ago: "Do not murder, because you'll be judged if you do." Well, I'm telling you that you will be guilty just for getting angry with your brother. Nowadays, if someone calls his brother a "good-for-nothing fool," he can be hauled into court before the Sanhedrin. But anyone who says, "You fool!" is really risking hellfire.

We're talking about a whole different approach to living here. Suppose you are in the temple offering a gift, and you remember someone has something against you. You should leave your gift waiting at the altar while you first go and make things right with that person. Then come back and give your gift.

When you're on the verge of a lawsuit with an enemy of yours, settle as fast as you can. Otherwise you might end up before a judge who will have you thrown into prison until you lose all your money.

Let's move on to the next one of the Ten Commandments. You know what it says: "Do not commit adultery." I want you to think of it this way—if you have lust inside even though you don't actually go to bed with that person, you've committed adultery in your heart. Have the right kind of morality on the inside so that you would rather tear out your eye or cut off your hand than commit sin. After all, isn't it better to lose an eye or hand than go to hell with your whole body intact?

It's written in the Law that you can get a divorce with the proper legal document. It may be legal, but that doesn't make it right. Anyone who gets a divorce, unless it's because of marital unfaithfulness, causes his wife to become an adulteress. And marrying an adulteress makes you an adulterer yourself.

Another law says, "When you swear by an oath, make sure you do what you said you would do. Keep promises you make to the Lord." Some people are pretty creative in the oaths they take, swearing by heaven as God's throne or earth as God's footstool or Jerusalem as the city of God. Others say, "I swear by my own head that I'll do what I promise" (as if we can even control which hairs grow in black or white!). Simplify your promises. Don't swear by anything. Just say yes that you are going to do something and then do it. Just say no, you're not going to do something and then don't do it. Don't let Satan twist your words into fake promises that you don't really intend to keep.

Another common old saying is "eye for eye; tooth for tooth." Don't be so determined to get even. When someone hits you in the face, don't hit him back, even if you have to let him hit the other side of your face. When someone sues you for your coat, just let him have it—throw in another piece of clothing to be extra generous. And when someone makes you walk a mile, go two miles. Be generous. Give when asked and lend when requested.

"Love your neighbor and hate your enemy" is another common expression that many live by. But I tell you that there is a better way: love your enemies, do good to people who hate you, bless people who curse you, and pray for people who persecute you. When you live out this kind of love, you will be called the children of your Father in heaven. Treat others the way you would want them to treat you. Consider the example of the Father who causes his sun to rise on evil people as well as on good people; he sends rain on the righteous and the unrighteous.

After all, what credit do you get for loving those who love you? Everybody does that—even sinners. It's not a big deal when you do good to those who have been good to you. Sinners do the same. Lending to a borrower who is sure to pay you back really isn't all that noble. Don't sinners lend to sinners if they are sure of repayment? Instead, love your enemies, treat them well, and even lend to those who probably won't pay you back. This kind of love brings a great reward because you'll be like the Most High God who is kind even to those who are ungrateful and evil. Be like God—merciful to all.

DON'T BE A HYPOCRITE!

When you do good and righteous acts for others, be careful not to show off in front of everyone, because that will disqualify you from God's reward. It's hypocritical to pretend you are being like God and then draw attention to yourself and seek praise. Even if you have seen hypocrites in the synagogue or out on the street, don't be like them.

They receive all their reward from human praise. You keep your good deeds a secret and trust the Father to reward you later.

It's the same when you pray. You've seen those who love to pray out loud on the street or in the synagogue so that everyone will see and hear them. They are hypocrites who are showing off and praying to get the reward of human recognition. It is far better if you hide out in your room with the door closed, praying to the invisible God. Trust God the Father to see and hear your secret prayers and fully reward you in his own way at the right time and place.

And when you're praying, be careful what you say. Don't talk nonsense like pagans who think prayers are better heard when they are long. Your Father doesn't need a long prayer with a high word count; he knows what you need even before you start praying.

Here's an example of how you should pray:

> Our Father in heaven,
> hallowed be your name,
> your kingdom come,
> your will be done
> on earth as it is in heaven.
> Give us today our daily bread.
> Forgive us our debts,
> as we also have forgiven our debtors.
> And lead us not into temptation,
> but deliver us from the evil one.

If you really forgive those who sin against you, your heavenly Father will forgive you. On the other hand, if you won't forgive others, then don't expect your Father to forgive your sins.

To avoid showing off like a hypocrite, be careful what you look like when you fast for spiritual purposes. Some actually make their faces look sick so that observers will give them praise for fasting. You should make your face look clean and healthy so others won't know you are fasting. As long as the Father knows, that should be good enough for you. Remember: God sees and knows and will properly reward you.

AVOID MATERIALISM

Don't stockpile possessions here on earth where moths eat cloth, rust corrodes metal, and thieves break in and steal our valuables. Instead, stockpile treasures in heaven, where there aren't any moths, rust, or burglars. Put your valuables where you want your heart to be, because that's what's going to happen anyway. Our hearts and our treasures usually stick together.

Your eye is the "light of your body." In other words, without your eyes your whole body and life are in darkness. If your eyes are good, they illumine everything else for you to see.

The eye is the lamp of the body. If your eyes are focused on what is good, that's what your body will see. But if your eyes are bad and focused on the wrong things, your whole body will be full of darkness. So focus on generosity and not on stinginess, and that's the way your whole life will be lived.

No one can serve two masters or follow two leaders. If you try, you'll just end up hating one of them and loving the other. You have to make a choice. It's the same with your loyalty to possessions or God. You have to choose which is most important. You cannot serve both God and money.

LIVING WITHOUT WORRY

Don't worry about how you are going to live life—what you'll eat, drink, or wear. These things are necessary, but there is more to life than food and more to our bodies than what we wear. Compare yourself to the birds you see flying around—they're not like farmers who sow, reap, and store in order to eat. Your heavenly Father takes care of them. Don't you know that you are much more important to God than the birds? Besides, worrying won't make you taller or add hours to your life.

Do you worry about clothes? Look at the lilies growing out in the fields. They don't manufacture clothes to wear, but they look beautiful the way God has dressed them. King Solomon himself never looked so good! God dresses up these flowers that have really short lives and get burned when the field is set on fire. Poof! They're gone. Well, if God does such a great job for lilies, you can count on him clothing you. Come on, have more faith! You don't need to worry and say, "What are we going to eat?" or "Where are we going to get clothes to wear?" That's the kind of talk that comes from unbelieving pagans. Be assured that your Father is watching out for your needs. So don't worry about tomorrow! There's a much better way: make God's kingdom your top priority. Do everything God's way. Then you don't need to worry, because God will take care of everything you need.

Let tomorrow worry about itself. Every day has enough trouble of its own without borrowing future worries.

Attitudes Toward Others, Toward God

Don't be a condemning judge of others, so that you won't be judged and condemned yourself. Instead, forgive others and you will be forgiven. Give to others and you will generously receive. Just as you judge others, you will also be judged. The same standard will be applied to your life that you apply to others' lives.

Maybe an illustration will help you to understand. Can someone who is blind lead someone else who is blind? Won't they both fall into a hole? Or compare to a teacher and a student—don't students often end up a lot like their teachers? So then, when it comes to making judgments about other people, be very careful. Don't be like a blind man who can't see where he is going, and don't be the kind of teacher who teaches students the wrong way to judge.

Picture yourself trying to get a tiny speck of sawdust out of somebody's eye while you have a wooden plank stuck in your own eye! How can you possibly say to that other person, "Let me get that speck out of your eye for you." Come on, you would be a complete hypocrite. Get that plank out of your own eye first, and then you can help the other guy.

None of this is to say that there isn't a place for appropriate and necessary judgment. Just don't be a hypocrite, criticizing others without first considering your own problems. When it comes to those necessary judgments, you should avoid giving what is sacred to un-believing dogs or what is precious to pigs. If you don't make this judg-ment, you'll risk being trampled and attacked by those dogs and pigs.

ASKING GOD FOR WHAT YOU NEED

Go ahead and ask God and he'll give to you. Seek and you'll find. Knock on God's door and watch it open up to you. After all, if your son asked for bread, you wouldn't give him a stone, would you? If your daughter requested a fish, would you give her a snake? Of course not, so you certainly can count on your heavenly Father—who is bet-ter than any earthly parent—to give good gifts to his children who ask him.

To sum all this up in just a few words: do to others what you would have them do to you!

TAKING THE NARROW WAY

You have a choice to make. You may choose the life of God's king-dom or make up your own laws and live your own way. I invite you to take the right way even though it is through a narrow gate. The wide gate along the broad road is on a path to destruction. A lot of people make that choice, but they are wrong. It's far better to be counted among the lesser number that takes the small gate along the narrow road that leads to life.

You will need to watch out for false prophets who promote the big gate and wide road. They dress up like sheep but are really dan-gerous wolves in sheep's clothing. If you watch carefully, you'll be able to tell who they are by the fruit they bear. Grapes don't come from thorn bushes or figs from thistle plants. Good trees don't have bad fruit, and bad trees don't have good fruit. You can tell a tree by its fruit. It's the same with people—evil fruit means an evil person; good fruit means a good person. What overflows from someone's heart comes out of that person's mouth. When trying to figure out who is a false prophet and who is a true prophet, remember that you can recognize them by their fruit.

Just because someone says to me, "Lord, Lord," doesn't mean they are going to be citizens in the kingdom of heaven. The only way into the kingdom of heaven is to do the will of my Father who is in heaven. It's not just saying the right words. When the day of decision comes there will be many who tell me, "Lord, Lord, didn't we prophecy, cast out demons, and perform miracles in your name?" I'll tell them in clear terms, "I never knew you. Get away from me, you who lived by your own laws instead of the laws of God."

In conclusion, I want you to think of what I've told you today as a rock-solid foundation for living in the kingdom of God. Every one of you who has heard what I've said and then does what you've heard is like the person who wisely builds a house on the rock. When the storm comes with wind, rain, and floods, that house stands strong because of the solid foundation. On the other hand, every one of you who has heard what I've said today and doesn't do any of it is like the person who foolishly builds a house on sand. When the storms hit this house, it comes crashing down.

———— ❂ ————

When Jesus finished his sermon, the crowds sat there in amazement over all he had said. They had learned more about God and life that day than at any other time in their lives. What amazed them most was the authority with which Jesus taught. Jesus told the truth with conviction from God and made them want to believe and do everything he said.

The crowds who followed him up the mountain followed him back down, wondering what he would say and do next.

CHAPTER FIVE

The local centurion had given a very large financial contribution to build the synagogue at Capernaum, and the elders of the synagogue insisted that Jesus grant him special treatment. Jesus' popularity meant he couldn't see everyone, but a large donor was considered to deserve a move to the head of the line.

No doubt the centurion was indeed a special man. His title came from the early organization of the Roman army, when soldiers were arranged in groups of one hundred (a "century") and the commander of the hundred was called a centurion. §

This centurion was a kind man, concerned about the poor health of one of his slaves. Owning slaves was not unusual among Roman citizens; up to one third of the population of some major cities were slaves. They were legally the same as possessions, with no human rights. § But the Capernaum centurion was different. He highly valued his terminally ill slave and was willing to do anything possible to save his life.

Making him even more unusual was the fact that he had come to love the nation of Israel. Many Roman officers hated Israel. The Jewish territories were classified as a hardship

§ The title continued even after the number changed. It came to describe the officer equivalent to a captain in a modern army—in charge of a company consisting of at least two platoons. As the centurion in charge of the Roman military presence in and around Capernaum, he was the ranking Roman officer of the area and had the authority of a local emperor. People had to do whatever he said.

§ An owner could overwork, abuse, or even kill a slave without getting into legal trouble. Sick and old slaves were particularly at risk because they had little economic value. Some slaveholders would just put them out when they no longer could work—not emancipated, just evicted. Such slaves were left with little more than desperation and death.

assignment. Seasoned soldiers with battle experience were the ones ordered to keep Roman rule in the volatile politics of Israel. Jews demonstrated antipathy toward the Roman occupation army, and many Roman soldiers were cruel and hateful toward Jews. Not this centurion. Perhaps it was because he was one of the many decent people of the ancient world and he had grown tired of Roman morals and polytheism. He saw a better way in Judaism with high standards and belief in one God. It was enough to make him give a very generous sum for the construction of the Capernaum synagogue. Not that he made that much on only a centurion's salary, but many officers came from wealthy families and had private funds.

When the centurion heard that Jesus was back in town, he asked the elders to request a miracle. He had to wonder if Jesus would even talk to him, since he was a Gentile, so he used the elders as a go-between. The elders of the synagogue pled with Jesus, "This Roman loves the nation of Israel and gave a big contribution to build the synagogue, so he deserves a miracle." Jesus agreed to go and started out with them toward the centurion's home.

As Jesus neared the house, the centurion sent some of his friends to say to him, "Lord, you really don't need to trouble yourself. Despite what the synagogue leaders told you, I don't deserve to have you come under my roof. That's why I didn't come directly to you myself. I know I'm not worthy of you or your time. But I also know that if you will just say the word, my servant will be healed. I know how it works—I am an officer with soldiers under my command. If I tell one of them to go, he goes. If I order another one to come, he comes. If I tell my servant to do something, he does it."

Jesus was amazed by the centurion's message. He stopped and turned to the crowd around him. "Take a good look at this Gentile," he said. "I want you to know that I've never found great faith like this before. Not even in Israel." He never did go to the house, but when the men with the message returned to the centurion, the dying slave was perfectly well.

A little later Jesus left Capernaum for a small rural village called Nain. It was a day's journey there and another day's journey back, but the distance didn't deter the crowds. His disciples and a large group of followers went with him the entire distance, filled with noisy enthusiasm all the way.

As they approached the village gate, they met another large crowd. A funeral procession, complete with professional mourners wailing, hired musicians playing funeral dirges, and a dead man being carried to burial, came toward Jesus. The mother of the deceased, a widow, was sobbing uncontrollably. § Now she was alone. There was no husband to grieve with her. No son to take care of her.

Jesus' heart went out to her. His own mother was a widow. He gently told the woman, "Don't cry." Then he reached over and touched the bier carrying the body wrapped mummy-style in white. The shocked pallbearers stopped, and the two boisterous groups fell silent, for it was against religious law for anyone other than the burial preparers to touch a dead body. Then Jesus said with authority, "Young man, listen to what I'm going to say to you. Get up!" The crowds now gasped in wonder. Was this man a fool or did he actually have the power to bring a dead man back to life?

§ Death of a family member is always difficult but especially for a mother who had lost her only son that day. In English there is a word for a child who loses his parents (orphan), a husband who loses his wife (widower), and a wife who loses her husband (widow), but there is no word to describe a parent who loses a child.

They gasped again when the dead man sat up and talked. Jesus gently gave him back to his mother. "A great prophet from God is here in our midst," the people exclaimed. "God has come to help his people." The news of the dead man brought back to life spread near and far.

When Jesus performed miracles, he usually added teaching, and when he taught, his audiences often wondered about his connection to John the Baptizer. Before John was executed, he had been imprisoned in one of King Herod's dungeons. Although previously a man of great conviction and courage, he too had questions about Jesus. Was it possible he wasn't the Messiah after all?

John was allowed to have visitors, and he asked a few of his friends to find Jesus and ask him if he was really the promised Messiah or if they should wait for someone else.

Jesus was neither offended nor defensive when he heard John's question. He simply encouraged the messengers to look at the evidence. "Go back to the prison and tell John what you've heard and seen," Jesus instructed them. "The blind receive sight, the lame walk, those with leprosy are cured, the deaf hear, the dead are raised, and the good news is preached to the poor." To encourage John's faith under pressure, Jesus added, "Blessed is the man who doesn't fall away from his faith on account of me." He knew that when John heard what was happening, his faith would be strong again.

Now that John was dead, some of his followers were trying to decide if they would switch their allegiance to Jesus. "What did you expect to see when you went out into the desert looking for a prophet? A reed blowing over in the wind? No? Then what did you go out to see? A man all dressed up in fancy clothes? No, those who wear fancy clothes are in royal palaces. Then what did you go out to see? A prophet? Of course you expected to see a prophet, and no ordinary prophet at that! When you went into the desert to see John, you met the one about whom the Scriptures give God's promise: 'I will send my messenger ahead of you, who will prepare your way before you.'

"I'm telling you the truth," Jesus continued. "No one greater has ever been born to a woman; yet the lowest citizen in the kingdom of heaven is greater than he is. From the time John the Baptizer started preaching until now, people have been trying to force themselves into the kingdom of heaven. Now I'm telling you that John is the one you've read about in the sacred writings by the Prophets and in the Laws of Scripture. He is the fulfillment of the promised coming of an Elijah to get things ready for the Messiah.

"I hope you're listening to this," Jesus exhorted his audience. "It's really important!"

Affirming the greatness of John, Jesus also made it clear that John was only one prophet in God's progression that led to something and someone far greater. The response among his listeners was divided between the believers (who accepted John's message and were baptized by him) and unbelievers (Pharisees and experts in the law who rejected John's message and had not been baptized by him).

Speaking directly to the skeptics in the audience, Jesus used an everyday example to challenge them to believe. "What analogy explains this generation? They are like children sitting in the marketplaces and shouting out, 'We played the flute for you, but you didn't dance; we sang a funeral song, and you didn't mourn.' And when John fasted from food and drink, they criticized him, saying, 'He has a demon.' Now when the Son of Man eats and drinks, they complain, 'This man is a glutton and a drunk, who hangs out with tax collectors and all kinds of sinners.' "

Jesus then used a popular proverb to summarize this teaching. "But the wisdom of what a person says is proved right or wrong by his or her actions."

The mental picture for the listeners was that of two groups of children. Group one tried to engage group two by playing happy music on a flute, but group two just stood there and refused to dance. So the children in group one played a sad funeral song, but group two just stood there and refused to pretend they were crying. They simply wouldn't play either way. The skeptics wouldn't believe when John preached repentance with austerity, Jesus was telling them, and they wouldn't believe when Jesus preached faith with joy.

Unbelief deeply troubled Jesus. He was aggravated by people who saw his miracles and heard his teachings but refused to change their ways or believe his message. The crowds began to see another side of the teacher from Nazareth as he denounced the cities where he had focused much of his attention. He compared proud Jewish towns to neighboring cities they considered quite pagan, such as Tyre and Sidon. He even compared them to the ancient city of Sodom that was destroyed by God for unbelief and immorality two thousand years earlier.

Jesus said, "Woe to you, Korazin! Troubles to you, Bethsaida! If the miracles you've experienced had been performed in Tyre and Sidon, they would have repented long ago in sackcloth and ashes. But let me tell you, it will be more tolerable for Tyre and Sidon on the Day of Judgment than it will be for you. And you, Capernaum, do you think that you will you be lifted up to the skies? No, you will go down to the depths. If the miracles performed in your town had been performed in Sodom, it would still exist. Let me tell you, Capernaum, that Sodom will be better off on the Day of Judgment than you will be."

Before they had time to react to these condemnations, Jesus broke out into a prayer. While addressed to God, the prayer was also a teaching for those in the crowd who did believe. There was a possibility that believers might think Jesus had lumped everyone in the unbeliever category, and he wanted to affirm the people of simple faith while clearly condemning the skeptics. Jesus prayed, "Praise to you, Father, Lord of heaven and earth, because you have kept these truths hidden from the religious elite and revealed them to little children and ordinary people. Yes, Father, that's the way you wanted it to be."

The prayer continued with an explanation of Jesus' own special relationship to God and how he extends that relationship to his believers. "Absolutely everything has been committed to me by my Father. He is the only one who really knows the Son. And the only one who really knows the Father is the Son and any other whom the Son decides to tell about the Father."

Here was a fascinating series of contrasts: belief and unbelief; Jesus' new way and the old religious way. Jesus summed it all up by comparing yokes. §

"Everyone who is tired and burdened, come to me, and I'll give you rest," Jesus invited. "Take my yoke on your shoulders and you'll learn from me a way of life that is gentle and humble of heart. Your souls will be rested and strengthened. You'll quickly discover that my yoke is light to bear and easy to wear."

The common people of Galilee loved Jesus' miracles and message. Those in the religious elite were increasingly provoked and angry. But not all of them. Some were curious and open to learn more about Jesus. One open-minded Pharisee named Simon (a common name) invited Jesus to his home for dinner, and Jesus accepted. §

§ Yokes, of course, are wooden frames by which two farm animals are joined at their necks for working together. However, rabbis used the term to refer to their whole system of teaching and lifestyle. For example, the yoke of the Pharisees was difficult because of all the rules to learn and live by that they laid on the people.

That night a woman showed up who wasn't on the guest list. It was surprising that Simon the Pharisee allowed her into his home, because her sinful life was well known around town. Prostitution was fairly common, often because of economic necessity. Whatever the

§ Houses often were built in a square around a courtyard. Formal meals were served in the courtyard with dinner guests reclining on couches around a low table. They lay on their sides, heads propped up with their left hands, feet bare and using their right hands to eat. When renowned teachers or celebrities were invited to dinner, the home often was opened to the public. The host provided cushions around the perimeter of the courtyard so that open-invitation visitors had a place to sit, watch, and listen. If the guest of honor was a celebrity, the home was usually packed with spectators.

reason for her behavior, she would have known she was living an immoral lifestyle and was looked down upon by the respectable religious people of the community. She had heard Jesus and was drawn to his message of compassion and forgiveness. She wanted very much to see him or she never would have risked an appearance in such company. She wore an alabaster jar of expensive perfume on a cord around her neck as a form of jewelry.

She pressed her way through the crowd until she stood right behind Jesus § as he was eating dinner. Stationed by his feet, she began to cry. She attempted to weep in silence, but her emotions took over until she was sobbing, her tears flowing. Everyone now could hear her but probably pretended not to notice out of embarrassment. Her tears were so profuse they

§ Only young girls wore their hair down; adult women bound up their hair for everyone except their husbands. Loose flowing hair was considered a sign of sexual impropriety.

dripped off her face onto Jesus' bare feet. Realizing what had happened, she fell to her knees and did something a woman never was supposed to do in public—she reached up and unfastened her long hair so it cascaded down in front of her. § Then she used her long hair like a towel to dry Jesus' feet.

It was a shocking sight. Most guests didn't want a woman like her there in the first place. First she made a scene with her crying, and then she broke one of the customs of society when she let her hair down. Even worse, who would use hair for a towel in any culture, especially to wipe a stranger's dusty feet?

As if all of this were not enough, finally she held Jesus' feet and kissed them.

Then she took out her alabaster container and poured perfume on Jesus' feet. § It was as if this woman lost track of everyone and everything except Jesus.

§ Alabaster is a soft stone, comparatively easy to carve into a container. Perfume was very expensive and used on special occasions or as the family's emergency savings account. It was never to be wasted.

At first no one said anything. Perhaps the guests and servants thought the host should handle the situation, and the host was waiting for Jesus to react. But Simon certainly had his private thoughts: "So this man is supposed to be a prophet? If he were, he would know what kind of woman is touching him—that she's a sinner." A true prophet should know something this important without being told.

Jesus sensed what Simon was thinking and said, "Simon, let me tell you something."

"Tell me, teacher," Simon responded.

§ A denarius was a coin equivalent to one day's wages for a typical worker.

"Two men owed money to a creditor. One owed him five hundred denarii, § and the other owed fifty. Neither one had the money to pay him back, so he canceled both of their debts. Now, here's the question: which one of them will love him most?"

Simon cautiously replied with the obvious answer, "I suppose it would be the one who had the bigger debt forgiven."

"Good answer!" Jesus said.

Then Jesus turned toward the woman and said to Simon, "Do you see this woman? Let's make a comparison here. I came into your house as an honored guest, and you did not give me any water to wash my feet, but she wet my feet with her tears and wiped them with her hair. You didn't give me a welcoming kiss, but this woman hasn't stopped kissing my feet. You didn't put oil on my head, but she has poured perfume on my feet. Therefore, Simon, her many sins have been forgiven, for she loved much. But whoever has been forgiven little loves little."

These were stinging words for Simon to hear in front of his guests. A good host would have offered water to wash Jesus' feet; roads were dusty and foot washing was a common courtesy. A good host would have greeted Jesus with a kiss; that was the standard cultural greeting. A good host would have put some olive oil on Jesus' head, also the common custom.

Then Jesus turned from Simon and spoke directly to the woman for the first time: "I forgive your sins. Your faith has saved you; go in peace."

Simon stayed silent, but the other guests began to murmur to one another, "Who does he think he is? Does he think he can even forgive sins?"

After this Jesus became more mobile, moving from town to town around Galilee. Those who believed grew in their faith. Those who didn't believe grew in their opposition.

The makeup of the crowds changed as he traveled around, but the twelve disciples were almost always with him no matter where he went. During these next weeks around Galilee several women joined the inner circle:

• Mary Magdalene was from the town of Magdala (this society

often lacked surnames but identified those with common first names by their town of origin, father's name, or a nickname). She was possessed by seven demons until Jesus called them out of her. After that she became a devoted believer and follower.

- Joanna, the wife of Chuza, an official of Herod Antipas. She was part of the royal court because her husband held a high and trusted position in the government.

- Susanna and some others.

These women were among the most generous financial supporters of Jesus. He no longer worked in the Nazareth carpenter shop and had no accumulated wealth. Like other first-century rabbis, Jesus depended on the generosity of benefactors.

As people polarized over who Jesus was, his closest followers were eyewitnesses to increasingly antagonistic exchanges between Jesus and his enemies. One of these encounters happened when a demon-possessed man who was blind and mute was brought to Jesus. Jesus healed him and he could both see and talk. The seekers in the crowd were enormously impressed and asked, "Could this be the Son of David?" §

§ Another religious reference to Jesus being the Messiah from God.

Neither the Pharisees nor any of Jesus' immediate family were present for this miracle, but they had quick evaluations when they were told what happened. His family said, "He is out of his mind!" and decided they needed to take charge of him and bring him back home to Nazareth. The Pharisees said that Jesus was demon-possessed: "The only reason he can drive out demons is because he works for Beelzebub,§ the prince of all demons!"

§ Beelzebub was a popular nickname for Satan (the word means "Lord of the Flies").

Clearly the accusation of demon-possession was more serious than the accusation of insanity—Jesus' miracles and teaching easily convinced most people that he was sane. But the demon-possession accusation acknowledged that he exercised extraordinary supernatural power when he healed the man who could not see or speak.

However, they were claiming that it was evil power Jesus used—he ordered demons and they obeyed him because he was himself a superior demon.

Once again Jesus knew their thoughts and answered them before they were spoken publicly. He told them that their thinking didn't make sense because Satan would never drive out demons; that would be self-defeating. "Divided kingdoms are self-destructive. The same is true of cities and families that are divided—they are wrecked. If Satan drives out Satan, he is divided against himself. How can Satan's kingdom stand if what you accuse is true? Besides, if I drive out demons by Beelzebub, how do your people drive them out? So then, they will be your judges. But if I drive out demons by the Spirit of God, then God's kingdom has arrived here in your presence.

"Or let me explain it this way. How can anyone enter a strong man's house and steal his possessions unless he first ties up that strong man? Only then can he rob his house." Jesus looked around the group.

"Whoever is not with me is against me," he said, "and whoever doesn't help makes things worse. Listen to what I'm going to say because it is really important. God will forgive every other sin and blasphemy except blasphemy against the Holy Spirit. Someone who speaks against the Son of Man will be forgiven, but anyone who speaks against the Holy Spirit will never be forgiven.

"Grow a good tree and you'll pick good fruit. Grow a bad tree and you'll pick bad fruit. The fruit you pick tells you whether the tree is good or bad. You are a pack of poisonous desert vipers—that's why everything you say is poison. Mouths speak what flows out of hearts. If someone is full of good, good comes out; if someone is full of evil, evil comes out. Be sure of this, that everyone is someday going to be judged by God for every thoughtless and careless word spoken. Your words are going to acquit or convict in God's courtroom." Jesus had called them all to accountability. Crediting Satan for the work of God, they were calling good evil. Jesus' concluding warning was serious:

they were at risk of never being forgiven for their sins.

Some of the Pharisees and teachers of religious law came to Jesus with a proposal. They seemed open and earnest, saying, "Teacher, we would like to see you perform a miracle." By now Jesus had given up on them. Their criticisms, attacks, and unbelief wouldn't change even if he did a miracle for them.

He answered, "You know who asks for miracles just to be entertained? The members of a wicked and adulterous generation ask for a miraculous sign! Well, you're not going to get a miracle except the sign of the prophet Jonah. Just as Jonah spent three days and three nights in the belly of a large fish, so the Son of Man will spend three days and three nights in the heart of the earth. The people from Jonah's generation who lived in Nineveh will stand up at God's final judgment and condemn this generation. And do you know why? Because they repented at the preaching of Jonah. And now someone much greater than Jonah is here, so this generation has a bigger reason to repent. Do you remember the Queen of the South who traveled all the way to Jerusalem to hear the wisdom of King Solomon? She will stand up at God's judgment to condemn this generation because she came so far to hear Solomon's wisdom and you won't listen to my greater wisdom that can be heard right here in front of you." §

§ Jesus was referring to a pair of famous stories in Israel's ancient history. Jonah was God's prophet sent to the large city of Nineveh to call for repentance from sin. He was swallowed by a large fish en route and miraculously preserved from death. Also, the Queen of Sheba traveled to Jerusalem to hear the wisdom of Solomon but learned a lot less than Jesus was teaching.

Although the subject was serious, Jesus added some wit to the conversation. This is the way Jesus made them laugh and learn. "When an evil spirit moves out of a person, it looks everywhere for a new home and can't find one. Then it says, 'I'll just go back to the house I left.' When it arrives, it finds the house vacant, neat, and clean. Then the evil spirit puts out an invitation to seven of its friends that are spirits worse than it is. They all move in together. The poor person is worse off than at the start. And that's just the way it is with this whole generation of people in this country."

———— ❋ ————

The stress on Jesus was enormous. To teach truth and do good he had to deal with criticism and threats everywhere he went. His enemies negatively interpreted almost everything he said and did.

His celebrity status drew even his family into the controversies. They really hadn't had much contact with him since he moved his home from Nazareth to Capernaum, but they were convinced that Jesus was out of control and needed help. If he wasn't going to come to them, they had to go to him. So his brothers talked their mother into coming along, and they all went to where Jesus was teaching.

Unable to get through the crowd packed around him, they sent a message to Jesus. One of Jesus' disciples told him, "Your mother and brothers are outside looking for you." Contrary to expectations, he declined to see them, asking, "Who are my mother and my brothers?" Then he answered his own question, pointing at his most loyal followers in the circle around him. "These disciples are my mother and my brothers! Anyone who does God's will is my brother and sister and mother."

But Jesus couldn't keep teaching like this. The constant mix of friends and enemies in every audience was calling for a different approach.

CHAPTER SIX

J esus loved to tell stories, and parables were his favorite kind to tell—memorable comparisons to everyday life. Details were included, but they were seldom central to Jesus' message. Parables usually had just one main point and perhaps a few sub points of lesser importance.

Some parables were so clear with obvious meaning that every listener immediately caught the point. Some were less clear, almost like a code, intended for Jesus' followers to understand while his enemies were confused. This approach kept his critics controlled so Jesus' time was less consumed by the argumentative harassment of his opponents. A few of those stories were so obscure that Jesus had to take his closest followers aside and explain what he meant. Certainly he was following an ancient Jewish teaching tradition. The Old Testament psalmist wrote:

> My people, hear my teaching;
> Listen to the words from my mouth.
> I will speak in parables;
> I will reveal things hidden for a very long time.

It was later on the same day that had been so combative with both the Pharisees and his own family that Jesus went to the lakeshore to teach. The crowds were so large that he again boarded a boat to teach the people lining the shore. He told them nine parables about the kingdom of heaven, describing the new order he had come to establish.

PARABLE OF THE SOILS

A farmer went out to plant seed. As the seed was scattered, some hit the road and birds quickly came and ate it. Some fell on rocks with very sparse soil; it grew fast, but the hot sun wilted the new plants because they didn't have decent roots. Some fell where there were lots of weeds growing; the seed took root, but the plants were strangled to death by the weeds. The rest of the seed was scattered on good soil, where it grew very well, producing a harvest of thirty, sixty, or a hundred times as much as was planted.

Now, let me tell you what this parable means. When the message about God's kingdom is heard but not understood, the devil and his demons swoop in to grab the seed that was sown in the hearer's heart. That's the meaning of the seed on the road. When the message is heard and happily received by a listener without roots, that listener doesn't last very long. That's the meaning of the seed in the shallow soil. When the message is heard and choked out of the listener's life by worries about life and the distractions of wealth, the listener doesn't grow and is fruitless. But when the message is heard and understood, it is like the fertile soil that produced a bountiful crop.

The main point of the parable: The same message receives different responses from different people.

PARABLE OF THE SPROUTING SEED

Let me tell you another parable to explain what the kingdom of God is like. In this story the farmer scatters seed on the soil and doesn't do much else to make it grow. Day after day and night after night it grows, whether the farmer is asleep or awake. The farmer can't figure out what makes it grow. It grows all by itself from seed to sprout and from sprout to full-grown grain ready to harvest.

The main point of the parable: Spontaneous growth of the Word of God in a responsive life is inevitable even if we can't explain it.

PARABLE OF THE WHEAT AND WEEDS

The kingdom of heaven is like a farmer who sowed good seed in a field. When everyone was sound asleep, an enemy came and scattered weed seed in with the wheat seed and then sneaked away. When the wheat sprouted and grew tall, the weeds were almost as big.

The farmer's servants asked, "You sowed only good seed, didn't you? Where did all these weeds come from?"

"An enemy planted weed seeds," the farmer explained.

The servants responded, "Should we go and yank up all these weeds?"

"Oh no," the farmer answered. "If you pull out the weeds, you might wreck the wheat. Let both grow together until the harvest. Then I'll tell the harvesters to first gather, bundle, and burn the weeds and then harvest the wheat and bring it into my barn."

The main point of the parable: It may be difficult to tell who is good and who is evil in this life, but God will make that clear in the final judgment.

PARABLE OF THE MUSTARD SEED

The kingdom of heaven is like a mustard seed planted by a farmer in one of the farm fields. You know it is the smallest seed that farmers around here ever plant, yet it grows into a bush so big it looks like a tree. When it's full-grown the birds think it is a tree and scores of them perch on the branches all at once.

The main point of the parable: God's work may start small but grows large in time.

PARABLE OF THE YEAST

The kingdom of heaven is like yeast that a woman kneaded into a big ball of flour until it totally permeated the dough.

The main point of the parable: God's kingdom starts little but saturates and changes that which is large.

PARABLE OF HIDDEN TREASURE

The kingdom of heaven is like treasure hidden in a field. The man who found the treasure didn't own the field, so he put the treasure back where he found it. Then he went home happy and sold everything he owned and used the money to buy the field and claim the treasure.

The main point of the parable: God's kingdom is worth more than everything we have, and finding it brings great joy.

PARABLE OF THE FINE PEARLS

The kingdom of heaven is like a merchant shopping for high-quality pearls. When the merchant found one that was perfect, every asset was turned to cash in order to buy that perfect pearl.

The main point of the parable: God's kingdom is worth looking for and more valuable than everything else.

PARABLE OF THE NET

The kingdom of heaven is like a net lowered into Galilee Lake until it filled with fish. The fishermen hauled the full net onto the shore and sorted the fish. They kept the good ones and threw the bad ones back in.

This is the way it will be with people at the end of this age. Only then it will be angels who sort the evil people from the righteous people, tossing the evil ones into the incinerator, where there will be lots of crying and misery.

The main point of the parable: Don't worry about trying to figure out who is good and who is evil. It's up to God to make that judgment.

PARABLE OF THE HOUSE OWNER

Coming to his final parable of the day, Jesus asked the crowd, "Have you understood all these things?" In very generous overstatement they shouted back, "Yes!" Giving them the benefit of the doubt, Jesus told them one more parable.

> Teachers of God's truth who have learned and understood about God's kingdom are like the owner of a house. The house owner has an important responsibility that comes with home ownership—to open up the storeroom and bring out good supplies that are old and good supplies that are new.

The main point of the parable: Those who understand Jesus' teachings should tell them to others.

WHY PARABLES?

The disciples came privately to Jesus and asked everybody's question, "Why do you use parables to teach?"

He explained,

> The secrets of the kingdom of heaven are for you to know but not for those who are unbelieving enemies. Those who have some of God's truth will be given more, until they have abundance. But those who don't have much will lose what they have.
>
> In answer to your question, this is why I use parables to teach. The people think they see, but they really don't; they act like they are listening, but they don't really hear or understand.
>
> They don't know it, but these unbelievers are actually fulfilling a prophecy from Isaiah that says, "You are always listening but never understanding. You are always looking but never see." The hearts of these people have become hard so that they are practically deaf and have shut their eyes so they

don't see. Otherwise they might catch themselves seeing, hearing, understanding, and even repenting so that I would heal them.

But let's talk about you. You are blessed because you open your eyes to see and your ears to hear. You want to know the truth? The great prophets and godly people of past centuries yearned to see what you see and hear what you hear. They couldn't, but you can!

Think about this. Nobody lights a lamp and then puts a dark cover over it or hides the lighted lamp under a bed. Of course not! Anyone who lights a lamp puts it on a table to give light to whoever enters the room. The truth is that sooner or later everything that is now hidden will be brought out into the open and exposed in the light for everyone to see. So listen carefully: Whoever has now will be given more later; whoever doesn't have now will later lose out.

They heard this explanation, but then his disciples particularly requested further decoding of the parable about the wheat and the weeds. Jesus explained,

The farmer who sowed the good seed is the Son of Man, and his seed is those who belong to God's kingdom. The field is the world in which we all live. The weeds are those who belong to the devil. The enemy who sowed those weed seeds is the devil himself. The harvest is the end of the age. The servants who harvest are angels.

Just as the weeds are yanked up and burned in the incinerator, that's what will happen to evil unbelievers at the end of this age. The Son of Man will send out his angels to weed out of his kingdom everything and everybody who does evil. The angels will toss them into the incinerator where there will be crying and misery. At the same time the righteous people in God's kingdom will shine as bright as the sun. If you can hear this, listen to what it means.

This had been a long and demanding day. The crowds were still large, but Jesus was tired and ready to move on. He dismissed the people and gave orders for the boat to cast off and set sail for the other side of the lake.

CHAPTER SEVEN

It was getting dark, and Jesus was exhausted. He needed rest whether the people were ready to call it a day or not. Ignoring the pleas of the crowd to stay, Jesus told his disciples to row across the lake to the other side. Other boats joined the small flotilla moving over the calm surface. As they headed south, the sky darkened and the shoreline disappeared while the noise of the crowd slowly quieted as the people dispersed.

Jesus was paying little attention to the other boats or to the crew of the boat he was in. Right after he instructed them to cross the lake, he moved to the elevated stern of the wooden boat, where the helmsman usually sat to operate the rudder. He reached under the seat and pulled out a cushion for his head, coiled his body so he would fit on the small area, and fell sound asleep.

An unexpected wind suddenly swept down from the hills, probably peaking at over forty miles per hour. § The veteran fishermen knew the danger well. All of them had stories about ferocious storms and near drownings, and all of them knew someone who had died in such storms. The safest place to fish was close to Capernaum. Not that the lake was very large, but every fisherman who had been in a sudden storm preferred to stay within close rowing distance of the shore.

§ The below-sea-level elevation of Galilee Lake makes it susceptible to unpredictable storms that churn the lake into large swells and waves that sometimes swamp small wooden fishing craft.

Their worst fears turned into outright terror that night. They were in the middle of the lake. Waves were crashing over their boats. Every effort to bail was futile as the rain and waves filled the boats faster than they could throw the water out. It must have felt as though all forty-two inches of annual rainfall were pouring down at once.

Jesus slept through it all. His disciples risked being thrown overboard when they grappled their way to the back to shake Jesus awake. One shouted to him, "Master, Master, we're going to drown!" Another yelled, "Teacher, don't you care if we drown?" A third cried, "Lord, save us! We're going to drown!" They were frightened, and their fears were well founded. These experienced fishermen knew the dangers all too well.

Jesus woke up and said, "Why are you so afraid? Don't you have faith?" It wasn't that he failed to see the storm, but he didn't fear the storm as they did. He rose to a sitting position, calmly looked around at the waves outside the boat and the panic inside it, and then spoke with an authority as if he had everything completely under control. He rebuked the wind and the waves, saying in a booming voice, "Quiet! Be still!"

The wind immediately began to die down. The waves flattened. The lake turned so calm that the stars reflected on the surface. All the boats lay still in the water, and no one spoke. Fear of drowning had been replaced by a greater fear of supernatural power. They had never seen or heard anything like this before. When they finally found their voices, there was trembling in their words as they asked one another for some explanation to make sense of what had just happened. They said, "Who is this? Even the wind and the waves do what he tells them." This seemed somehow different from the miracles they had seen on shore—miracles for others, miracles more individualized, miracles they thought they somehow understood. They had no mental category for an event or a person like this—someone who could tame the weather with a word.

Their question went unanswered. They rowed in silence through the night to the eastern shore of the lake.

When the boat arrived on the southeastern shore, they were all glad to get out and walk on solid ground, even if it was Gentile country. §

If they expected calm on land, they were mistaken. As soon as Jesus stepped out of the boat, two demon-possessed men rushed toward him. They were so violent that travelers avoided this road. This was the domain of these men, and all visitors were threatened until they fled. The two were both scary, but one clearly was dominant—the one who came right up to Jesus.

§ Gadara was one of ten Greek-culture communities called the Decapolis ("Ten Towns"). It was the kind of place many Jews preferred to avoid. The actual city was about six miles southeast of Galilee Lake, but the shoreline was still part of the district.

This strange man was a mess. Completely naked, he lived in nearby caves that were used as burial tombs. When he ventured out, it was to frighten and attack the ordinary citizens of the area. The local police had tried to restrain him by shackling his hands and feet and placing him under twenty-four-hour guard, but it never worked. His power was supernatural, breaking every chain they used on him and overpowering all the guards assigned to him. Day and night this man shouted and screamed, often cutting his skin open with sharp stones. Like a wild rabid dog, he terrorized the entire town where once he had lived.

But he was no wild animal. As uncontrollable and frightening as he looked, this man was intelligent and insightful. Actually, he had spiritual insight. The man and Jesus saw and spoke to each other at the same time. Jesus said, "Out, evil spirit! Come out of this man!" While Jesus was saying this, the man ran right at him, fell to his knees at Jesus' feet, and shouted at the top of his voice, "What do you think you're going to do to me, Jesus, Son of the Most High God? Leave me alone. Swear to God that you won't hurt me!"

Without any introduction he knew Jesus' name. While his own disciples were still trying to figure out who Jesus was, this wild man seemed to know. From his statements, he knew Jesus was no ordinary preacher or religious leader. He was the Son of the Most High God.

Jesus immediately took charge of the situation, much as he had

§ "Legion" was a six-thousand-soldier unit of the Roman army. That was probably not his actual name. He was referring to the demons living in him and considered them so numerous that Legion was chosen as a descriptor. If this was literally the case, he had been taken over by six thousand demons.

during the storm the previous night. He asked, "What's your name?" The man identified himself by a strange name in keeping with the strange man he was. He said, "My name is Legion." §

Jesus combined compassion for the man with anger against the myriads of demons that had done this to him. Jesus was determined to cure this wild man and set him free from his spiritual oppression. When Jesus ordered the demons out, they talked to him, begging not to be thrown into the abyss, the hell that was their ultimate destiny. They actually offered a short-term alternative. "If you make us leave, put us in those pigs over there," they said, referring to the herd of about two thousand swine feeding on a high bluff overlooking the lake.

When Jesus agreed, the demons exited the man and entered the pigs. Had the demons somehow outsmarted Jesus? The pigs broke away from the pig farmers and stampeded through the fence and over the cliff into the lake, where they all drowned. Jesus had used their own suggestion to get them to leave the wild man voluntarily, which quickly deprived them of any living host.

This man's good fortune was very upsetting to those tending the pigs. They had just lost a large fortune in livestock. The herders ran into Gadara and reported what happened. A mob of townspeople responded by running out to see for themselves. What they found stunned them. The man they all knew and feared was sitting there with Jesus, fully clothed and completely sane. His countrymen should have been delighted, but they were frightened. Perhaps it was a fear that the same supernatural power would be unleashed on them. Whatever the cause of their fear, they pleaded with Jesus to get back in the boat and leave their region.

Jesus didn't need to stay where he was not welcome. He again boarded the same boat and told the men with him to push off. The man who was recently healed begged to go along. Jesus said no and told him, "Go back home to your family and friends. Tell them what happened. Tell them about the mercy of the Lord that set you free." This sounded like a contradiction with what he had been telling those he healed on the north side of the lake. But this was a different place and situation. On the north side, Jewish authorities were threatening Jesus, but on the south side there were few Jews and no threats. It wasn't that he didn't want people to know who he was or what he was doing. He was holding off the threats of the religious leaders who were out to kill him until he had done everything he wanted to do. Jesus wanted to keep his destiny on his own schedule.

The man did what Jesus asked and became something of a traveling preacher, going around to the cities of Decapolis telling how much Jesus had done for him. Because so many people knew him from before and now saw the change, they listened and were amazed.

With Jesus again in the boat, his men rowed all the way across the lake, back toward the north shore. Because noise carries well across open water, they could hear shouting and singing, along with yelled petitions for healing and other help before they could see the crowd on the lakeshore.

Usually no one person could penetrate such a mob, but Jairus was different. As leader of the Capernaum synagogue, he was well known and highly respected. When he walked toward Jesus, the people split like a river around an island. Jairus was wealthy and influential. It was he who chose who read the Torah each Sabbath at the synagogue and who gave spiritual leadership to the community.

Jairus came to ask Jesus for a favor. Jairus was used to being asked for favors himself. It was surprising he even would come, because Jesus' popularity with synagogue leaders was falling quickly while his popularity with the crowds was rising. Jesus had previously been at the top of the list of the "most sought after" synagogue teachers, but now that some of the Pharisees were discrediting him, Jesus was not being invited any longer. But Jairus came to Jesus for personal rather than political or religious reasons. His twelve-year-old daughter was dying.

This father was desperate. Jesus was her last chance. When a man's daughter is dying, he harbors few thoughts of pride or protocol. Like most loving fathers, Jairus was willing to do anything, including public begging, if it might save his only daughter's life. Jairus fell at Jesus' feet and pleaded for him to come. "My little girl is dying. Please come to my house so you can touch and heal her and make her live."

Jesus agreed to come and immediately followed Jairus toward his home while Jesus' disciples walked close behind and the entire crowd formed an entourage. The air was filled with excitement, but then the crowd started to behave like a mob. When they swept through the narrow streets of Capernaum, no one was willing to let others get ahead of them. They shoved and jammed together. Jesus was so pressed by people that he could hardly walk and was nearly being crushed.

It was enough to make Jairus panic. Time was running out. His daughter was dying and Jesus was barely moving because of the tight quarters. Jairus tried to hurry others along, ask for space, keep Jesus walking forward, but none of it was working.

§ The law said that a woman with her condition could not attend religious services nor could anyone she touched or who touched her. For religious purposes she was classified as unclean.

In the crowd was a woman who had been sick for a dozen years. Though not dying, she suffered from a chronic menstrual flow that left her physically emaciated and socially isolated. §

She had consulted many doctors, but nothing she had tried had given her any relief. Her money was gone, and she was worse than before.

The woman pressing forward to reach Jesus had little in common with Jairus. He was one of their religious leaders, wealthy and respected. She was poor, outcast, and isolated, and no one knew her name. But the two did share one characteristic—they both were desperate. She had been so sick for so long that she didn't have much hope left. She was worn out from her illness and from the way people treated her. She wanted Jesus' help, but she was not looking for his recognition. She dreaded public attention. She didn't want to look anyone in the eye, not even Jesus. So she reached through the press of the crowd and with simple, breathtaking faith, she touched Jesus, hoping that it would be enough. She thought, "If I can just touch his clothes I will be healed." And immediately she was healed. The bleeding stopped. She felt it. She knew it. That was the happiest moment of her life.

Jesus stopped and spoke with such authority in his voice that the crowd fell silent. "Who touched me?" he asked. Their responses were laughable—everyone around him denied touching him. The truth is they had been bumping into him every step down the street. While they were all denying that they had touched him, Peter was honest enough to say, "Master, the whole crowd has been jostling and touching you!" Peter must have thought Jesus was joking. But Jesus knew there are ordinary touches and there are extraordinary touches. "Someone touched me; I felt the power going out of me." Only one person had touched him with a finger of faith. She had connected to Jesus like none of the others. She truly believed. And the power of God flowed through that connection to heal her body.

Jesus did not let her remain anonymous. "Daughter, may your heart be encouraged! You truly believed, and your faith has healed you." Knowing she was identified, she fell trembling at Jesus' feet and admitted that she was the one. Her story poured out of her. Her words were to Jesus, but everyone heard. She told why she had come and why she had touched him and how she had been instantly healed. Jesus told her, "Go in peace and be free from your disease."

This public announcement meant that she would be welcomed back into the fellowship of the synagogue. Superstition was chased away. It was not magic she had experienced from touching a piece of clothing; it was the power of God received by faith.

While Jesus was still talking with the woman, messengers ran up, out of breath, and told Jairus, "Your daughter is dead." Then one of them added sarcastically, "I guess there's no need to bother this teacher anymore!"

Jesus acted as if he didn't believe what the messengers had said. He turned to Jairus and told him, "Don't be afraid; have faith. She's going to be healed," and continued walking on to Jairus' house. He ordered the crowd to wait behind and took with him Jairus, Peter, James, and John. When they arrived at the house, it was chaotic—family, friends, and neighbors were wailing and crying. The funeral flute players had already arrived and started their mournful tunes. Immediately taking charge, Jesus asked, "What is all this noise about? The girl isn't dead. She's asleep." They laughed at him, but Jesus told them, "Be quiet. Stop wailing. Get out of here." He sent every wailer out of the house and then led the girl's mother and father to the motionless girl's side.

§ Aramaic for "Little girl, get up!"—the same words most parents used to awaken their daughters every morning.

At that moment time stood still for her parents. At the bedside, they were conflicted between shocked grief and seemingly unreasonable hope. The three disciples stood in silence at the far side of the room. Jesus took the girl's hand and said to her, "*Talitha koum!*" §

The twelve-year-old stood up and walked across the room. Jesus suggested that she be given some food to eat. Her parents were astonished and beside themselves with joy. Jesus told them to keep this to themselves and not tell anyone else. But bringing someone back from the dead wasn't the kind of secret that could easily be kept.

Caution and warnings for secrecy followed Jesus' miracles more and more. He was no longer going to give signs to critics and unbelievers. Miracles were only for those who already believed or were open to believing. His enemies insisted on spinning and twisting the good he did into something evil and controversial, so Jesus repeatedly told recipients of his miracles not to tell what had happened.

Two blind men followed the crowd of Jesus' admirers as best they could. At times they were clumsy and had trouble keeping up, but everyone knew them and where they were because of their persistent shouting: "Have mercy on us, Son of David!" When Jesus entered a house along the way that day, the two men were swept inside by the others who were cramming through the front door. To their own amazement they both ended up in front of Jesus, and he asked them, "Do you really believe that I can make you see?"

"Yes, Lord," they enthusiastically affirmed.

Jesus reached out both hands to simultaneously touch the men. As he touched their eyes he said, "Just as you believe...see!" and they both could see! He was emphatic in warning them, "Make sure you don't tell anyone about this." But they were too excited to keep such an event to themselves and spread the story of what happened all over the region.

Right after this came another wonderful healing, but it ended up triggering a further accusation against Jesus. While Jesus was leaving the house where the blind men were healed, a demon-possessed man who couldn't talk was brought to Jesus. It was obvious what he needed, and Jesus simply drove the demon out of the man so that he could speak. The crowd saw it all. They told one another, "This is a first! Miracles like this have never before been performed in Israel." The people in the crowd were tilted toward faith, but some Pharisees were once again provoked and told everyone, "The only reason he can exorcise demons is because he works for the devil."

Jesus didn't defend himself against their criticism because he knew it wasn't going to do any good, but it did underscore the importance of limiting news about the miracles.

A year earlier when Jesus was in Nazareth, the people had tried to kill him, prompting Jesus to flee and move his headquarters to Capernaum. It had looked like he would never go back, but Jesus gave Nazareth one more visit.

Jesus and his followers arrived in town midweek. It was a modest homecoming for someone so heartily welcomed everywhere else he went. It was an opportunity for him to stay at the house where he grew up, greet people in the streets, and stop by the shops he knew so well. On the Sabbath, he entered the synagogue much as he had done almost every weekend of his life. When there was a time in the service for synagogue members to speak, Jesus stood and taught. He was weaving quotes and explanations of the Old Testament into a mesmerizing presentation. The people were amazed at how good he was at this, but this amazement caused skepticism instead of praise. "Where does he get this stuff?" they asked. "What's the deal with his wisdom and miracles? He's the carpenter, isn't he? He's a local nobody. His mother is Mary and his brothers are James, Joseph, Judas, and Simon, right? Those are his sisters right over there."

As they were asking each other, "Who does he think he is anyway?" Jesus said, "Everybody in the world honors a prophet except the people in his own hometown!" Unlike in many other places, Jesus didn't do many miracles in Nazareth. There were only a few sick people here and there that he touched and healed.

When Jesus left Nazareth, it was for the last time. He was not only finished with Nazareth but nearing the end of his travels in the province of Galilee. He was moving on.

Town after town, village after village—Jesus visited them all. His audiences were usually large. His dozen disciples were always with him. Other followers stayed with him for days and weeks at a time before they would get weary or have to return to responsibilities in their hometowns.

The message was similar in every synagogue as well as at the impromptu gatherings on village streets and rural hillsides—the good news of the kingdom of God, along with the healing of every sickness and disease.

Often Jesus would pause and just look out over the hundreds of people who came to see him, his heart filled with compassion and love for them. So many were so harassed and helpless, like sheep that had wandered from the fold and had no shepherd to watch out for them. With a tremor in his voice, he would turn to his disciples and almost whisper words that the rest of the people didn't hear, "The harvest is huge, but there aren't many harvesters. Pray that God will send out more workers into his field."

Jesus pulled his twelve disciples aside and gave them supernatural powers to do what he had been doing, giving them authority to drive out demons, heal diseases, and preach the kingdom of God. He divided them into teams of two and sent them to the villages he hadn't yet personally visited. His instructions were specific:

- Don't go to Gentiles or Samaritans. Focus on Jews who are lost.
- Preach this message: "The kingdom of heaven is near."
- Heal the sick, raise the dead, cleanse those who have leprosy, drive out demons.
- Give to others as generously as you have received from God.
- Don't take money or supplies. Everything will be provided along your way.
- When you enter a town, find some good person to stay with. Bless the people and home where you stay. If no one welcomes you, just move on. God will judge that town later.
- I am sending you out like sheep in wolf territory. You're going to need to be as shrewd as snakes and as innocent as doves.

These instructions were specific to their first venture in representing Jesus and extending his ministry without having him there. It wasn't that these rules would apply to all future missions or to all other followers of Jesus. This was only the beginning.

Jesus didn't want them to see his popularity without counting the cost. Because of their association with him, persecution was inevitable. Even family members would turn against them. They were to use such harassment as a teaching opportunity among the people to whom Jesus was sending them.

Jesus warned them, "Be on your guard against those who will turn you over to the local councils and have you beaten in local synagogues. Because of your relationship with me, you will stand before high-ranking government officials—from governors to kings. Whether they are Jews or Gentiles, you will be my representatives to them. You will be arrested, but don't worry what to say, because the Holy Spirit will give you just the words you need when that time comes.

"How bad will it get? Family members will betray one another so that they are executed—brothers against brothers, fathers against children, children against parents. Everybody may hate you because of me. But you and every other disciple who sticks with me to the end will be saved. If the persecution gets really bad in one place, leave and go somewhere else. You won't get to all the cities of Israel before I come to be with you.

"Think of it this way. No student is superior to the teacher or servant to the boss. It's good enough for the student or servant to just be like the teacher or boss. So if someone accuses me of being Beelzebub, the devil, you'd better get ready for them to say the same about you.

"But I don't want you to be afraid of those who criticize and attack you. Sooner or later they will be exposed for who they are and what they do. No secrets! Teach my lessons to everyone. The truth is that they may be able to kill your body, but they can't hurt your soul. They aren't the ones to worry about. Save your respect and fear for God, who has the power over souls and bodies. God is the one who can send someone to hell, not some human officials. And the good news is that God loves and watches out for you. Think about how little a couple of sparrows are worth—not much! Yet God takes care of these little birds. If he does that for them, you can rest assured that he will take far better care of you. He even keeps track of how many hairs you have on your head. So don't be afraid; you're worth a whole lot more than any sparrows.

"Whoever acknowledges me before others I will also acknowledge before my Father in heaven. But whoever disowns me before others I will disown before my Father in heaven.

"Just don't think that the only reason I came to earth was to make everything peaceful and nice. My message also brings a sword. It's like that quote from the Jewish prophet Micah: I've come to turn 'a man against his father, a daughter against her mother, a daughter-in-law against her mother-in-law. A man's enemies will be the members of his own family.'

"In ordering your relationships, I must be first. Anyone who loves his father, mother, son, or daughter more than me isn't worthy to be called my disciple. You can't put family first and me second or last. To be a worthy disciple, you'll need to carry a cross on a lot of days and you'll need to follow me every day. It may not be easy, but it will be good. You'll discover that anyone who finds his life without me actually loses it, and anyone who focuses his life on me actually finds it." §

§ Jesus' warnings did not sound as extreme to his first-century disciples as they may sound to modern people in less hostile cultures. Their danger was great. The society was polarized and often violent. The threat of death was real.

But not all of Jesus' words of commission to his disciples were grim. He said, "We're in this together. Those who welcome me will welcome you, and those who welcome you also welcome me. Those who welcome prophets and other righteous people share their rewards. For example, if someone gives a single cup of cold water to one of my disciples, that person will receive a reward from God."

———— ❋ ————

No, Jesus was not exaggerating when he talked about threats of death. John the Baptizer was a tragic example. His public condemnation of Herod Antipas had cost him his life.

John was dead, but Herod could not stop thinking about him. When he heard reports about Jesus' popularity and miracles, he wondered if John had come back to life. Herod sought counsel. Some advisors said, "John the Baptizer has been raised from the dead, and that explains all these miracles that he is performing." Others said, "He is Elijah." Then there were those who were diplomatically vague, claiming, "He is a prophet, like one of the prophets of long ago." When Herod heard these explanations, he decided the first answer was the right one—Jesus was John the Baptizer come back to life. With fear and fascination, he determined to meet and talk with Jesus face-to-face.

With all this royal attention, Jesus was becoming famous through all the layers of society. He was moving from being a local populist among ordinary people in small towns to a national celebrity.

Jesus was also moving beyond Galilee, which had so long been the center of his teaching and healing.

CHAPTER EIGHT

They were so filled with excitement and stories of miracles they all were talking at the same time—Peter, John, Thaddaeus, and the others. It became almost impossible to hear what each disciple was saying.

Jesus decided to find another place for their debriefing, and he told the twelve, "Let's move along out of here. Come with me, and we'll look for a quiet place to get some rest." They threaded their way through the crowd and down to the lakeshore, boarded boats, and rowed away to search for some peace and quiet. But by the time they crossed the lake and landed, there was an even larger crowd waiting to meet them. Leaving jobs and homes and street corner conversations as the word spread, some had set out at a run. Others saw the group of men coming across the lake, figured out what was happening, and hurried to the scene.

Jesus' band of twelve no doubt were feeling irritated. They were tired of so many people following them and wanted time to relax and have Jesus to themselves. They were ready to row to a different landing or float out in the water where the crowds couldn't reach them. But Jesus looked with love and care at the people who had come with hopes for healing and teaching. His shepherd's heart drew him to the people and them to him.

While Jesus delighted in teaching the truth about the kingdom of God and healing those suffering with all kinds of diseases, he knew he and the twelve couldn't continue on like this. The crowds were too thick. He was drawing too much political attention. His men were feeling neglected. It was time to do things differently, although the change would have to wait for another day. The people were hungry, it was late in the afternoon, and they were on the outskirts of nowhere.

The twelve disciples, though bone-weary from the previous weeks of travel, teaching, and healing, did some investigation on their own while Jesus was dealing with the people. They calculated the crowd to total around five thousand men plus women and children and knew it could turn into an unhappy mob when dinnertime and darkness arrived. Besides, they were hungry themselves and they wanted to get Jesus alone to report on what they had done to fulfill his earlier orders. It must have seemed obvious to them that Jesus was so caught up in the people and their individual problems that he was unaware of the growing difficulty facing them as the sun went down in the west. As a group they pushed through the crowd and interrupted Jesus. "This is an out-of-the-way place, and it's getting really late. Send these people away so they can spread out to area villages and buy themselves something to eat." Jesus looked at his disciples and replied, "You give them something to eat." He seemed to be looking right at Philip, who was from that side of the lake, maybe implying that Philip should know where to find food.

§ It was a quick mental calculation: two hundred denarii to buy enough food for one bite per person. At the going wage of one denarius per day for a working person, it would take eight months' wages for ten thousand bites.

Feeling defensive, Philip did not want to take responsibility for them. He told Jesus, "Even if we had eight months' wages, it wouldn't be enough money to buy one bite of bread per mouth!" § It simply was far too expensive.

Andrew was watching and listening, trying to figure out how he could help. By Philip's calculations, it couldn't be done. Andrew tried to find a way. His suggestion didn't seem to have much potential, but he told Jesus, his voice tentative, "I found a boy with five little barley loaves and a couple of small fish, § but that's not going to feed all these people." It wasn't

§ Barley was the poor person's bread. Primarily used as animal feed, barley was looked on with disgust since it was dry and didn't taste very good.

much, but the child was willing to share what he had. Those close enough to hear must have smiled and wanted to laugh. The boy's resources were cute but pointless!

Jesus didn't laugh. He said, "Bring the boy's lunch here to me," and he told his disciples to

The two fish were the little perch that swarmed in Galilee Lake. The fish were pickled soon after they were caught and thus were preserved for later consumption.

seat the crowd in small groups on the grass. No doubt the twelve were at least bewildered if not annoyed. The crowd slowly hushed and sorted themselves into groups of fifty to a hundred each. It was surprisingly quiet, and Jesus' voice carried well. He held the five loaves and two fish in his hands, looked upward, and prayed a prayer of gratitude. The loaves were small, about the length of Jesus' hand. He broke each one of them in pieces and did the same with each of the fish. Then he gave the pieces to his twelve disciples and told them to start handing them out to the people.

What began with skepticism grew into awe and satisfaction. No matter how much the twelve doled out, there was always more. The impromptu supper guests ate until everyone was full and didn't want any more. Jesus told them, "Gather the leftovers. Don't waste any food." At the end of the day, a dozen baskets were full to overflowing with pieces of bread and fish.

Previous miracles had been personal. This miraculous meal was for everyone. The hushed awe quickly shifted into shared adrenaline. With exuberant praise for Jesus, some began to say, "This Jesus has to be the Prophet of God." He was a new Moses—like the original Moses who miraculously fed the people of Israel with manna, bread that God sent from the sky every day. Only the God-sent Messiah could have done this. "He should be king!" enthusiastic voices cried.

Jesus wasn't responding to their political enthusiasm, and the mood started to shift. They were going to make him king by acclamation. Force him to the throne. After all, anyone who could feed a crowd of thousands with a boy's lunch could recruit, mobilize, and feed an army stronger than the Romans. They had been waiting for this opportunity for half a millennium, and they weren't going to let Jesus decline.

Immediately Jesus gathered his twelve disciples and hurried them into the boat with orders for them to leave him and row to Bethsaida on the western slope of Galilee Lake near Capernaum. Jesus dismissed the crowd and—with an escape that itself bordered on miraculous—slipped away from the people and climbed up alone on the nearby mountainside to pray.

Jesus prayed alone in his wilderness retreat for about nine hours while his men were making their way across the lake. It should have been a quick and easy journey, but the winds blew against them. They kept the sails down and rowed into the waves. Already exhausted from an intense day, they made only three-and-a-half miles between eight in the evening and five in the morning. When Jesus finished praying, he looked down from the mountain and saw them struggling to keep the small wooden craft afloat out in the middle of the wind-swept lake.

He walked down the mountain toward the water and kept right on walking—on the water—out toward the fishing boat. It seemed like he was going to walk right past them when they saw him on the lake. They were already frightened by the storm, but they were terrified when they saw a human form atop the waves. A few of the men were speechless, but the majority shrieked in fear. "It's a ghost!" they shouted to one another. Jesus heard them and smiled. "Be courageous!" he said. "It's me, Jesus. Don't be afraid."

There was comfort in knowing it wasn't a ghost, that it was Jesus, but this was one more supernatural encounter they had no prior experience from which to understand. With impetuous enthusiasm, Peter was the one who responded to Jesus' encouragement. He called, "Lord, if it's really you, let me walk over to you on the water."

"Come on!" Jesus invited him. Peter rolled over the side of the boat and walked on the water toward Jesus. At first he just looked at Jesus and took steps as if he were on dry ground. Then he must have remembered where he was and realized what he was doing. He panicked and started to sink, screaming, "Lord, save me!" Jesus instantly reached out his hand and grabbed Peter, telling him, "Ran low on faith, did you? Why the doubt?"

Jesus and Peter stepped into the boat, and the wind died down. They immediately reached the shore at Gennesaret, not far from Capernaum, but the others in the boat were still trembling with shock and amazement. They worshipped Jesus and told him, "You really are the Son of God!" Somehow they must not have been all that impressed by the feeding of the crowd, but they were dazzled by the walk on water.

The early-rising local fishermen were working on their nets when they recognized Jesus and sent word to the nearby villages that Jesus had been sighted. This quickly produced another crowd of patients looking for a cure. Most of those who came that day were too sick to walk and had to be carried on mats by family members. As Jesus walked from Gennesaret to nearby villages, similar crowds of the chronically ill gathered with hopes for a cure. When the lines were especially long, the people suggested a shortcut to his healing power, asking permission to just touch the edge of Jesus' cloak rather than have him heal them one at a time. This worked, and those who touched his clothes were equally healed. In ways it was a better-than-usual day, because his enemies were leaving him alone. Not that they weren't still critical of him, but even his critics liked the benefits of his miracles.

Most days were starting to look like the previous ones. Long hours. Large crowds. Growing fame. Endless lines of needy people. The training of those he had recruited to spread his message and power was getting pushed to the back. If Jesus was going to go beyond being a one-at-a-time healer and turn his work into a movement, he needed time and privacy for teaching and training the twelve.

----------- ❄ -----------

The tide of popular acclaim started to turn the next day. It all began innocently enough with little indication that morning of how the day would end.

When the light of dawn turned into full day, the crowd from the miraculous meal started looking for Jesus once more. In talking with one another, they began to piece together the facts. There had been only one boat on the shore, and they saw it leave without Jesus. So by midmorning a small flotilla of fishing boats based in Tiberias had landed on the shore near the grassy area of the previous night's miracle. But Jesus was nowhere to be seen. They assumed that he had somehow escaped them and headed back toward Capernaum on the northern shore. Another stampede began as they rushed into the city of Capernaum, where they found Jesus. They asked, "Rabbi, what time did you get here?"

Without answering their question, Jesus said to them, "You know, the real reason you're looking for me isn't because of my miracles but because you ate the loaves and had your fill." This was an interesting indictment, because Jesus had confronted others for always wanting to see a miracle. He went a step further with these inquirers, saying that they were more interested in free food than even divine miracles. "Don't work for food that spoils," he told them, "but for food that lasts forever, which the Son of Man will give you. He has the full endorsement of God the Father." Even more noteworthy than the title Son of Man was the claim that he bore the seal of God the Father.

Someone asked, "Okay then, what do we need to do in order to get in on what God is doing?" Jesus told him, "Being part of God's work means you must have faith in the one he has sent."

It's difficult to know the motive behind the next question. Either they asked in ignorance or were close to taunting Jesus. Several of them asked, "What miracle are you going to do so that we will believe? Our ancestors ate manna in the desert that God miraculously sent down from heaven." Perhaps they were tapping into an old Jewish belief that manna would return to Israel at the coming of God's kingdom. These were the same people who were fed by a boy's small supply of bread and fish. They had already seen this miracle of authentication yet they were asking for another one. §

Jesus responded to their question but tried to bring them back to the greater issue of their belief. "Let me tell you the truth one more time," he told them. "The true bread of heaven doesn't come from Moses but from my Father in heaven. And the 'bread' isn't really bread but the Messiah whom God sent from heaven to give eternal life to this world." He kept bringing them back to the fact that all supernatural miracles come from God, not from Moses or any other miracle worker. He was leading the conversation so they would see him as the one God empowered for miracles—the new Moses. He baited the hook with "the bread of God," and they bit. A chorus of, "Sir, from now on give us this bread!" began.

§ Strangely, the example they cited was a miracle from nearly fifteen hundred years earlier when Moses had been the agent of God in supplying a daily breadlike substance called *manna* to feed their ancestors during the forty years they traveled through the desert between Egypt and Palestine. Perhaps their point was that Moses' miracle fed three million people, not five thousand, and lasted for forty years, not one meal. Whatever they were saying, they were overlooking the significance of what had happened the night before.

Finally, Jesus had them set up to hear his major claim: "I am the bread of life. Anyone who comes to me will never go hungry, and anyone who believes in me will never be thirsty. As you've heard before, even though you've seen me, you do not believe. It's all about God the Father who gives followers to me, and I never reject anyone he gives to me. I came down from heaven to do his will, not mine. His will is for me not to lose any he has given me but to raise them up to be complete at the end of time. My Father's will is that everyone who believes in his Son will have eternal life. Even those who die will be raised back to live forever at the end of time."

His listeners caught on right away, and many didn't like what they heard. He was telling them that he came from God as the bread that gives eternal life, and that life after death depended on him. The religious leaders best understood this teaching and most reacted against it. Grumbling to anyone who would listen, they said, "Isn't this just Jesus, the son of Joseph, whose parents we know? What is he talking about when he says, 'I came down from heaven'?"

They were annoyed with Jesus, but he instructed them to stop grumbling to one another. Jesus continued, "Let me tell you one more time. No one can come to me unless drawn to me by God the Father, who sent me from heaven. And those who come to me will be raised to life by me at the end of this era. Your own prophets wrote, 'They will all be taught by God.' Everyone who listens to the Father and learns from him comes to me. No one else has seen God the Father except the one who came from God. You do not believe this, but it's the truth! Anyone who believes has everlasting life. I am the bread of life. Your forefathers ate the manna in the desert, but they eventually died. I'm offering you the bread that comes down from heaven; whoever eats this bread doesn't die. I'm talking about me. I am the living bread that came down from heaven. Anyone who eats this bread from heaven will live forever. This bread is my flesh, which I will give for the life of the world." Here was a further assertion that he came from God and is the source of eternal life.

The crowd struggled to understand much of what he was saying. Jesus was saying things that were very difficult to understand at the time and made sense only later. His listeners started debating his meaning, ending with sharp arguments. One summarized the debate well when he demanded, "How can this man give us his flesh to eat?"

It was a good question, but Jesus' answer only confused them more. He said, "I'll tell you the truth one more time. Unless you eat the flesh of the Son of Man and drink his blood, you won't have life in you. Whoever eats my flesh and drinks my blood has eternal life; I will raise him up at the end of time. For my flesh is real food and my blood is real drink. Whoever eats my flesh and drinks my blood remains in me, and I in him. God the Father is alive, and I'm alive because of him. That same life goes to anyone who feeds on me. Like

I told you, your ancestors ate the manna you were talking about and they died, but everyone who feeds on the living bread of God will not die but live forever."

It was one of the most memorable exchanges in the history of Capernaum. But Jesus' words would not be adequately explained until much later and farther away, in Jerusalem. For the time being, the whole thing remained a mystery.

Some of Jesus' fringe followers could not tolerate any more of this. They concluded, "This is a hard teaching. Who can believe it?"

Jesus only pushed them harder, publicly confronting their grumbling and asking them, "Does this offend you? What if you see the Son of Man ascend to heaven? The Spirit gives life; the flesh ultimately counts for nothing. My words to you are spirit and they are life. Yet some of you just won't believe." What would it take to convince them to become true believers? He wondered if they would believe were they to see a reverse miracle and watch him return to heaven.

The increased directness of Jesus came from his realization that there were some who were going to believe and others who would eventually turn against him and betray him. He was starting to sort out who his friends were and who his enemies were. Or as he told them, "This is why I told you that no one can come to me unless the Father has helped."

Hundreds turned their backs on Jesus and walked away. Though they had been taught and healed and fascinated, they were not going to follow someone making claims they could not accept. He obviously cared about these people and was troubled by their departure. He turned to his twelve closest followers and asked, "You don't want to leave too, do you?" The emotion vibrated in his voice.

Peter, often the first to speak—impetuous, bold, winsome, and sometimes impertinent and foolish—wanted to reassure Jesus. "Lord, who else would we go to? You have the words of eternal life. We know you and we believe that you are the Holy One of God." While many were turning their backs in disbelief, Peter was announcing greater belief. To describe Jesus as "the Holy One of God" was a bold escalation of faith.

"Have I not chosen the dozen of you? Yet one of you is a devil!" Jesus fired back. It was yet another puzzling declaration, a mix of affirmation and a seeming non sequitur. Why would Jesus brand one of his own disciples as a devil? Maybe he glanced toward Judas Iscariot as he answered Peter, although probably not. Here was another item in the growing list of teachings to be explained and understood at a later date.

The term *disciple* started to take on a new meaning that day. Instead of identifying the thousands who were attracted to Jesus, it began to refer to the hundreds who totally believed in Jesus. And it particularly meant his team of twelve. But whatever the description, a turning point had been reached. The crowds thinned. The critics had more fodder for their accusations. Jesus' popularity had passed its peak.

DISCIPLES

Disciple simply means "learner" or "pupil" and describes a common relationship to first-century teachers. The Greek philosophers gathered their disciples as did the Jewish rabbis. Jewish religious leaders ultimately considered themselves to be disciples of Moses, not merely their local teacher.

On the outer fringes of followers around a particular leader, disciples were merely inquisitive seekers. As seekers grew in understanding and commitment, the description of *Disciple* came to mean a loyal follower who adopted the teacher's ideas and lifestyle. Some disciples even echoed the teacher's voice, gestures, appearance, and teaching style.

Jesus' biographers have used the term in different ways, almost like concentric circles. There were sometimes thousands of seekers, but the circle shrank to hundreds who considered themselves devoted followers of Jesus. His closest circle of twelve disciples eventually came to be known as *apostles*, meaning "ones who are sent." They represented the strongest group of people who totally believed in Jesus and his teaching.

During the first generations of the Christian church, *disciple* became a synonym for *Christian*. A Christian disciple was more than a curious student; the disciple absolutely believed in Jesus as Savior and Lord.

Months had passed since Jesus' last trip south to Jerusalem, but the religious establishment in the capital had not forgotten him. Reports were coming to them from Galilee, and they were alarmed at what they were hearing. Popular and powerful, Jesus and his teachings risked upsetting the Romans, who were always on the watch for rebellion. Most of all, Jerusalem's religious leaders feared that ordinary people were turning to Jesus for spiritual guidance rather than to the synagogues, traditions, and the established religious hierarchy. Their suspicions fed into wild speculation about where all this was going. Yet they didn't want to further alienate the crowds by publicly attacking the popular Jesus. They had a problem and knew it. The only idea they could come up with was to trap Jesus into a public discourse that might expose him as a charlatan and heretic. Then the Jewish population would turn against him and these religious leaders would look like heroes who were faithful to God and the Jewish law. Once this approach was decided, they waited for Jesus' next visit to their strongest turf, Jerusalem in Judea, but he didn't appear. So they appointed a delegation to travel north to Galilee, which could be a risky proposition since Galilee was Jesus' native province, where he had stronger support.

What they didn't realize was that Jesus was deliberately avoiding Jerusalem and the surrounding areas in Judea, primarily because of threats against his life. They also didn't know that Jesus' popularity was already weakening in Galilee.

When the delegation arrived in Galilee, they found Jesus and his disciples walking in the countryside eating leftover barley bread and pieces of fish without first washing their hands. The issue was not germs but defilement. Their concern wasn't sanitation but tradition. Pharisees insisted that hands be ceremonially washed to be right with God. There wasn't water for purification readily available out in the countryside where Jesus and his followers were eating, but it was the principle that provoked this controversy. Jesus wasn't following the Pharisees' rules for washing. Since they were looking for issues, this became an instant opportunity for criticism. Their previous tactic of undermining Jesus over Sabbath laws hadn't been all that successful, so they decided to accuse him of being disrespectful of Jewish traditions. This might strike a more responsive chord among the masses. §

§ Religious Jews were especially careful to thoroughly wash their hands, wrists, and forearms before touching food. It was part of an array of rules that had multiplied over the centuries and was passed down as oral tradition. Anyone who failed to wash before eating was called unclean, in a spiritual more than a physical sense. Besides the sanitary benefits, the frequent washings were a way of reminding the faithful that they were ritually unclean before God. They extended the washings beyond their skin to dishes and utensils. Everything had to be washed.

The delegation bypassed the disciples and directly asked Jesus, "Why don't your disciples wash their hands before eating? Do they ignore the tradition of the elders? Do they always eat with unclean hands?" Clearly it was a trap. The only two possible explanations they could imagine were that these men were deliberately defying tradition or they were ignorant of tradition because Jesus, their rabbi, had failed to properly teach them.

CLEAN AND UNCLEAN

Like other Middle Eastern cultures, the Jews had a system of ritual purity and impurity. In order to properly worship the holy God at the temple, a person needed to be ceremonially clean (that is, religiously prepared for the ceremony).

Ritual purity was not the same as moral or physical purity. It simply meant that a person was clean of defilements that were religiously defined. The list of defilements that made a person unclean was long: touching a dead body; eating nonkosher food; eating meals with Gentiles; entering a Gentile's house; sexual functions (emissions, menstruation, intercourse, etc.); giving birth; having leprosy or touching someone with leprosy; and many others, including contact with persons who were considered ritually unclean for one of the reasons listed. Obviously, many were normal, natural, and frequent parts of everyday life that are not immoral or sinful.

Purification was required before a Jew could go to the temple to properly worship God. Usually this purification was relatively simple and brief. Sometimes purification was automatic after a day of waiting. Sometimes it required some type of sacrifice. Often a person was ritually purified through ceremonial washing.

Everyone was constantly moving in and out of states of ritual cleanness and uncleanness. One could hardly avoid living in a house with a woman during her monthly cycle, touching someone who had touched a corpse, doing business with Gentiles, etc. Being unclean wasn't considered unusual, surprising, or immoral. However, in order to worship God at the temple, cleansing was required.

Many Jews rarely or never came to the temple in Jerusalem because they lived so far away. Ritual purity was not a significant concern for them. On the other hand, devout Jews living in Jerusalem often went to the temple every day, so naturally, ritual purification was a frequent concern for them.

The Pharisees took the process a significant step further. They wanted to bring the standards for temple purity to everyday life. This was no easy task. It meant that they washed often, avoided dealing with Gentiles, stayed away from tax collectors who did frequent business with Gentiles, minimized contact with women, and avoided people who were themselves ritually unclean. Many of the Pharisees meant well and were admired for their efforts, even by those who didn't measure up to the same standards.

To many Pharisees, it seemed that Jesus was flagrantly ignoring their zeal for ceremonial purity. Jesus was emphasizing moral purity rather than ceremonial purity, and he denounced those who raised ritual and external purity above moral and ethical purity.

Instead of arguing about his disciples' hand-washing, Jesus confronted the delegation and those they represented. Quoting the prophet Isaiah, Jesus said to them, "You men are such hypocrites! Isaiah got it right when he prophesied about you, 'These people honor me with their lips, but their hearts are far from me. They worship me in vain; their teachings are but rules taught by men.' You've abandoned the commands of God and substituted human commands instead." Jesus chose not to debate the theories of their traditions; he described them as hypocrites and exposed their behavior as being inconsistent with the laws of God that they claimed to diligently obey.

Jesus went to the epicenter of Jewish law, the Ten Commandments. These were the laws about which the delegates were most confident in their compliance. It was a direct attack when Jesus went on to tell them, "You have a fascinating way of abandoning the commands of God in order to substitute your own traditions. For example, Moses said, 'Honor your father and your mother' and 'Anyone who curses his father or mother must be put to death.' You have twisted things to the point where you say that if a man says to his father or mother, 'Any help you expected to receive from me is Corban, § then he can quit doing anything for his father or mother. That way you cancel the word of God by your tradition that you have made up over the years. And this is just one example of many things you do just like that."

During this verbal exchange there were plenty of witnesses, and their numbers were growing by the minute. Jesus decided to include the bystanders in the lesson and called the crowd to hear, but it was still pointedly intended for the delegation from Jerusalem. He said to them all, "Listen to me, everyone, and under-

§ Jesus referred to a legal loophole created by the Pharisees. They went to the temple and declared all their money, possessions, and time to be "Corban," which meant that it was a gift donated and dedicated to God. Then they would say that they had no money, possessions, or time of their own to take care of their elderly parents. This way they were relieved of responsibility for parents in a society where the elderly were heavily dependent on their adult children. This made them appear to be generous and devoted to God while actually being selfish, irresponsible, and breaking the intent of the law to honor parents.

stand this. Nothing external can make someone 'unclean' by going into him. Rather, it is what comes out of a person that makes him 'unclean.' "

Jesus' disciples were raised to respect Pharisees and rabbis and were unsure how to deal with the tense dialogue they had heard. "Do you know that the Pharisees were offended by what you said to them?" they asked him.

Jesus told them, "Any plants that my heavenly Father didn't plant will be uprooted. Leave the Pharisees; they are blind guides. If a blind man leads a blind man, both of them will end up walking off the road into a ditch."

They understood Jesus' disdain for the hypocrisy he had just confronted but were still trying to figure out what Jesus meant prior to that. Peter spoke up for everyone and asked him to explain the parable to them.

Jesus told Peter and the others, "You're really not smart enough to understand this yourselves? Isn't it obvious that nothing that goes into someone from the outside can make him 'unclean'? What a person eats doesn't go into the heart but into the stomach and then out of the body." In saying this, Jesus was turning upside down some of the traditions they had been taught all their lives. Then Jesus became very specific. "What comes out is what makes someone 'unclean.' Out of the heart come evil thoughts, sexual immorality, murder, adultery, greed, malice, deceit, lewdness, envy, slander, arrogance, and foolishness. It is the inside evils that make a person 'unclean.' "

Racial and religious animosity between Jews and Gentiles ran deep throughout the region. When Jesus headed forty miles northwest to the area of Tyre and Sidon (in modern Lebanon), he was entering a region most Jews avoided all their lives. §

§ The city of Tyre had dominated the area for hundreds of years. Since conquered by Alexander the Great in 332 BC, it was predominately Greek in culture and language, though now ruled by the Romans. King Herod had built a pagan temple for the people to worship their gods.

Jesus' journey to the Mediterranean coast was more of an escape from Galilee than an excursion into hostile territory. Both he and his disciples needed time together and a respite from the crowds and the conflict. Jesus should have been little known and completely unrecognized once he left his Jewish homeland and entered Tyre. But it was not to be.

They entered a house outside Tyre, intending it to be their place of secret retreat. The secret was quickly uncovered, and the curious began to show up. One woman from a Greek family, although she was locally born in Syrian Phoenicia, rushed to the home as soon as she heard Jesus was there. Without the usual standing-room-only crowds, she got to Jesus easily and quickly. She told him her daughter was desperately ill and pleaded, "Lord, Son of David, have mercy on me! My daughter is very sick, suffering from demon possession."

Jesus just looked at her without saying a word. The combination of her pleading and Jesus' silence became uncomfortable. His disciples didn't know what else to do but insist that she be sent away because "she keeps crying after us."

"God sent me to the lost sheep of Israel," he told her in Greek. She was a Gentile and outside his calling, he pointed out to her.

She wasn't deterred by Jesus' exclusion. Now that she had his attention and he had spoken to her, she fell on her knees right in front of him and begged, "Lord, help me!" Jesus looked down at her and calmly told her, "First let the children eat until they are full, because it's not right to take the children's bread and give it to their dogs." § The message was clear: the Jews were to come first to the table of divine blessing.

§ This was a rather disparaging response. Jews commonly referred to Gentiles as dogs and often had disdain in their voices when they used the term.

This woman wasn't about to give up. With quick wit and clever humor, she picked up on Jesus' metaphor and replied, "Yes, Lord, but the dogs eat the children's crumbs that fall under the table."

Jesus delighted in her response and told her, "Woman, you have great faith! I grant your request." He sent the woman home to her daughter. She was still lying in bed, though she had been healed when Jesus spoke.

There was a significant message in this encounter, a message later understood in its far-reaching implications: Jesus was primarily committed to his own Jewish people but fully intended to expand his message and kingdom to everyone else as well. The kingdom of God was coming to the whole of humanity, and not just to the Jews.

LANGUAGES OF JESUS

Many languages were spoken across the first-century Roman Empire, and words were borrowed from one language and added to another. Also, languages changed over generations so they differed from century to century.

The New Testament was written in Greek because that was the *lingua franca* of the Roman Empire. However, most of the quotes and conversations reported in the New Testament were originally spoken in Aramaic.

Aramaic was the everyday language of Jews in Galilee, where Jesus grew up. It was the language of the Assyrians and Persians who conquered Israel generations earlier and introduced their language to the Jewish people. What started out as an unfamiliar tongue spoken by foreigners and diplomats became the ordinary language of the people. Distinct dialects developed so that the Aramaic of Galilee was differentiated from the Aramaic of Judea.

Hebrew remained the language of Jewish Scripture. It was learned even by those who did not speak it at home or in business. We know that Jesus could read Hebrew because he publicly read from the scrolls in the synagogue. He also dialogued with the religious leaders in the temple, where knowledge of Hebrew was important.

Greek was the spoken language of the Roman Empire, used for literature, commerce, and diplomacy. It is not difficult to imagine Jesus learning basic Greek from Roman merchants in the area of Nazareth when he was a child. As an adult he communicated with the Roman governor Pilate, whose primary language was most certainly Greek.

Jesus and his disciples traveled twenty-some miles north to Sidon, distancing himself even further from Galilee. But it turned out to be only a brief stop in the northern of these twin cities. They turned south and journeyed through Galilee, skirting the lake but not stopping for any length of time. They went beyond Galilee to Decapolis— from one Gentile territory, through Jewish Galilee, and into another Gentile territory. They climbed back up the mountainous terrain where Jesus had prayed alone through the night after the miraculous meal serving the thousands, only this time his disciples were there with him. It was one more opportunity for the thirteen of them to be together without the pressing crowds.

The respite didn't last long. Word spread that Jesus was back, and large crowds began to gather. They came for healing—the blind, disabled, and mute, along with many others with illnesses. Those who couldn't reach Jesus on their own were carried by others.

One of the first to arrive was a man who was deaf and nearly mute. He could make sounds, but it was almost impossible to understand him. Jesus met him and ushered him away for a more private meeting. The men who had brought him asked Jesus to place his hand anywhere on the man with the hopes that Jesus' touch would heal him. Jesus used a different method for this healing. First he put his fingers into both of the man's ears. Then Jesus spit on his own hand and touched the man's tongue with his fingers. Finally, Jesus lifted his head up as if he were looking right at God in heaven, and a long sigh came from him before he said, "*Ephphatha!*" § It was immediately obvious that

§ This means "be opened" in Jesus' native Aramaic language.

the man could hear but even more dramatic when he spoke with clarity and coherence.

Jesus told those who saw this miracle to keep it under wraps. He was still trying to minimize the political attention that his healings inevitably drew. But, again, his instructions made no difference. People couldn't seem to help themselves. Whether they repeated what happened in public or whispered it as "a secret just for you," word quickly spread. The crowd, already large, kept growing. Jesus healed for hours. People were amazed. They were stunned. They were overwhelmed. No one had ever witnessed such supernatural power. Gentiles were now openly praising the God of Israel. As one of them summed it up, "He has done everything amazingly well. He even gives hearing to the deaf and frees the tongue of the speechless to talk."

The more Jesus healed, the more sick people arrived. What started with one deaf and mute man grew to a mass of thousands, including those who were sick and those who accompanied them. It turned into a healing marathon that lasted for three full days. Amazement and celebration were everywhere, but fatigue and hunger were also settling in. During one of the periodic breaks when Jesus sat down to rest, he gathered his disciples in a close circle around him and told them, "I feel sorry for these people who have been here for three days and don't have anything to eat. If I send them away hungry, they will pass out on the way because some of them have so far to go home."

The twelve didn't expect a repeat of the tremendous meal Jesus had hosted the last time they were in Decapolis. After they heard him confront the wrong motives of those who were fed during the day-after meeting in Capernaum, they assumed there would be no more miracle meals. They asked, "Do you know where we could buy enough bread to feed this crowd out in the middle of nowhere?" It sounded like a rhetorical question, but Jesus answered with another question, "How many loaves do you have so far?"

They counted what they had available and reported back to Jesus that they had seven loaves of bread and a few small fish. Much like the last time, Jesus had the people sit down on the grass and he spoke a prayer of gratitude. He started breaking the bread and fish into pieces and told his disciples to distribute the simple meal to the crowd. A few hours later all the people were fed to satisfaction, and there were seven basketfuls of broken pieces left over. They had fed four thousand men, plus the women and children who accompanied them, for a total of more than ten thousand who were fed!

Jesus and the disciples went back to the boat and left the Gentile-populated east coast of the lake and headed toward the Jewish-populated area of Magadan and Dalmanutha. Another unpleasant encounter ensued, and this time some of the Sadducees joined with the Pharisees to harass Jesus. Under normal circumstances they were enemies with different opinions about almost everything, but they found common ground in their hatred of Jesus.

They had conspired to try another entrapment, starting out with a request for a miracle. They had convinced themselves that they could attack Jesus at his point of greatest strength, using his supernatural power to trip him up.

Jesus was not going to perform miracles on command, especially for his enemies. Instead he responded to them with an analogy set in local weather forecasting. "In the evening, you say, 'Red sky at night, fishermen's delight,' and in the morning, 'Red sky at morning, fishermen take warning.' You are good at forecasting the weather from the color of the sky, but you can't interpret the signs of the times. An evil, adulterous generation is always looking for more miracles, but the only one you are going to get is the sign of Jonah." §

§ They knew well the story of Jonah being swallowed by a huge fish and coming out alive three days later, but they had no idea what this had to do with their request for a miracle. Jesus would wait to make sense of this prediction— another item on the "wait and see" list.

This conversation was going nowhere. He wasn't going to change their minds—they had already decided not to believe in him, in his miracles, or his teaching. Jesus abruptly ended the dialogue and walked back to his usual boat for another ride northeastward across the lake. On good days with gentle winds, the sails were used instead of the oars and crossing the seven-mile-wide lake could take less than an hour.

The twelve had forgotten to bring food—again. All they had was one loaf of bread for all thirteen of them. This time Jesus was not going to make it into a meal, but he did use that single loaf as an object lesson. He told them, "Be on your guard against the yeast of the Pharisees, Sadducees, and Herodians." Trying to figure out what he meant, they whispered back and forth that he was talking about their forgetfulness in bringing food for their travels.

Jesus easily overheard their conjectures and asked them, "Why are you talking about not having bread?" He shook his head. "Can't you see or understand what I say? Are your hearts hardened? Do you have eyes that are blind and ears that are deaf? Have you already forgotten when I broke the five loaves for the hungry crowd? How many basketfuls of pieces did you pick up?"

"Twelve," they answered, feeling a bit subdued.

"More recently, when I divided up the seven loaves for the thousands, how many basketfuls of leftovers did you pick up?"

"Seven," they replied.

"Do you still not get it?" Jesus asked them.

Actually, they finally did understand. He wasn't talking about lunch. He was talking about leaven. Leaven or yeast is the ingredient that permeates flour and makes bread rise when baked. Jesus was warning them against the defective thinking of the Pharisees, Sadducees, and Herodians (members of a political party that supported the rule of King Herod). These three groups were quite different from one another, but all held something in common. They refused to believe the truth Jesus taught without constant verification with miracles; they were predisposed against belief. Jesus was warning his disciples not to be like them, not to let their disbelief permeate their thinking the way yeast permeates bread. The only way they were going to see a clear picture of Jesus as the Messiah was to avoid the false thinking of disbelief.

It wasn't that Jesus was rationing out his miracles. He loved showing God's power, especially in healing the sick. But he didn't want the miracles to overshadow the spiritual truth he came to present. He didn't want people to be so captivated by the miracles that they overlooked God.

Then he coupled his warning about miracle-seeking with another miracle—just to keep the balance.

When the boat landed at Bethsaida, some people brought a blind man who asked Jesus for his healing touch. Using a slightly different tactic than other times, Jesus took the man by the hand and led him down the path until they were just outside the village. This time he spit a small amount of saliva on each of the man's eyes. He put his hands on the man and asked him, "Do you see anything?"

The man answered, "I see people, but they look like trees walking around." He was partially cured.

Jesus stood behind him and reached around in front of him to put his hands on both of the man's eyes again. This time everything was clear; his sight was now totally normal. Jesus told him to go home on his own, to avoid the village, where others could see him. This miracle was to give sight to the blind man and insight to his disciples. It wasn't meant for the crowds or for the critics.

There would be more miracles, but next there needed to be more teaching.

CHAPTER NINE

"Who is this Jesus?" was the question on many lips. Many people just couldn't figure him out. In some ways he seemed so ordinary—a local boy who grew up in Nazareth; a man whose appearance didn't stand out in the crowd. He laughed and cried, slept and sweat, got hungry and ate. Yet he also was so above average with his amazing miracles, articulate arguments, and keen intellect. Some days he looked and sounded like just one more Jewish worker with a Galilean accent. Other days he acted and talked as if he were God himself. When asked to identify himself or give an explanation to clear up confusion, his answers were often hard to understand, a sort of doublespeak that was difficult to decipher.

During a visit to one of the villages in the region of Caesarea Philippi, Jesus gathered his twelve disciples for a private prayer meeting. Between prayers he asked them, "Who do the people in these crowds say I am?"

They replied, "Some say you are John the Baptizer come back from the dead. Others say Elijah, and still others say that one of the prophets of long ago has come back to life."

This was a small sampling of the rumors and guesses of those who came to see Jesus. Elijah was a prophet who was taken directly to heaven without dying, so maybe he was still alive and had come back again after a nine-hundred-year absence. Most of the famous Hebrew prophets had died at least four hundred years earlier; some had been dead for a thousand years or more. John the Baptizer was a recent prophet, although to identify Jesus as a man who had recently been beheaded was rather bizarre.

Jesus' query really was a lead-in for his more important and personal question to his closest friends: "What about you? Who do you say I am?"

This wasn't a new question. These disciples of Jesus were often asked this by others. The twelve had discussed it among themselves myriads of times before. But this was the first time Jesus had directly asked their opinion. It was a turning point in their relationship and in Jesus' movement toward the fulfillment of his life mission.

Trigger-tongue Peter, as usual, was quick to respond. With brash boldness he asserted, "You are the Messiah, the son of the living God." The others no doubt were stunned. They had wondered but never dared actually say it to Jesus. Peter thought they had danced around the issue long enough and it was time to clear the air. He was convinced that Jesus was the Messiah sent from God. If he was wrong, Jesus would correct him.

§ "Church" is the English translation for the Greek work *ekklesía,* which means a community or congregation. Jesus was anticipating future followers gathering together in his name—similar to the Jewish synagogues but new and different. The concept of the church was further developed and explained by later New Testament writers.

"God bless you, Simon son of Jonah, because you didn't figure this out from human knowledge; my Father in heaven is the one who told you," Jesus affirmed. "And now that you have said who I am, I'm going to say who you are. You are Peter, 'the Rock,' and on this rock I will build my church, § and the gates of Hades aren't strong enough to keep it down.§ I am going to give you the keys to open up the kingdom of heaven. What you tie down or set free here on earth will be tied down or set free up in heaven." The tone of Jesus' voice and words clearly communicated that this was very important. He used the formal name, Simon bar Jonah, and then played on his nickname—Peter means "rock" and this was a rock-solid declaration. Looking to a future

§ "The gates of Hades" was a Jewish way of referring to death. The "gates" keep the dead imprisoned. Jesus' church would become so powerfully alive that it would be stronger than death itself, he was telling them.

his followers didn't yet see, Jesus anticipated a worldwide church he planned to establish and saw Peter and his statement at the foundation. It was the first mention of the church that would dominate these men's lives and become Jesus' central strategy and lasting legacy.

At this point the disciples didn't know what a church was. Jesus promised supernatural authority linking spiritual actions on earth with eternal outcomes in heaven. He revealed himself here as more than a teacher and miracle worker; he was a visionary.

Like so many times before, Jesus now warned his disciples not to tell anyone that he was the Messiah. Not that it wasn't the truth or that the people wouldn't find out later. But Jesus had a plan and a timeline, and he still wasn't ready to go public. The timing wasn't open-ended, though; there was less than a year left. These twelve now knew he was the Messiah. It was time to let them in on his plan. He knew it was going to be a shock, and they would need months to get used to it before others found out. No parables or codes or veiled references this time.

Jesus plainly told them what to expect:

- He was headed to Jerusalem, where he would suffer at the hands of the Jewish leaders.
- He would be rejected by the elders of Israel, the chief priests of the temple, and the teachers of religious law.
- He would be crucified.
- Three days later he would come back to life again.

Peter, alarmed by Jesus' predictions, took Jesus aside to confront his upsetting description of what was going to happen. He rebuked Jesus, saying, "Never, Lord! This will never happen to you!" While Peter may have been distressed by Jesus' statements, Jesus could not allow Peter's response to stand. Speaking to Peter in a voice he intended to be heard by the other eleven, Jesus said, "Get behind me, Satan! You are a stumbling block to me. When you talk like that you are not thinking God's thoughts; you're thinking ordinary human thoughts that are wrong." Jesus' intensity nearly knocked Peter off his feet. He had meant to affirm and protect Jesus. He thought he would be a hero for what he'd said. Instead he was addressed as if he were the devil himself.

No one said another word. Peter didn't know what to say, and Jesus just walked away in silence. But the exchange was on his mind when Jesus later summoned his disciples and the nearby crowd to a teaching time. No miracles this day; just a forceful line in the sand. Jesus told them all, "If anyone chooses to follow me, he must deny himself and take up his cross and follow me. You need to understand that whoever wants to save his life will lose it, but whoever loses his life for me will find it. What good is it if someone gains the whole world yet loses his soul? What is worth more than your eternal soul? The day is coming when the Son of Man is going to come to earth in his Father's glory with his angels and will reward everyone according to what he has done. The truth is that some who are standing here right now won't experience death without first getting to see the Son of Man coming in his kingdom."

§ Jesus had witnessed a crucifixion when he was eleven years old. A man named Judas the Galilean led an insurrection against Roman rule. He attacked the imperial armory at Sepphoris, only four miles away from Jesus' home in Nazareth. The Roman response was swift and severe. Sepphoris was burned to the ground, and all of the citizens were sold into slavery. The two thousand rebels were crucified on the same day on crosses that lined the road near Nazareth. Jesus' memory had been etched with the horror of crucifixion.

If they were serious about their commitment, it would not always be cheering crowds, marvelous miracles, and free food. Jesus was announcing that he expected them to suffer and die if that's what it took to follow him. He promised great rewards in his kingdom but potential pain and problems in the process. It was another teaching that would make more sense later, especially the part about the cross. Some of them had seen crucifixions. § When he told them that following him would mean carrying a cross of their own, he was talking about a high price for loyalty.

The fuller meaning of the cross was a year away, but the prediction that some of them would see him in the majesty and glory of the kingdom of God was only a week away. §

The next week Jesus climbed one of the highest mountains in the region and invited Peter, James, and John to accompany him. The climb was strenuous, starting at the warm lower elevations and rising to the peak at an altitude high enough for snow to be on the ground. When they reached the summit, Jesus organized a four-man prayer meeting. He did the lion's share of the praying while the others started to fall asleep, probably from a combination of altitude, exhaustion, and not yet understanding why they were there.

§ Another event Jesus may have been referring to was forty days after his resurrection, when his followers saw him ascend into heaven in a cloud and angels appeared with an announcement about Jesus' eventual return to earth.

Jesus quietly slipped away from them—not far, maybe ten yards. The color of his face changed to shine like the sun. His clothes looked as white as light. He became brighter and brighter. He still looked like Jesus—still human, but something much more unearthly. Spiritual. Supernatural. The three disciples were awakened like a sleeping child whose nap is suddenly interrupted by the bright flash of nearby lightning. When they looked at Jesus, they had to blink and shade their eyes at the brilliance. It was more intense than looking directly at the sun on a cloudless summer day. What they saw was the Jesus they knew in a form they had never experienced. And with Jesus there were two other men whom they figured out were Moses and Elijah. Lacking any experience to analyze or categorize what they saw, they looked and listened in stupefied silence. The three brighter-than-life men were talking about Jesus' coming death in Jerusalem.

At first the witnesses were so mesmerized that they lost track of time. Then when they recognized that the mystical meeting was coming to an end, they didn't want it to conclude. Peter proposed to Jesus, "Rabbi, it is so good for all of us to be here. Let's build three dwellings—one for you, one for Moses, and one for Elijah." He spoke more out of enthusiasm mixed with fear than reason. Jesus didn't even respond to Peter's idea.

What happened next was even more bewildering than the heavenly brilliance of the three men. The group on the mountaintop was enveloped in a bright cloud—like a fog of sunlight. The voice of God spoke from the cloud and said, "This is my son, whom I love! I am totally delighted with him! Listen to him!"

The voice knocked them off their feet, and Peter, James, and John lay facedown on the ground and shook with fear. They became so paralyzed by what happened that they couldn't look up or arise.

Jesus walked over to them and touched each one. "Get up," he calmly told them. "Don't be afraid." Still trembling, all three looked around before trying to stand. All they saw was Jesus. They stood, but they remained utterly awestruck by what they had seen and heard. When Jesus started back down the mountain, they followed in silence.

"I don't want you to tell anyone else what you saw today. Keep it a secret until the Son of Man has been raised from the dead," Jesus told them as they walked. This time they kept his secret—not only because he asked them to but because they couldn't come up with a description or explanation that the others would understand or believe. They were in awe of all of Jesus' previous miracles, but this was beyond everything else. It was like they had gone to heaven and seen God himself.

What they couldn't tell others they could discuss among themselves. These three disciples now shared a new bond forged in their supernatural mountaintop encounter. As they walked together, their fear began to subside, and normal conversation resumed. When they finally were able to talk about it, they were particularly concerned with what Jesus meant by his time limit. He had told them to keep quiet until he was raised from the dead, but they didn't know what that meant or when it would happen. All three believed in a future resurrection from the dead to be experienced by everyone who has died—a date with God for eternal judgment. But they didn't think Jesus was talking about that resurrection but something sooner and more personal.

The three asked Jesus questions in order to connect their previous religious teachings with what they were learning from him. They remembered a prediction from the fifth-century BC prophet Malachi: God would send Elijah back "before the great and dreadful day of the Lord comes." So they asked Jesus, "Why do those who teach us the Scriptures say that Elijah must come before the Messiah?"

Jesus answered, "Because that's the way it will happen. First Elijah comes to restore and get everything ready for the Messiah. But I have news for you. Elijah has already come! The trouble is they did not recognize him and ended up doing him in. They are going to do the same to the Son of Man, who is also going to suffer death." This time they knew what he meant. John the Baptizer had fulfilled the prophecy of Malachi, and Jesus was headed for suffering just as John had suffered.

At the bottom of the mountain, a crowd was waiting for Jesus to resolve a new controversy. Tempers were heating up in an argument between the other nine of Jesus' disciples and several teachers of the law. The crowd gathered to witness the debate, but when some of them saw Jesus, they started running toward him. Within minutes the whole crowd surrounded him. Jesus asked what the argument was about, but didn't hear a clear answer with everyone talking at once.

As if all this wasn't chaotic enough, a father in the crowd pushed others aside and fell on his knees in front of Jesus. He implored, "Teacher, I beg you to see my son and have mercy on him. He is my only child. He has seizures and great suffering. Some kind of a spirit seizes him, and he suddenly starts screaming until the spirit takes his speech and throws him on the ground. He foams at the mouth, grinds his teeth, and becomes stiff as a board. The problem is chronic—the spirit is destroying him. I pleaded with your disciples to drive it out, but they couldn't help."

It was obvious that the child needed help, but Jesus also was concerned about the attitudes of those in the crowd. "All you unbelievers, how long do I have to stay around and put up with you?" he asked the crowd. His heart was drawn to the sick child and the desperate father, so he said, "Bring your boy for me to see."

Transporting the boy triggered another one of the seizures. Somehow when the spirit in the child saw Jesus, it threw him into a convulsion. He hit the ground, thrashing about and foaming at the mouth.

Jesus asked the father how long this had been going on. "Since he was a baby," he answered. "It has often thrown him into fire or water, nearly killing him. If there is anything you can do, please take pity on us and help us." As he spoke, his face and voice combined hope with the exhaustion of constantly being on call for his son's entire life.

" 'If there's anything I can do?' " Jesus quoted the father. "Everything is possible for someone who believes." The father, afraid that his doubt might have alienated Jesus, quickly said, "I really do believe! Please help me overcome my unbelief!"

People were running toward the crowd, hoping to see a miracle. Instead of waiting for them, Jesus spoke quickly before any more came. He rebuked the evil spirit in the boy, saying, "You deaf and mute spirit, I order you to come out of him and never come back again."

A chilling evil-spirit scream came out of the boy's mouth, another convulsion violently shook him, and the evil spirit left the boy, who now lay rigid and still on the ground. Those standing around were saying, "He's dead." But Jesus leaned over, grabbed the boy's hand, and pulled him to his feet. The boy was fine, standing in front of Jesus and his father, calm and healthy.

Anxious to escape the growing crowd, Jesus headed indoors with his disciples close behind. They wanted to know how he had healed the boy when they couldn't. Lowering their voices so they would not be overheard, they asked Jesus, "Why couldn't we drive out the evil spirit from that boy?" Jesus told them, "You really want to know? It's because you have so little faith. The truth is that if you have faith as small as a mustard seed, you can say to this mountain, 'Move from here to over there,' and it will move. Nothing will be impossible for you to do." Sensing their next question, "What exactly are you telling us to do?" Jesus told them, "This kind of evil spirit is especially difficult and can come out only by prayer."

The weeks passed quickly until Jesus had only six months left to live, and he knew it. Every day and hour counted, and he wasn't going to allow the throngs to control his schedule. There were twenty-six weeks remaining to teach his followers and get to Jerusalem for the final countdown to his death. His plan was to leave the area of Caesarea Philippi in the northeast and travel through his home province of Galilee and then on to Jerusalem in the southern province of Judea, making every effort to avoid crowds and controversy.

As they entered Galilee, Jesus again told his disciples, "The Son of Man is going to be betrayed into the hands of enemies. They will kill him, and after three days he will rise." Even though his little band had heard him say this before, they just did not understand. It didn't fit with his power and popularity. But no one had the nerve to ask Jesus for an explanation. They really didn't know what to ask.

Jesus led them back to his Capernaum headquarters, but the townspeople didn't know where he was staying. When several of the temple tax collectors couldn't find him, they settled for Peter, confronting him about past-due taxes. Unlike Matthew, who collected taxes for the Romans, these tax collectors worked for the temple and collected religious taxes to subsidize the sacrifices used in the worship liturgy. The tax rate was two drachma per year, normally collected every spring. Jesus and his group had been out of the area when the taxes were due so the collectors wanted them to pay now, even though it was autumn.

"Doesn't your teacher pay the temple tax?" they asked Peter. Always quick to defend Jesus and think later, Peter told them matter-of-factly, "Yes, he does!" although he probably didn't know.

Peter headed back to Jesus' house to tell him what happened. As soon as they saw each other, before Peter had a chance to explain, Jesus asked, "What do you think, Simon? When kings collect taxes, do they go after their own sons or the rest of the citizens?"

Peter must have been nonplussed for a moment, even after all the supernatural things he had seen Jesus do. But realizing Jesus already knew what had happened, Peter answered, "The rest of the citizens."

"Then the sons are exempt," Jesus said to him, telling Peter that he was exempt from the temple tax. Peter no doubt wished he had known this back in the marketplace and hadn't been so quick to say that Jesus paid the tax.

"But let's not offend them," Jesus added. "Go down to the lake and cast your fishing line. Take the first fish you catch; open its mouth and pull out a four-drachma coin. Take the coin and give it to them to pay my tax and yours."

Peter, shaking his head in amazement, did what Jesus said. He caught the fish, found the coin, and paid the taxes. He had been at the center of another miracle. When he returned to the house, he had an exciting story to tell to the team of disciples.

They had come to know each other well. Usually they got along, but familiarity brought differences and tensions. During their travel back to Capernaum, the twelve had debated who was the greatest among them. Like many arguments, it had multiple beginnings. Peter, James, and John climbed the mountain with Jesus—the other nine didn't. Every time Peter spoke first, he seemed as if he were the leader of the group. And now he had found the coin in the fish and experienced a miracle that was exclusively his. A mood of jealousy and competition controlled the discussion, and it became a heated argument.

They didn't think Jesus heard them as they had walked from Caesarea Philippi, and they were embarrassed in the Capernaum house when Jesus asked them, "What were you arguing about back along the road?" No one answered.

Finally several of them broke the silence with a question for Jesus, hoping to get the pressure off of them: "Jesus, tell us who is the greatest in the kingdom of heaven."

Jesus was gentle with them. He asked them to sit down around him on the floor, and he seized the teaching opportunity—perhaps one of their most memorable lessons from their years of listening to Jesus.

"The way for someone to be first is to become the very last and the servant of all," Jesus told them. They listened intently...and humbly. Waiting for Jesus' next words, they were interrupted by a small neighbor boy walking into the house. Jesus knew they were thinking "Get this child out of here! We're having an important conversation with our teacher."

Jesus called the child over to him and put the little boy right next to him, clearly communicating that the place of honor went to the neighbor boy. § He told the men, "Listen to this truth! Unless you change and become like little children, you'll never enter into the kingdom of heaven. So anyone who humbles himself like this boy is the greatest in the kingdom of heaven. Anyone who welcomes a little child like this one in my name welcomes me. Anyone who welcomes me welcomes the God who sent me. You want to know who is the greatest? It is the person who is least among you all."

§ In their culture the honored place in relation to a king, teacher, or other important person was at the right side. One of the greatest honors royalty could bestow on a subject was to have that person sit or stand at his right in the king's court or some other public ceremony.

There had been many teachings they didn't understand until long after Jesus spoke them, but this wasn't difficult to grasp. If they wanted to be great they shouldn't seek the place of honor but become like children, who don't have social prestige. Become like the neighbor boy in his simplicity and humility. It was one of Jesus' counterintuitive teachings, a turning of ordinary human thinking upside down.

The crowd went home. The twelve men sat around Jesus in the house. Defenses were down. Conversation was comfortable. It was just the way Jesus planned it—teaching and learning that would last for a lifetime.

"Teacher," said John, "several of us saw a man driving out demons in your name. We told him to stop, because he was not one of our group."

"Don't stop him," Jesus said. "No one who does a miracle in my name is likely to turn around the next minute and say something bad about me. Let's assume that whoever is not against us is for us. The truth for you to learn today is that anyone who gives you a cup of water in my name, because you belong to me, will certainly never lose his reward.

"And if anyone causes one of these little children—" Jesus paused as he touched the head of the child—"one of these little children who believes in me to sin, he'd be better off if he were thrown into the ocean with a large millstone tied around his neck. Grief and troubles are exactly what people in this world deserve because of the things they do that cause people to sin! Such things must come, but woe to the one through whom they come! If your hand causes you to sin, cut it off. You're better off going through life with one hand missing than going to the endless fires of hell with two hands. And if your foot causes you to sin, cut it off. You're better off going through life maimed than to walk into hell with two feet. And if your eye causes you to sin, pluck it out. You're better off entering the kingdom of God with one eye than to look around hell with two eyes and see that it's a place where 'their worm does not die, and the fire is not quenched.' Everyone will be salted with fire. Salt is good, but if it loses its saltiness, how are you going to make it salty again? Stay salty and be at peace with one another."

He had their attention. The point was powerful. Side with Jesus! Do what is good! Avoid influencing the innocent to sin! Avoid sin at any cost! Be like salt—good for taste and good as a preservative against decay!

Turning back to the little boy, Jesus said, "Make sure that you don't look down on one of these little children. They have angels in heaven who look into the face of God the Father." He looked around at the twelve men watching him intently.

"What do you think? If a shepherd owns a hundred sheep, and one of them wanders off, won't he leave the ninety-nine sheep safely in the fold and go looking for the one that is lost? And when he finds it, you know that he is happier about that one sheep than he is about the ninety-nine that did not wander off. It's the same way with your Father in heaven. He's doesn't want one of these little ones to get lost."

In rapid succession, Jesus had sided with the underdogs of society—the marginal, the young, and the lost. He taught his followers to use their strength for the benefit of the weak.

While Jesus dreamed and planned for his followers to be transformed by him and his message, he also anticipated inevitable human conflicts. He wanted his church to have Christians who were unlike the rest of society, even though not always perfect. This meant that when they sinned, they would take a different approach to dealing with their sins and conflicts.

Jesus taught his disciples, "If someone sins against you, go and talk one-on-one about what was done. If that person listens and positively responds to you, you have won your brother or sister over and salvaged your relationship. But if that person refuses to listen, take one or two other disciples along so that the issue will be heard by two or three witnesses. If there is a refusal to listen to them, tell it to the church to see if that will help. In an extreme case where someone refuses to listen even to the church, treat that person as you would an unbeliever such as a pagan or a tax collector." Jesus wanted his followers to deal with their problems in a kind and compassionate manner. However, those who were unresponsive to compassion and kindness wouldn't be allowed to continue in their misbehavior. If need be, they would be excluded from the church until they changed their ways. This was more than human psychology and good advice. Jesus was convinced that his followers would be the connection between earth and heaven after he was gone.

He had talked with them before about teamwork and pulling together, but he repeated it for emphasis. "I've said this before, but I'll tell you again: if two of you on earth agree about asking God for something, it will be granted to you by my Father in heaven. When two or three come together in my name, I'll be there too."

Some of the twelve listened like students who were preparing for a test. Others, like Peter, personalized almost everything Jesus said. Peter really wanted to learn and to live Jesus' way. He now asked Jesus about forgiving those who had sinned against him. Peter knew well the traditional Jewish teaching that an offended person should repeatedly forgive the offender—up to three times. After three offenses, they reasoned, a victim risked simply enabling the abuser. But Peter knew that Jesus was usually more generous than Jewish tradition, so he proposed doubling the number plus one. Peter asked, "Lord, when another disciple sins against me, how many times should I forgive him? Up to seven times?"

Jesus told Peter to forgive seventy times seven times, but he didn't literally mean 490 times and no more but rather no limit. While Peter and the others listened in stunned silence, Jesus explained his mandate for forgiveness with a story about how the kingdom of heaven on earth truly works.

§ A talent was both a measure of weight and of money. In monetary terms, Jesus didn't specify if the ten thousand talents were of bronze, silver, or gold, although it would be an exceptionally large amount of money in any case. The amount combines the largest Greek numeral with the largest denomination of money. It was an amount beyond the wildest dreams of an ordinary person.

"Imagine a king who decided to settle all his financial accounts among his servants. Starting at the top, a man who owed ten thousand talents was brought into the presence of the king. § Because he was unable to pay, the king ordered all of his possessions sold and that he and his family be sold as slaves. It wouldn't pay off the debt, but at least the king could recoup some of his money.

"The debtor dropped to his knees and begged for mercy. He asked for an extension on the debt and promised to pay back everything he owed. The king knew that the man couldn't come up with ten thousand talents in ten lifetimes of extensions. Since the king was a generous and compassionate master, he felt sorry for the servant and did something that caught everyone by surprise—he canceled the entire debt and let the man go free, even allowing him to keep his house and other possessions.

"As the forgiven servant was leaving the palace grounds, he ran into a colleague who owed him a hundred denarii. § He demanded immediate payment of the small debt and actually began to choke and shake the man to get his money. Frightened and panicked, the small-time debtor fell to his knees and begged for more time, promising full repayment.

§ The denarius was the basic Roman coin and the typical pay for a day's work by a laborer in Israel. A hundred denarii represented a hundred days of pay for a worker. Although not an insignificant amount of money, it was relatively little, certainly when compared to ten thousand talents.

"The first servant felt no compassion. He called the police and had the man thrown into jail until he could come up with the denarii he owed.

"All this was done out in the open where everyone could see and hear. The rest of the palace employees were so shocked by what happened that they reported the whole incident back to the king. The king ordered the first servant back to his throne room and confronted him with his inconsistency. 'You are an evil man!' he declared. 'I forgave your huge debt because you asked, but you wouldn't forgive a mere hundred denarii a few minutes later. I'll tell you what. Your debt is reinstated, and you are sentenced to stay in prison under torture until you pay back the whole amount.' "

Jesus' point was obvious. "This is how my heavenly Father will treat each of you unless you forgive your brother from your heart," he told Peter and the others. If God was willing to forgive their lifetime of sins, they should be willing to forgive any sins against them without keeping count. And if they failed to forgive, it showed they had not experienced God's forgiveness.

Their stay in Capernaum wasn't long. It was still Jesus' northern headquarters, but he was spending increasingly less time there as he counted down the final months of his life. Once again he gathered his closest followers and started walking. Their destination was Jerusalem, and their route was the main road through Samaria. §

§ Some Jews were anxious about travel through Samaria. Years later, in AD 52, there was a massacre in Samaria of Jewish tourists who didn't take the longer route between Jerusalem to the south and Galilee to the north. But normally the long route was actually more difficult and dangerous.

A man who practiced religious law walked alongside Jesus and assured him that his commitment to Jesus was sufficient for any route. "Teacher," the man said, "I will follow you wherever you go."

Jesus warned him that his bravado was underestimating the challenge: "Foxes have holes and birds have nests, but the Son of Man doesn't have a place to sleep at night."

As the lawyer reconsidered his promise, Jesus turned to another fellow traveler and told him, "Follow me!" Having witnessed what happened to the lawyer, this man deferred a final answer, saying to Jesus, "First let me go and bury my father." Those listening no doubt thought this was a good answer, because Jewish culture gave high priority to a son's responsibility to care for his father's burial. Jesus' response might have seemed harsh: "Let the dead bury their own dead. If you want to follow me, your assignment is to go and proclaim the kingdom of God." This man's father wasn't dead yet, and burials almost always took place on the day of death. So it wasn't very likely he would be walking alongside Jesus if his father had just died. This man was putting off his decision to follow Jesus indefinitely. His father might live a long time. Jesus told him to stop worrying about his father's burial and join the cause of God's kingdom right now. §

A third would-be follower of Jesus offered his excuse before Jesus had a chance to invite him. He said, "I will follow you, Lord, as soon as I get back from saying good-bye to my family." Jesus had heard enough excuses. "Go back home if that's what you want to do, but remember that no one who puts his hand to the plow and looks back is qualified to serve in the kingdom of God."

§ There is another understanding of this conversation. There were typically two burials of those who died. The primary burial took place on the day of death. One year later, after the body had been reduced to a skeleton, the bones were removed and placed in limestone chests known as ossuaries, and there was a secondary burial. The entire year was considered a period of mourning with limited participation in the social life of the community. This man may have wanted to tend to his father's second burial and follow Jesus later.

Even among his followers, Jesus was hearing a variety of excuses to abandon him. Seeing the erosion of people and revealing their personal disbelief, Jesus' own brothers told him in front of others, "You should leave here and go to Judea. Show your disciples there some of your miracles. If you want to be a popular leader, you need to quit hiding and show yourself off to the whole world!"

Jesus' family misunderstood his goals and schedule. Jesus told his brothers, "The right time for me isn't now. But you don't care about that, because for you any time is right. You just don't get it because the world doesn't hate you, but it's different with me. The world hates me because I testify that what it does is evil. You go on to the Feast yourselves, but don't expect to see me there until the right time has come." So he stayed up north in Galilee for a little while longer. While it wasn't yet "the right time" for Jesus, it indeed was getting closer. He was headed back to heaven by way of Jerusalem; the countdown had begun.

Jesus waited until his brothers had left and then secretly went south. Several scouts had gone ahead into Samaria to arrange lodging. It was a simple task that turned sour when the local villagers found out the purpose of Jesus' journey. Since Samaritans believed God was to be worshipped on Mount Gerizim rather than at the Jerusalem temple, they refused to welcome Jesus' entourage. James and John were angered by their inhospitality and wanted to pray fire down from heaven to destroy their village and all its people. Jesus rebuked James and John, insisting that they just find another place to stay.

CHAPTER TEN

They all tried to figure out Jesus. Some were early believers like Peter and John, who said, "He's a prophet of God." Others were early enemies, including a few Pharisees and synagogue rulers. They said, "He deceives the people." But most were simply curious. Thousands were attracted to his miracles, even though they were unsure how he did them. Crowds gathered to hear his teaching even if they hadn't decided if they agreed. Some thought he was the political Messiah they had long awaited. Others were simply grateful for the food he provided, the healing they received, or the child he helped. Whatever the reason, the rumors about Jesus were rampant. But they were often only whispered because many were afraid of the authorities and what their reaction might be to sympathetic attitudes about Jesus.

What began as curiosity became strong convictions among some. Thousands became serious followers. One hundred twenty signed on as disciples. A dozen were in his band of closest supporters. At the same time, his critics and enemies multiplied. Most, but not all, were political and religious leaders—those entrenched in the establishment. Among those who made up their minds against Jesus were Pharisees, high priests, those around them, and a majority of the religious council called the Sanhedrin. Some were reacting from misunderstanding and others from malice. Either way, they perceived Jesus as a threat to their traditions and power—his popularity could lead the people against the established leaders of Israel. They decided to at the least discredit him or maybe even kill him. They could not tolerate him much longer.

WHY JESUS CONFLICTED WITH THE RELIGIOUS LEADERS

Some of the religious leaders were Jesus' friends and supporters, but conflict with others caused frequent tension. It wasn't all their doing. Jesus talked about them and to them in terms that made them angry and defensive. His accusations were direct:

- They had not rightly taught the Scriptures; thus, they had not prepared the people of Israel for the coming of the Messiah.
- They had supplanted right teaching with traditions.
- They had not set good examples as leaders for the people to follow.
- They had repudiated Jesus as the Messiah and turned people against him.

The religious leaders—including some of the Pharisees, Sadducees, Herodians, chief priests, synagogue rulers, and members of the Sanhedrin—certainly didn't see the situation in the same way. They thought they were proper teachers and leaders. They had convinced themselves that their traditions were faithful to God and the Scriptures and that Jesus was not the Messiah but an imposter—either a self-appointed charlatan or, worse, an agent of the devil.

Such opposing positions were the fuel for conflict, especially when everyone was convinced that the stakes were high—God, truth, kingdom, Israel, and eternal life. Jesus relentlessly pounded at their teachings and traditions; they increasingly resented Jesus until they decided he had to be killed.

Jesus' strongest support came from the northern province of Galilee. His greatest opposition was centered in the southern province of Judea, especially Jerusalem. To be sure, not everyone in Galilee was for him nor was everyone in Judea against him. In addition, there was less polarization throughout the central provinces of Samaria and Perea.

When the opposition became even stronger, he withdrew from Jerusalem until the politics and conspiracy cooled, returning later. All of this was connected to his sense of timing for his mission and eventual death in Jerusalem.

When Jesus and his followers arrived in Jerusalem in the fall of AD 29, the Feast of Tabernacles was about to begin. Although similar to the harvest festivals of many nations, the annual Jewish celebration wasn't rooted in pagan religious mythology but in Hebrew history.

Also called the Festival of Ingathering and Festival of Booths, § it commemorated the years of wandering in the wilderness when the nation escaped slavery in Egypt and journeyed to the promised land of Canaan.

The festival itself included lots of rejoicing as people celebrated God's provision and protection. Special daily sacrifices were offered at the temple, starting with thirteen bullocks on the first day and one less on subsequent days until seven were sacrificed on the seventh and final day. On the eighth day, called the Great Day of the Feast, one bullock, one ram, and seven lambs were sacrificed in a separate ceremony.

§ During those forty years, the people lived in tents and booths. The annual fall festival required every Israelite to build temporary shelters out of boughs and branches and then to live in these temporary shelters for the week of the feast. The feast began on the fifteenth day of the seventh month of the Jewish year and lasted for seven days. It was one of the three annual mandatory-attendance festivals for all male Jews in Israel.

Although this feast was celebrated throughout Jewish history, some changes and additions came through the years, including a ceremony of pouring water. This was not prescribed in the Old Testament law but was added as an expression of gratitude for God's provision of the rain that made the harvested crops possible.

This year there was broad expectation that Jesus would come to Jerusalem for the feast. The religious leaders kept asking where he was, but it wasn't until halfway through the week that he made his first public appearance and began teaching at the temple. He quickly drew a crowd, impressing everyone with his style and content. Jesus had not attended a recognized rabbinical school or studied with a well-known rabbi, and the educated people were stunned and wondered to one another, "How does this man know so much without a formal education?"

Jesus decided to give a public answer. "My teaching isn't my own. It doesn't come from a rabbi who tutored me; it comes from God who sent me. Those who choose to obey God will quickly recognize whether my teaching is from God or I made it up. Many teachers are in it for personal honor, but any teacher who promotes the honor of God is a teacher of the truth. Moses gave you God's law, right? Well, none of you keeps the law you received. So why are you trying to kill me?"

From the crowd came shouts that he was demon possessed. They accused him of being delusional. Some asked, "Who is trying to kill you?" Jesus' statement alerted his enemies to the fact that he knew what they were planning to do.

Jesus ignored the question and returned to teaching, dealing particularly with the most common criticism raised against him—that he was a Sabbath breaker because he healed on the weekly day of rest. His defense was brilliant as he exposed his critics for doing exactly what they accused him of doing. He said, "I did one miracle on the Sabbath, and you are all upset. Yet you perform circumcisions on the Sabbath and say that it is all right because it came down from the patriarchs and Moses. § Stop judging everything from first impressions and try making a right judgment for once." Certainly, he argued, if it is legal to injure for the sake of good on the Sabbath, it must be legal to heal for the sake of good on the Sabbath.

§ Jesus referred to the ancient Jewish rite of circumcising male babies when they were eight days old, even if it was the Sabbath, and the resulting injury to the baby.

The temple court was a forum for public dialogue and debate. Speakers were not afforded the luxury of uninterrupted lecture. People talked, shouted, argued, interrupted, and arrived and departed at will. While Jesus was teaching, one man in the crowd remembered the rumor he had heard about the leaders conspiring to kill Jesus and said, "Isn't this the man they supposedly are trying to kill? Here he is, speaking publicly, and no one is saying a word to him. Maybe all our religious leaders have decided he's the Messiah after all!" Another man interjected, "He's not the Messiah. He can't be, because we know where this man is from. When the Messiah comes, no one will know where he comes from."

Jesus heard them and raised his voice over the buzz of comments from the crowd. "Yes, you know me, and you know where I am from. But I'm not here on my own. The true God sent me. You don't know the true God, but I do because I came from heaven and was sent by him." This passed over the heads of some, but a few knew that he was again claiming to come directly from God. They tried to grab him to quiet him, but Jesus wasn't ready yet, and there were too many in the crowd who liked what he taught and looked to him as their Messiah. These believers said, "When the Messiah really does come, will he do any more miracles than this man?" If Jesus wasn't the Messiah, how could anyone be?

The Pharisees weren't persuaded. The comments from the crowd convinced them all the more that Jesus was dangerous and had to be silenced. Conspiring together with the chief priests who had police power, the temple guards were sent to arrest Jesus. When they arrived, Jesus was telling the people what sounded to them like a riddle: "I am here with you for only a little while, and then I will return to the one who sent me to you. You will look for me, but you won't be able to find me because you won't be able to go where I'm going." A typical statement from Jesus that simultaneously told his followers he was headed to heaven while allowing his enemies to infer that he was going into hiding to avoid arrest.

Some of the Jerusalem leaders put their heads together to decide what he meant. "Where could he possibly go that we couldn't find him? Do you think he might leave this country and go teach the Greeks somewhere else in the Roman Empire? What did he mean when he said, 'You will look for me, but you won't be able to find me' and 'You won't be able to go where I'm going'?" Their best guess was that Jesus was hinting at a move outside of Palestine to another part of the empire where Jews lived in Greek cities with Greek culture and language. This could be a way of getting rid of him without really having to deal with him. In any case, they called off the planned arrest. They would wait out Jesus.

On the last day of the Feast of Tabernacles, the authorities were carefully monitoring Jesus' movements and words. They were spread around the temple crowd during the water-pouring ceremony when Jesus shouted to the crowd, "If anyone is thirsty, let him come to me and drink. Just as the Scriptures promise, whoever believes in me will have streams of living water flowing out of him." He made himself and his offer the center of the ceremony. The authorities didn't understand this any more than they had understood his last public declaration. Most who heard didn't grasp Jesus' hidden meaning.

John was there and later explained, "By this Jesus meant the Holy Spirit, who would later be received by all who believed. Up to this time the Spirit hadn't come into people because Jesus hadn't yet ascended to heaven and been glorified." Jesus' statements were increasingly like pieces of a puzzle that would make sense on a future date when they were placed in position with one another and the whole picture could be seen.

Even when they didn't get the full meaning of what he said, some sensed the supernatural authority with which Jesus spoke. They responded, "This man is definitely the Prophet." Others went much further, declaring, "He is the Messiah!"

With less enthusiasm and plenty of skepticism, others asked, "How can the Messiah come from Galilee? Doesn't the Scripture say he will come from David's family and be born in Bethlehem?" They obviously didn't know he had been born in Bethlehem. Since he spoke with a Galilean accent, they assumed he was born in Galilee.

So once again, different people had opposite responses and the crowd was divided. Some wanted to crown him the Messiah and others wanted to seize him for trial as a threat to society and peace. Because there were so many on both sides, no one had the courage to do either for fear of coming out on the losing side of a fight. The religious police observed all of this and returned to the temple leaders to give their report.

When the police returned without Jesus, the chief priests and Pharisees were upset. "Why didn't you bring him in?"

They were completely unprepared for the police officers' answer: "None of us has ever heard someone speak the way this man does." They had been so mesmerized by Jesus' teaching that they couldn't arrest him as ordered.

"You mean he has tricked you too?" the Pharisees exclaimed. "Have any of the leaders or any of the Pharisees believed in him? Of course not! Those people in that crowd don't know a thing about God's law—there is a curse on them."

What they didn't acknowledge was that there were Pharisees who did believe in Jesus. Nicodemus was one of the most prominent Pharisees who had secretly met with Jesus and tilted toward becoming a disciple. Without revealing his own experience, Nicodemus simply asked, "Does our law condemn anyone without first hearing what he has to say and finding out exactly what he is doing?" He was calling on his colleagues to play by their own rule of a just hearing.

The response was mockery. "Nicodemus, are you from Galilee too? Check it out, and you will find that prophets don't come out of Galilee." The reactionary retort ignored Nicodemus' question and denigrated the people of Galilee.

The day ended in a stalemate. The religious leaders were as anti-Jesus as ever, but Jesus was still free from arrest. The Pharisees and chief priests called it a day and headed home. Jesus left the temple and camped out for the night on the nearby Mount of Olives just outside Jerusalem's east wall.

Jesus awakened early and returned to the city just before sunrise. By dawn he was standing in the temple's large outer courtyard as the sun rose above the horizon. A crowd gathered surprisingly early that morning, maybe realizing that yesterday's tension could erupt into a new day's confrontation. Jesus sat to teach as more people gathered to listen. Those who came to see a memorable conflict were not disappointed.

While Jesus was teaching, the religious teachers and Pharisees pushed through the crowd, interrupting Jesus and forcing a bedraggled-looking girl to stand in front of him.

The spokesman for the group threw down the gauntlet with his prepared statement: "Teacher, this woman was caught in the actual act of adultery. According to the Law, Moses commanded us to stone such a sinful woman. What do you say should be done to her?"

§ The Old Testament law that prescribed stoning for adultery is in Deuteronomy 22:23-24. The law specifies the conditions of the crime to include intercourse between a man and a female virgin who is engaged to be married. The sex must have taken place within a city where she could have screamed for rescue but did not (thereby implying that the sex was consensual). The penalty after conviction is for both the man and the woman to be stoned to death.

It was a trap—a very clever and sophisticated trap. Old Testament law prohibited adultery and required execution as punishment. § But this situation was more complicated than at first it might seem. The basic law in Leviticus 20:10 applied to married people. Death was the penalty, but the method of execution was not specified.

Because the accusers were setting a trap for Jesus, they didn't want an easy way around the law on some technicality. The law under which the accusation was made required an engaged virgin. Since many women at the time were getting married in their teen years, this could well have been her first sexual experience.

Death by stoning was so rare at the time that it was virtually nonexistent. Under rabbinic law two or three eyewitnesses to the adulterous sexual intercourse had to offer identical independent testimony. The chances of having multiple eyewitnesses to such an intimate illegal act were close to zero. It sounded like a prearranged sin of seduction with the witnesses carefully stationed in advance.

Under the Roman laws of occupation, certain police and judicial powers were assigned to the local Jewish authorities, but capital punishment was not one of them. For a stoning to be legal, the order of a Roman magistrate was required—again, highly unlikely.

The legal problems actually made the case better for Jesus' opponents. They had him either way; it really didn't matter whether he ordered her release or execution. If Jesus called for her release, he appeared uncommitted to the Old Testament law and subject to a religious indictment in a Jewish court. If Jesus called for execution by stoning, he was defying Roman law and subject to arrest and trial in a Roman criminal court. And there was the political risk of a law-and-order decision, which could jeopardize Jesus' popularity with the crowds, who felt oppressed by such laws and drawn to Jesus by his love, tolerance, and compassion.

They indeed had him in a trap. And what about the woman? Embarrassed. Ashamed. Publicly exposed. Humiliated. Possibly destined to die. And where was the other guilty party, the man?

The accusers had brought their rocks. Their hands were heavy with the weight of stones chosen to kill. The crowd stood silent—awed, confused, wondering what was going to happen.

Jesus bent down to the ground and began to write in the dirt covering the temple courtyard. The fact that he was literate may have surprised some of his enemies—many in this time and place could neither read nor write.

The crowd could see what was happening but most would not know what Jesus was writing even if they were near enough. Perhaps Jesus was writing the sins of the accusers. The words in the dirt really didn't matter at the moment.

Finally Jesus spoke. "Whoever among the accusers is without sin should go ahead and throw the first stone." §

§ The law required that the first stones be thrown by the eye-witnesses who testified at the capital trial.

Silence.

Jesus stooped over and wrote again. Perhaps this time the witnesses farther away assumed he was adding each of the accuser's names to the list of sins already written.

Silence, except perhaps the sound of a *thud* as a rock fell from one accuser's hand and hit the ground. *Thud*, a second and third one. One by one, from the oldest to the youngest, the trap-setters and self-appointed judges drifted away through the crowd.

Silence.

Jesus and the woman were left. She could not have known what he would do next. Her fate was in his verdict. Her accusers had gone but Jesus remained—perhaps to be her accuser instead of the religious leaders? As Jesus rose from his stooped position and stood straight, he asked, "Young woman, where did they all go? Has no one condemned you?"

"No one, sir," she said.

"I don't condemn you either. Go home now and don't do this again." §

§ Jesus' encounter with the woman and her accusers is reported in chapter eight of the Gospel of John, although most scholars agree it was not part of the original edition. It is probably a well-known true story added by a later editor.

———— ❋ ————

The crowds came back after sunset that night to see the lighting of the giant candelabra. It was late September, when the nights were cool as the season changed from summer to fall. Like every other night of the feast, the people crowded into the temple's Court of the Women, a large inner court used for public assembly. In the center of the court there were four tall candelabra erected especially for this festival. The light symbolically reminded the Jews of an earlier chapter in their national history when God led their ancestors through the wilderness with a pillar of fire. In a city that was mostly dark at night with little artificial light, the flames from the candelabra illuminated home courtyards across the city. Men of Israel danced and sang psalms of joy before God as part of their worship. The fires burned all night throughout the week of the feast.

The holiday crowd was packed tight into the courtyard. Conversations buzzed among people who could barely see one another in the darkness. The priests walked to the huge, well-fueled candelabra carrying small flames to ignite the oil. Suddenly the fires erupted and lit the night like noon on a clear summer day. Although an annual event, the lighting of the candelabra was always enough to make the people gasp and cheer in awe at the brightness. When their exclamations quieted, Jesus said in a clear voice, "I am the light of the world. Whoever follows me will never walk in darkness. Whoever follows me will have the light of life."

The Pharisees quickly challenged him. "Stop this right now. You talk like you are your own witness, and that just doesn't work." It was a challenge based on a legal technicality that was more suited to a court of law than a large public courtyard. But, having been caught by surprise, this was what first came to their minds. They were arguing a fine point of Jewish law regarding eligibility to testify, insisting that a testimony was not valid unless collaborated by an independent witness.

Jesus answered, "It is perfectly valid for me to be my own witness because I know where I came from and I know where I'm going! You are the ones who aren't valid, because you have no idea where I came from or where I'm going. Your problem is that you make your judgments by human standards, but I don't do that. When I judge, my decisions are always right because I don't judge by myself; God sent me and stands with me in all my decisions.

"You want to discuss legal technicalities?" he further challenged them. "All right, let's go to your own law that requires two witnesses as the test for truth. I have two witnesses. Number one, myself, and number two, my Father who sent me."

While the crowd, standing outside after dark, was neither prepared nor disposed for a courtroom-like debate, the Pharisees knew this was an argument they weren't going to win and immediately tried to change the subject. They asked Jesus, "Where is your father?" He had said his father was his witness. They were beginning a slanderous line of attack that would come with a later punch line.

A surprisingly long dialogue followed between Jesus and his critics. It rambled over a series of subjects with many hidden barbs and clever responses. For his enemies, it was an attempt to trip him up; for Jesus, it was an opportunity to teach on a broad range of important topics.

"You don't know me or my Father," Jesus answered. "If you really knew me, you would know my Father as well." He was standing near the temple's offering box when this conversation took place. Since the authorities were trying to arrest him, perhaps the Pharisees were hoping to keep him talking until the police arrived, but no one actually tried to take him that night.

Picking up on an earlier theme, Jesus announced, "I'm going away. You'll try looking for me, but you'll end up dying in your sin while searching because you can't come where I'm going."

The last time he said this they thought he was moving to Greece. This time they thought he might be talking about suicide. "Will he kill himself? Is that why he says we can't come where he is going?"

Jesus kept talking. "You are from below; I am from above. You are from this world; I am from heaven. I said that you will die in your sins if you don't believe I am God's Son, and that's exactly right—you will indeed die in your sins."

"Who are you?" someone in the crowd shouted out.

"Haven't you been listening? I'm exactly who I have been claiming all along! You'd better listen, because I have much to say in my judgment of you. You need to understand that I came from my Father, that my Father is absolutely reliable, and that I am reporting to you what he told me to say to the world."

Jesus was, of course, talking about God, but they assumed he was talking about his human father. To clarify, Jesus intentionally provoked the Pharisees by referring to himself as the Son of Man. "You may not understand now," he said, "but when you have lifted up the Son of Man, then you will know that I am exactly whom I've claimed. Then you'll know that I haven't been making up all these words I've spoken to you. Let me tell you one more time: what I am saying comes straight from the Father. He sent me. He hasn't abandoned me. Everything I do pleases him." This made sense to a lot of listeners, who believed Jesus right then and there, deciding he was the Messiah from God.

Jesus told them, "If you stick with my teaching, you are really my disciples. Then you will know the truth, and the truth will set you free."

A few of them seemed confused by this proclamation of freedom, insisting, "We are Abraham's descendants and have never been slaves of anyone. How can you possibly say that we will be set free? What you say doesn't make sense." Of course, Jews had been slaves to regional empires from Egypt to Assyria, Babylon, Persia, and Greece. At the moment this conversation was taking place, Jerusalem was occupied by a Roman garrison. But this dialogue wasn't about Israel's history of defeats and occupations. They all knew that Jesus was focused on the personal issue of enslavement to sin.

"Let me tell you the truth," he continued. "Everyone who sins is a slave to sin. Slaves don't have legal standing in the family, but a son is different. A son belongs to the family forever. So if the Son sets you free, you will be really free. I know you are Abraham's descendants. What doesn't make sense here is why Abraham's descendants would be ready to kill me for speaking God's truth. All I'm telling you is what I have seen in the Father's presence. You don't act like you are related to Abraham. You act like you belong to some other fathers."

The crowd insisted, "Abraham is our father," almost in unison. ❧ Ancestry is important in most cultures and certainly so in Jewish culture. Tracing parentage is an important part of personal identity.

They were neither prepared for nor pleased by Jesus' accusation that they weren't living up to their heritage as descendants of Abraham. It was a harsh blow. Jesus insisted that true children of Abraham were related to him by belief and behavior more than genetics. The way some

❧ The fatherhood of Abraham continues as a critical mark of identity and debate after another two thousand years of Middle East history and conflict. But the greater issue here is that there was a popular belief that all Jews were spiritually free because they were physical descendants of Abraham.

of them were treating Jesus was unlike Abraham and more like the way their fathers, grandfathers, and great grandfathers had treated God's previous prophets.

Stung by Jesus' criticism, some fought back with a personal attack on Jesus and a supernatural accreditation of themselves: "We aren't illegitimate children like you. The only father we have is God himself." Rumors had been going around that Jesus was the illegitimate son of Mary, not the son of Joseph the carpenter at all, publicly labeling him a bastard. In the same breath, they upped the ante on their own legitimacy. Whereas before they had claimed Abraham as their father, they now claimed God himself as their father.

Jesus was not panicked by the verbal escalation. "If God really were your Father, you would love me, because I came from God. You would love me because I'm not an independent, self-appointed teacher. God sent me. You know why this isn't clear to you? It's unclear because you are incapable of hearing the truth. Your real father is the devil himself, and you live to please him. He's always been a murderer, and he has never been willing to accept the truth. Lying is his native tongue. He's a father all right—the father of lies! So when I tell the truth, it sounds strange to you because you only like to believe lies. That's why you won't believe me. You don't prove me guilty of any sin. I tell the truth of God, and you just can't believe it. If you belonged to God you would hear what I have to say and believe every word. But you do not belong to God!"

The religious leaders didn't follow Jesus' logic and interpreted his words as name-calling. They thought they were responding in kind when they replied, "Wow! Weren't we obviously right when we said that you were a Samaritan and demon possessed?"

Jesus told them, "You were wrong. I am not possessed by a demon. The truth is that I honor my Father, and you dishonor me. I'm not seeking glory for myself. There is one who seeks glory, and he is the judge of all. I tell you the truth, all someone needs to do is keep my word and that person will never experience death." He had spun the conversation around to honoring and trusting God as the ultimate judge of truth and securing personal eternal life by believing in Jesus and what he said.

They attacked again. "No doubt about it, we now know for sure that you are demon possessed! Think about what you just said. Abraham and all the other prophets died, and yet you claim that anyone who keeps your word will never experience death. Who do you think you are? Are you supposed to be greater than our father Abraham?"

The heated discussion continued like volleys at a sporting event. "If I glorify myself, it really doesn't mean much," Jesus declared. "What means everything is that my Father, whom you claim as your God, is the one who glorifies me. You don't really know him, but I do. If I went along with all of you and said that I don't really know God, I'd be a liar—like all of you! All I'm doing here is telling the truth. The absolute truth is that I know God, and I keep his word. Your father Abraham that you're so proud of rejoiced at the thought of seeing my day. When God showed him, Abraham saw it and was glad."

They picked up on his last comment. "You aren't close to fifty years old, and you say that you have seen Abraham."

Jesus touched off a firestorm of emotion and anger, saying, "The truth is that before Abraham was born, I am!" They may have misunderstood some of his earlier statements, but they didn't miss any of the subtle meaning in Jesus' final statement. He was claiming to be more than two thousand years old. He was claiming to have lived before his present body was born. Then, when Jesus said, "I am," he was not just playing with verb tenses, he was using part of the holy and unspoken name for the God of Israel, Yahweh. §

Some in the crowd became so angry that they grabbed for stones to pummel Jesus to death then

§ Yahweh was a name considered too sacred to be spoken. Instead, Jews substituted words like "Lord" and "God." The name Yahweh comes from Moses' wilderness conversation with God at a burning bush fifteen hundred

and there. His statements were outrageously blasphemous in their view, and they considered it their duty to come to the defense of God and kill Jesus immediately. While they were reaching for rocks, Jesus slipped into the crowd and hid himself from his angry assailants. It was time to get out of Jerusalem and allow time for his enemies to calm down.

years earlier. The name is based on the Hebrew language state-of-being verb and roughly means, "I am that I am." It speaks to the eternality of God, who has forever existed in the past, present, and future. When Jesus said, "I am," his listeners heard him identify himself with Yahweh.

CHAPTER ELEVEN

A fter safely escaping Jerusalem, Jesus spent the next three months traveling through the surrounding province of Judea. He moved often to escape his adversaries, but that provided a good opportunity to teach his true followers.

Jesus appointed 36 two-person teams of his disciples to operate as advance agents for his travels. Each team was sent to a different village to prepare for a visit from Jesus himself.

There were hundreds of small hamlets throughout Judea. He could have used more than the thirty-six advance teams he recruited. As he told them, "There is plenty to harvest but a shortage of harvesters. Ask the Lord of the harvest, therefore, to send out more harvesters."

Recognizing the risks, Jesus told them, "As you go, remember to be careful, because I'm sending you out like lambs in wolf country." In his commissioning speech to them, he laid out his guidelines and expectations:

- *Travel light.* "Don't take anything but the basics."

- *Stay focused.* "Don't waste time chatting with everyone along the road."

- *Stick with the responsive.* "When you enter a house, give your blessing: 'Peace to this house.' If your blessing is well received, stay at that house and enjoy the hospitality, food, and drink. Free hospitality comes with your travels. Stay at the same house as long as you are in that town. When townspeople offer you food, eat what they offer. Heal the sick people and preach, 'The kingdom of God is near you.' "

- *Move past the unresponsive.* "When you come to a town that doesn't welcome you, tell them, 'We won't stay if we're not wanted. When we leave town, we'll even kick your dust off our shoes. But at least listen to this: The kingdom of God is near. And by the way, on judgment day you're going to be worse off than the town of Sodom.' " Jesus even named some of the unresponsive communities and told his teams what to tell them: "Misery on you, Korazin! Misery on you, Bethsaida! If the towns of Tyre and Sidon saw the miracles you've seen, they would have repented a long time ago. That's why it is going to be easier for them on judgment day. And the same goes for Capernaum, which thinks so highly of itself and is going to fall hard."

All things considered, it turned out to be a successful preaching tour. The seventy-two who traveled the towns of Judea came back from their first round buoyed with enthusiasm and joy. They reported, "Lord, even the demons obey what we say if it's in your name."

It was a good account—the powers of Satan and evil had been defeated. But Jesus warned them lest they get inappropriately proud of their success and miss the greater significance. He said, "I saw Satan drop like a streak of lightning from heaven. Now it's true that I've given you power and safety over snakes, scorpions, and the evil enemy. But that shouldn't be your biggest reason to rejoice. Rejoice that you belong to God!" These were good weeks for Jesus. In words that were half prayer and half teaching, Jesus said, "Father, Lord of heaven and earth, I praise you because you hid the greatest wonders from the smart, educated people and showed them to ordinary folk. Yes, Father, this really made you happy!"

Then Jesus said, almost as if he were talking to himself, "How wonderful that the Father has committed everything to me. I am the only one who really knows the Father. The only way others are going to know the Father is if I decide to reveal him to them."

When no one else was around, he told his disciples, "Blessed are your eyes that see what you are seeing. Prophets and kings only dreamed of seeing and hearing what you've seen and heard."

During those months of touring Judea, Jesus crossed paths with a lawyer who asked, "Teacher, what do I need to do to get eternal life?"

Jesus' memorable response included another question: "What does the Law say? What's your reading of it?" Like many of Israel's most devout Jews, the lawyer wore two small leather boxes called phylacteries strapped to his wrist and head. Inside were pieces of paper with parts of the Old Testament Law written on them. Jesus was asking him to read the answer to his question from his own phylacteries.

The lawyer answered, " 'Love the Lord your God with all your heart, soul, strength, and mind,' and 'Love your neighbor as yourself.' "

"Good answer!" Jesus said to him. "Do this, and you will live."

But the man wanted to justify himself, so he asked a follow-up question. "So who exactly is my neighbor?"

Jesus told him a story. "A man was going down the steep road from Jerusalem to Jericho when bandits abducted him. They stripped off his clothes, beat him up, and left him to die along the side of the road. A priest just happened to be traveling that same road, but when he saw the beat-up man, he passed him on the opposite side without offering help. A Levite from the temple staff came by later and did the same thing. Then a Samaritan came along, felt sorry for the man, and stopped to help. He cared for his wounds and then gave him a donkey ride to the nearest inn, where he nursed him through the crisis. In the morning he paid the innkeeper to give further lodging and care, saying, 'Take care of him for as long as necessary. The next time I come through here I'll reimburse you for any additional cost.' "

Then Jesus asked the lawyer, "Which of these three travelers do you think was a neighbor to the man who was beat up by the bandits?"

The lawyer gave the obvious answer, "The one who had mercy on him."

Jesus told him, "You go and do the same."

Not all of Jesus' days were spent debating critics, teaching crowds, and healing sick people. Over the years he had built a network of loyal followers who became good friends. Jesus often visited them and stayed in their homes for meals and lodging. Among them were three siblings named Mary, Martha, and Lazarus who lived in the village of Bethany. §

§ Bethany was about 1.8 miles (three kilometers) east of Jerusalem on the other side of the Mount of Olives, located along the road from Jerusalem to Jericho. The village's modern Arabic name is el-Azariyeh.

Jesus came daringly close to Jerusalem in order to visit his friends, risking arrest from the temple police. Mary was thrilled to have Jesus in her house. She sat on the floor next to his feet drinking in everything he had to say.

Martha, who was outside preparing food for the group of guests with Jesus, was also delighted to host Jesus. But she was unhappy that Mary wasn't helping her in the outdoor kitchen. Her irritation festered into anger until she finally walked to the courtyard and interrupted Jesus midsentence. "Lord, doesn't it bother you that my sister has left all the work to me? Tell her to help me!"

Jesus loved them both. He certainly wasn't ungrateful for Martha's work, but he was far more interested in talking with them than eating their food. "Martha, Martha," he graciously answered, "you get so worked up about so many things! But there's only one really important thing that will last, and that's what Mary chose." It could have come across as a rebuke to Martha, but clearly that was not what was intended. Jesus' manner was compassionate and disarming.

As much as Jesus enjoyed the company of his friends, it was too dangerous to linger in Bethany. Jesus soon was on the road again, traveling with his disciples. It was a good thing they were with him, because it would be one of those especially memorable days to learn from their teacher.

The topic was prayer. They had long been intrigued with the importance and practice of prayer in Jesus' life. Before important decisions, Jesus prayed. When they awakened early in the morning, they would see Jesus off by himself, praying. Before and after intense spiritual encounters, Jesus always prayed. While most of the time he prayed alone, in private, direct conversation with God, they also prayed together as a group. They could not help but be intrigued by the simplicity and faith of his prayers. They included intimacy and awe; familiarity and worship; asking and submitting; originality and Scripture. Every prayer seemed so natural and spontaneous, yet each was an eloquent masterpiece. They wanted to learn to pray the way Jesus prayed. So they came right out and asked, "Lord, teach us to pray, just as John the Baptizer taught his disciples."

It was as if Jesus had been waiting for them to ask. He told them that when they prayed they should say something like this:

"Our Father who is in heaven, holy be your
name!
Your kingdom come, your will be done, on
earth as it is in heaven.
Give us this day our daily bread.
Forgive our sins as we forgive those who sin
against us.
Lead us not into temptation, but deliver us
from evil."

THE LORD'S PRAYER

The Lord's Prayer has become one of the most famous, frequent, and familiar prayers of Christians, although some have suggested that it may be misnamed. It really should be called "The Disciples' Prayer," because it was given to them to pray.

The prayer is organized with parallel petitions: (1) May your name be recognized as holy; (2) May your kingdom come; (3) May your will be done. It is a prayer for the fullness of God's kingdom to come to earth.

First-century Jews often memorized prayers for recitation, most notably from the Psalms. First-century Christians followed a similar pattern.

The Lord's Prayer was probably intended more as a sample than a formula. The wording varies in the New Testament reports of what Jesus said, so it was not word-for-word the same every time. The purpose wasn't to memorize someone else's prayer but to learn a pattern that could be adapted and individualized. Most of the disciples probably heard this prayer enough times to memorize it, and they all made their own modifications. As it was recited by later Christians, they added a tribute of praise to God at the end: "Yours are the kingdom, the power, and the glory forever. Amen."

This was not the only time they asked nor was this their only lesson in the school of prayer. They had heard this prayer from Jesus before. Perhaps they would have been satisfied with a formula, but Jesus forced them to learn a related lesson. He might have told them, "When you pray, don't give up easily. Be persistent. Keep praying, because God likes persistence." But instead he told them a story.

The story is set in the context of Middle Eastern hospitality, where one had to feed and lodge friends if they asked. Jesus began, "Imagine that one of you goes to a friend's house around midnight, knocks on the door, and asks, 'Friend, could you lend me a few loaves of bread, because a guest just showed up at my house and we're out of food.'

§ The late hour presented a family problem because so many homes were just one room with a dirt floor and a fire to keep warm during the cool nights. The whole family—even the barnyard animals—slept together around the fire. The door was closed for privacy and safety. When a neighbor knocked on the door, the owner of the house was reluctant to answer because that might wake up the family and animals.

"Now imagine that the friend whispers back through the door, 'Go away. Leave me alone. My family and I are all in bed with the door locked and I can't help you.' § You keep knocking and asking until he gets up and gives you what you want—not because of your friendship but because of your bold persistence.

"So here's my prayer lesson for you: Keep asking and it will be given to you; keep seeking and you will find; keep knocking and the door will be opened. Eventually those who ask receive; those who seek find; and those who knock get in."

The message here wasn't that God resists prayers; it was that God rewards bold persistence. Jesus added to this teaching by comparing the goodness of human fathers to the greater goodness of God the Father. "What dad would give a snake when his son asks for a fish? Or a scorpion when asked for an egg? Even sinful fathers know how to give good gifts to their children. Well, then, it's obvious that your heavenly Father will give the Holy Spirit to those who ask him!"

Moving on through Judea, Jesus risked unwanted visibility by performing more crowd-drawing miracles. A man with a demon in him came to Jesus for healing; he couldn't speak. Jesus ordered the demon out of the man, and he immediately was able to talk. A crowd gathered to see what was going on, and they were most amazed at what happened. But there were some cynics who raised the old accusation against Jesus that he was empowered by Beelzebub and not by God. Others were willing to grant that his power came from heaven, but they wanted him to keep rolling out more miracles—for their entertainment more than for helping those who needed his healing touch.

One woman was so impressed with Jesus that she called out, "Blessed is the mother who gave you birth and nursed you." Not exactly what Jesus needed at that moment, but he decided to turn it into a teaching opportunity. "Thanks, but the ones who are really blessed are those who hear the word of God and obey it."

The crowd again was growing. Some probably hadn't heard the earlier call for Jesus to entertain them with more miracles. Changing crowds frequently necessitated repeat teachings. As before, he told them that no quantity of miracles would ever satisfy them. Their ancestors had been pleased with fewer and less spectacular miracles. Now they had bigger and better miracles from Jesus that weren't good enough for them.

Some probably considered Jesus audacious when he presented himself as performing greater miracles than prophets of the past. They would have been equally offended when he returned to one of his familiar themes, Jesus as the light of the world. He capped off this provocative teaching with the statement that his truth was the only sure way to light their minds.

Standing in the crowd that day was a Pharisee who invited Jesus to his home for a meal. This part of Judea was far enough from Jerusalem for Jesus to be relatively safe, but it was close enough for the Pharisee to have regular communication with others from the capital city. Unlike another Pharisee up north who earlier invited Jesus for dinner out of curiosity, this man invited Jesus to dinner with the purpose of entrapping him.

Jesus accepted the invitation, arriving in time for the evening meal. It was a familiar scene. As before, the guests reclined along the table, propped up by their left elbow and eating with their right hand. Other observers stood around the perimeter, there to watch and listen while the invited guests ate and talked.

As soon as Jesus reached for a nearby serving dish, the host expressed great shock that Jesus hadn't first washed his hands. Hand-washing was one of the required rituals. §

Recognizing that he was surrounded by a hostile audience, Jesus chose to speak directly to the real issue rather than defend his actions.

Looking at his host but addressing them all, Jesus said, "You Pharisees wash the outside of the cup and dish, but inside you are full of greed and wickedness. You are so foolish! Did not the creator of the outside create the inside as well? Tell you what, why don't you give the food inside the dish to the poor, and then everything will be clean for you?"

It turned out that the guests wanted to lis-

§ Not for sanitary reasons, because germ theory was still more than fifteen hundred years in the future. They washed their hands to be ceremonially clean. Quite a routine, they had multiple washings before every course of every meal. Large pots of special noncontaminated water stood around the courtyard. The minimum amount of water per hand was the capacity of an eggshell. Each hand was individually rinsed from the fingertips to the wrists. Palms were washed by rubbing the water into the palm with the fist of the opposite hand. Finally, water was poured over the entire hand once again, this time from the wrist to the fingertips. Omitting the slightest detail was considered to be unobservant and disrespectful of tradition.

ten, so it became a teaching session, with Jesus diagnosing the beliefs and lifestyles of those at the Pharisee's home.

GREED DISGUISED TO LOOK LIKE GENEROSITY

"Grief to you Pharisees, because you give God ten percent of your mint, rue, and all your other little garden herbs, but you forget to practice justice and the love of God. It's fine that you gave your ten percent, but you really need to practice justice and love for God as well."

LOVE OF RECOGNITION

"Grief to you Pharisees, because you love sitting in the most important seats in the synagogues and receiving honored greetings in the marketplaces."

DANGER TO OTHERS

"Grief to you, because you are like unmarked graves, which people walk over without knowing that they are stepping on graves in the ground."

One of the religion lawyers was offended and blurted out, "Teacher, you're insulting us with what you're saying." Jesus wasn't finished with his speech yet. He wove his response into his next point.

BURDENING OF OTHERS

"Grief to you religion teachers, because of the way you burden people with rules they can't keep and then don't do anything to help them."

PRETENDING TO HONOR THE REJECTED

"Grief to all of you, because you build tombs to honor the dead prophets but won't admit that your forefathers were the ones who killed those prophets. Because of this, the all-wise God said, 'I will send prophets and apostles, some of whom they will kill and others they will persecute.' Because of your lack of repentance, God will hold this generation responsible for the blood of every prophet God has ever sent in all of history—from A to Z, from Abel to Zechariah. That's right; I'm telling you that you are accountable for all of them."

HINDERING GOD'S TRUTH

"Grief to you experts in Jewish law. You had the key to God's knowledge and used it to lock everyone out—including yourselves!"

When the meal was over, Jesus stood up to leave. Not surprising, the emotions of the Pharisees and religion teachers were inflamed against him. They were either barraging him with questions or debating with one another over which questions to ask.

Jesus went from the smaller audience in the house to a large crowd that had gathered to see him and possibly to witness the confrontation between the popular preacher and the leaders of the religious establishment. As they pushed closer to see and hear, they began to trample one another.

Before engaging the potentially volatile crowd, Jesus huddled with his disciples, making sure they were the only ones who heard him. He told them, "You really need to keep up your guard against the yeast of the Pharisees. They are such hypocrites. There aren't any secrets that won't be revealed. What is said in the dark will be heard in the light, and what is whispered will be shouted.

"Like I've told you before, my friends," he continued. "Don't be afraid of those who can kill your body and no more. Fear should be saved for those who can send someone to hell. Sparrows are cheap—they're currently selling at five for two small coins. But no matter how cheap they are, God cares about them. He even cares about every one of the hairs on your head. All that is to say that you really don't have to worry about anyone or anything because you are in the care of God himself." Indeed, he had told them all this before back in Galilee, but they actually appreciated the times when Jesus repeated his teachings to them.

"That reminds me to tell you something else you've heard before. Anyone who acknowledges me here on earth I will acknowledge later before the angels of God in heaven. On the other hand, anyone who disowns me before people will be disowned before the angels of God. And anyone who speaks against the Messiah will be forgiven, but anyone who blasphemes against the Holy Spirit will not be forgiven.

"One more reminder. When you're brought before synagogues, rulers, and government authorities, you don't need to worry about how you will defend yourselves or what you will say. When the time comes, the Holy Spirit will tell you what to say."

During a short lull in the clamor from the crowd, one man yelled to Jesus loud enough for them all to hear, "Teacher, tell my brother to split the inheritance with me." Jesus replied, "Who appointed me to be your probate judge?" Then Jesus began a long speech, appearing to address the large gathering but really intending it for his disciples. He was a master at speaking to two different audiences on two different levels at the same time. "Watch out! Be on guard against greed, because there's a whole lot more to life than owning a lot of possessions."

Then he told them a story. "The land of a very rich man produced a good crop. He thought, 'What am I going to do? I don't have enough storage space for a bumper crop like this.'

"Then he had an idea. 'I'll tear down my barns and build structures large enough to store the grain and all my other possessions. And then I'll say to myself, "You have plenty of good things and lots of money set aside for retirement. Take life easy! Eat, drink, and be happy." '

"But God said to him, 'You fool! You're going to die tonight. Then who will get all the possessions and money you've saved up for yourself?' "

Jesus looked around at his listeners. "This is the way it is with anyone who stores up possessions and money for himself but isn't rich toward God."

He lowered his voice, not excluding the crowd but looking at his disciples as he said, "What I'm saying here is not to worry about your life, body, food, or clothes. Life is more than food, and the body more than clothes. Compare to the ravens. They don't sow or reap; they don't have storage rooms or barns, yet God feeds and takes care of them. You are so much more valuable than birds! You are totally in God's care, and besides, what's the point of worrying anyway? Has worry ever added an hour to anyone's life? Relax. Trust God to take care of you!

"Consider how the lilies grow. They don't worry or work hard. Yet lilies are more magnificent than Solomon dressed in his best. Now if that's the way God clothes lilies and other vegetation that doesn't last very long, you've got to know that he's going to make sure you are properly clothed. You have so little faith! Don't set your heart on meals and worry so much. That's what the pagans do, but they don't believe in God the way you are supposed to. Trust that God knows your needs. Just put God and his kingdom first, and he will take care of everything else.

"Please don't ever be frightened, my flock of friends. God wants to give his kingdom to you. Sell what you own and give to the poor. If you want to have a purse that won't wear out and always keeps your riches safe, deposit what you've got in the bank of heaven, where there are unlimited resources that are burglarproof and mothproof! Think of it this way: wherever your treasure is deposited, that's where your heart is focused as well.

"I want you to not only be on guard against what is evil but to be dressed and ready to go and do what is good. Keep your lights burning bright, like the staff of a mansion waiting for its owner to return from his wedding and asking to be let back in. An employee on the owner's staff who is waiting for his arrival will always be dressed and ready to serve. Think how good it is to have everything ready for him even if he comes home in the middle of the night. This kind of steady readiness is what any smart homeowner constantly expects of his staff, because he doesn't know if or when a break-in might occur. All this readiness applies to you, because you don't know when the Son of Man will come back to earth again. You need to be just as ready as you would be while waiting for your boss to come home or in case a burglar might try to break in. Always ready!"

Peter was confused. Who was Jesus talking to? "Lord," he asked, "are you telling this parable to us or are you telling it to everyone?"

Lowering his voice and focusing his eyes on his followers, Jesus answered, "Who do you think is the faithful and wise manager of the master's staff and budget? If the manager does a good job while the owner is away, what do you think he is going to do when he comes home and likes what he sees? You know the answer—the manager will get greater responsibilities. But suppose the manager thinks that the owner will be gone a long time and decides to get drunk, beat up the rest of the staff, and mismanage what has been entrusted to him. Then the owner unexpectedly comes home and sees the mess the manager has made. He's so angry and upset that he beats up the manager and demotes him to the lowest job available.

"Any servant who knows what the owner wants and ignores or avoids his will gets severely punished. By contrast, if there is a servant who doesn't know what his boss wants and does things contrary to that boss's will, he will get a lesser punishment. The principle is that much is expected of those who have been given much and a lot is asked of those who have been entrusted with a lot.

"I came to earth to start a fire. I wish it were already burning, but it's not yet time. I have difficult days ahead that I wish were behind me. I just don't want you to think everything will be easy and I'm just going to make everyone peaceful. The truth is that I am bringing division. From now on families of five will be divided three against two or two against three with fathers against sons, sons against fathers, mothers against daughters, daughters against mothers, mothers-in-law against daughters-in-law, and daughters-in-law against mothers-in-law."

Having laid out a clear picture of what God wanted from Jesus' followers as they lived out the kingdom of heaven here on earth, and

having told them how tough the coming journey would become, Jesus
turned back to the larger crowd. Raising his voice, Jesus told the crowd,
"When you see a cloud forming in the west you quickly say, 'It's going
to rain,' and it does. And when you feel the south wind blowing, you
say, 'It's going to be hot,' and it is. You are such phonies! You know
how to forecast weather but not what is really important in these
times. Why is that?

"Why don't you judge between yourselves what is right? Before you
go to court in a lawsuit that will end up with someone losing and going
to jail, figure it out between yourselves. If you pursue a lawsuit, the
judge isn't going to let you off until the last coin is paid." They had
become good weather analysts but not very good spiritual forecasters.

Jesus was telling them that if they were smart, they would listen
and reconcile with God before it was too late. People do that with
personal debt and local courts, he said; how much more important
to do the same with sin and the court of God.

It was late and time for everyone to go home and reflect on all
they had seen and heard. While some were leaving, others would not
quit. They had just heard the latest news out of Jerusalem and wanted
a theological understanding about what happened.

The news they told Jesus was about another brutal attack against
Jews ordered by Pilate, the Roman military governor. Once before,
Pilate's soldiers had entered the temple courtyard disguised as Jewish
worshippers. They threw off their disguises and bludgeoned to death
innocent people who were worshipping God. Now it had happened
again. The attacks were so brutal that human blood ran across the
temple floor, mixing with the animal blood from the temple sacrifices. The men who reported this to Jesus thought he would be especially interested since all those who were attacked were from Jesus'
home area of Galilee. Maybe he even knew some of them personally.

None of this came as a surprise to those who knew Pilate's style. Yes,
he had done some great good for Jerusalem, especially in keeping the peace
in an often volatile place. But he could be notoriously hardhearted and

heavy-handed. Human life, and especially Jewish life, wasn't highly valued by this veteran soldier. However, the question linked to the news report wasn't about the guilt of the governor but the guilt of the victims. It was commonly believed that people who suffered tragedies like this had it coming. They were being punished for their sins. §

Jesus responded to the tragic news, "Do you think these Galileans who were slaughtered were worse sinners than all the other Galileans who weren't killed? Of course not! But if you don't repent, you are all going to perish." Jesus made no connection between personal tragedy and personal sin. But, he warned his listeners, everyone can experience unexpected tragedy and should repent of sin and get right with God before tragedy strikes, or it may be too late. The eternal disaster would be greater than the immediate tragedy. He added another recent event to further make his point. Jesus reminded them about eighteen construction workers who had died when a tower under construction in Siloam fell on them. "Do you think they had greater sin than those in Jerusalem who didn't have a tower fall on them? No! But you need to repent if you don't want to perish forever." The conclusion is the same: no one knows when death may catch him by surprise, so everyone should repent of sin and get right with God right now.

Trying to switch their attention from tragedies to opportunities, Jesus told one of his favorite parables. §

That day's parable was set in a vineyard. Since topsoil was often thin and precious, gardeners used any extra space for other plantings. Fig trees were popular because they consumed little space and normally produced a crop within three years. Here's what Jesus said: "A man planted a fig tree in his vineyard and went to look for fruit on it. When no figs

§ This Jewish notion went all the way back to the Old Testament story of Job. Job was a righteous man who suffered financial collapse, the deaths of all his children, and calamitous health problems. Although he seemed like a good man, his friends assumed there must be great sins hidden in his life for God to allow or cause him to suffer so much.

§ Parables were quite different from the news stories that had started this most recent conversation. Parables are stories that are plausible but made up to teach a principle. Unlike news stories that could make many points, Jesus' parables were told to make one major point (although sometimes he included subpoints as well).

grew, he told the gardener, 'For three years now I've been checking for fruit on this fig tree, and there's never been any. Chop it down! There's no good reason for it to take up space and soil.' " Jesus' point was that his listeners should produce fruit for God in their lives. His implication was that if they weren't productive, God had every right to judge them and cut them down.

With typical compassion, Jesus added a postlude to his parable. " 'Sir, let's give it one more year,' the gardener suggested. 'I'll dig around it and fertilize it. Let's hope it will bear figs by this time next year. If not, then I'll cut it down.' " In other words, a merciful God gives second chances and extensions, although not forever.

The journey into Judea was increasingly intense. Jesus was visiting multiple villages, drawing large crowds, and facing mounting opposition from established religious leaders. Sabbath days were supposed to be for rest, but there was little rest for Jesus. Not only did he go to synagogues to teach, but people came to see and hear him. Since they were off work on the Sabbath and Jesus was easier to find at the synagogue, Sabbath days were particularly long and exhausting for him.

One Sabbath in a Judean synagogue, Jesus was teaching when the people's attention was diverted to a tragically deformed woman. No matter how many times the local people had seen her, they couldn't help but stare. For almost two decades she had been handicapped by a back so curved that she was bent over almost in half. She walked with great pain and difficulty. Her normal view was looking at the ground, although she no doubt preferred not to look people in the eye. It was enough misery to suffer from the deformity without the added pain of people's stares.

Medical remedies hadn't helped her. Her deformity wasn't from birth or from an accident or even from a disease—at least none of these were the primary reason she was so misshapen. It was supernatural. She was misshapen and deformed by an evil spirit. Who could explain such a thing?

While others stared at her that Sabbath, Jesus spoke to her. He asked her to come up next to him and said, "Woman, I set you free from your deformity." He touched her and immediately she stood up straight, praising God for her restoration.

It was an amazing and wonderful miracle that delighted almost everyone there, except the synagogue leader. He publicly reprimanded the woman, "There are six days for work. Why don't you come to be healed on those days, not on the Sabbath?"

Jesus couldn't allow the woman's joy to be quenched by this man's indignation. He addressed the synagogue leader and any who sided with him. "You hypocrites! You care for animals on the Sabbath. Don't you all routinely untie oxen or donkeys from their stall and water them on the Sabbath? So why shouldn't this daughter of Abraham, whom Satan has kept disabled for eighteen long years, be untied on the Sabbath day from the stall of deformity that has imprisoned her?"

It was a powerful answer that rebuked Jesus' critics and delighted the rest of the congregation. They were thrilled with the miracle they had seen and the practical approach to the Sabbath Jesus taught.

Then Jesus returned to his sermon. "What is the kingdom of God like? What's a good comparison?" he asked them. "How about a mustard seed? A man planted a mustard seed in his garden, and it grew into a tree big enough for birds to perch in its branches."

The tiny black mustard seed was the smallest seed used by farmers in the region, yet it grew to become a bush ten to twelve feet tall. That's what God's kingdom will be like, he told them—starting small and growing large.

Jesus took another favorite analogy from everyday life. When he was growing up, his mother baked bread every day. It was the same in all the households that were represented that Sabbath at the synagogue. The woman of the house would take some yeast that was left over from the previous day's baking and add it to the day's dough. "The kingdom of God is like yeast that a woman took and mixed into a big batch of flour until it worked all through the dough." Here he was telling them that the kingdom of God may be small, but it is so powerful that it can permeate and change all of society.

Three months of walking the hills and villages of Judea were coming to an end. It was time for Jesus to return to Jerusalem.

CHAPTER TWELVE

W as a return visit to Jerusalem really a good idea? The last time Jesus was there, his enemies had tried to kill him. But time had cooled the mood, and Jerusalem was where Jesus was headed. Actually, the city never was a totally safe place. Politics polarized the citizens. Power struggles were frequent. Romans were always ready to crush anything that smacked of opposition. Zealots prowled, ready to kill a Roman or two. It was hard to tell where the lines were drawn between personality, politics, and religion. The city could erupt at any time and often did.

But there were enough daily distractions in the capital city that the leaders and citizens had plenty to think about besides Jesus. He was going to give it another try.

As his entourage walked through the gate and entered the part of town known as the lower city, Jesus saw a man who had been born blind. § He had never seen the expressions of shame on the faces of his family, but he would have learned to perceive moods and attitudes in tones of voices that sighted people would never notice. His blindness was more than a physical disability; it was considered judgment from God.

A couple of Jesus' disciples used the man to pose a theological question. "Jesus," they asked, "whose sin caused him to be born blind—

§ With no other occupational option, those who were blind lived out on the street and learned at a young age to hold a hand open for alms. Blind children could be quite profitable as beggars because sympathy triggered generosity. As such children grew older, each became just one more blind beggar in a city that already had too many. Uncaring parents cut their losses and left their sightless children to survive on their own.

his or his parents'?" Their question exposed their assumption that disabilities were the direct cause of sin or that parental sins were played out in their offspring. The blind man had lived with this kind of question all his life. He was the daily victim of prejudice and discrimination. Many people who walked past his blind eyes and begging hands assumed that he was judged by God and had gotten what he deserved.

Everyone was surprised by Jesus' untraditional answer. He told them, "Neither! He isn't blind because he or his parents sinned. This happened to demonstrate the work of God in his life. As long as the sun is still shining, we must do the work of God who sent me. When it gets dark, no one will be able to work. As long as I am here, I am the light of this world."

Jesus lifted the discussion to center on the purposes of God rather than the reason for suffering. In this blind man's case, it really didn't make any difference why he was blind; he was on his way to becoming the subject for a supernatural display of God's healing power. At the end of the day, no one would care why he was blind, and everyone would praise God.

The blind man couldn't fathom Jesus' self-description as "the light of the world"—he had never seen light. But he could hear the saliva hit the ground and the brush of Jesus' clothes and the slight scrape of his sandals on the ground as he kneeled to pick up the spit-made mud. He heard the rush of air as Jesus stood again. He didn't anticipate Jesus' hand coming toward his face to smear the mud over both eyes. A crowd of onlookers had gathered, and they all heard Jesus tell the blind man, "Go, wash your face in the Pool of Siloam."

Siloam was the closest public water source in the southeast section of Jerusalem, and it is where the man would have gone to wash anyway. He certainly was very familiar with finding his way to the water without a guide or assistance. But this time was different. He must have hoped this wasn't a cruel joke. The compassion in Jesus' voice and the power of his touch was unlike any he had heard or felt before.

When he reached the pool and knelt next to the edge, he washed his eyes and face, and—he could see! For the first time in his life he saw the light, the pool, the people, and his own hands and feet and body. He headed home—probably not to the back alley, where he slept under a broken stairway, but to his parents' home and the neighborhood where he had grown up. He was greeting the merchants by name and waving to the women looking out the second-level apartments as they struggled to recognize him. Yes, he looked like the blind boy who had grown up nearby, but he couldn't be the same person, because this man could see!

It was more than enough to set the whole neighborhood abuzz. "Isn't this the same man who used to sit and beg?" Many said he was, but others said, "No, he just looks like him." They may have thought they were talking quietly enough that he couldn't hear, but a lifetime of super-sensitized ears helped him hear, and he shouted back with passion, "I'm the beggar. I'm the man who used to be blind."

"That's impossible," his old neighbors argued. "If you're the blind guy, come on, tell us how you can see."

He was more than glad to tell them what happened. "The man called Jesus made some mud and smeared it on my eyes. He told me to go to the Pool of Siloam and wash my face. So I went and washed, and now I can see!" he explained.

"Okay, if that's what happened, where is Jesus?" they wanted to know.

"I don't know where he is," he answered. "The last time I saw him, he was up the road from the Pool of Siloam in the lower city." But then he must have thought, *The last time I saw him? I never did actually see him!*

Since it was the Sabbath, the local Pharisees were meeting at the synagogue, so they were all together when they heard about the healing. Their religious gathering turned into a religious trial. The formerly blind man was brought into the synagogue, where he was again asked how he received his sight. He matter-of-factly told them, "He put mud on my eyes, and I washed, and now I can see." The Pharisees didn't need to ask who the healer was; it was obvious that Jesus was back in town. It didn't take long for these Pharisees to return to the fierce level of opposition of three months earlier. One of their leaders spoke for the majority when he announced, "This Jesus isn't from God. How could he be? He doesn't keep the Sabbath!"

§ The super-strict enforcement of Sabbath rest spiraled into a litany of prohibitions against cutting fingernails, carrying a handkerchief down stairs, lighting a candle, or helping the sick. It was permissible for a physician to stop a dying patient from getting worse but illegal to help a sick person get better. Blindness was not life threatening, so it could wait for treatment (or miracles) until after sundown on Saturday.

It was the same old controversy that had plagued Jesus for three years. Because the Ten Commandments called the Sabbath a day of rest, these devout Jews restricted work. The principle was good, but the practice became absurd. §

That day in the synagogue a minority of the Pharisees were conflicted. Despite the majority opinion against Jesus, they wondered how someone who was a sinner could make a blind man see. Rules aside, it certainly appeared that Jesus was from God. No one else had ever cured congenital blindness.

Unable to reconcile the differences among themselves, the Pharisees asked the man, "Tell us what you think about Jesus. It was your eyes he opened." The man told them, "Jesus is a prophet." Not that this man was an expert in such matters, but it seemed to him like a good first explanation.

Reluctant to believe that the man had ever actually been blind, some of the Pharisees sent for his parents. They were truly frightened when forced to testify. Ordinary people, they knew that a wrong answer could result in excommunication. Those claiming that Jesus was the Messiah were threatened with being thrown out of their synagogue. That meant exclusion from the religious and social life of the community. Their fear multiplied when Pharisees started asking questions so fast that they barely had time to answer: "Is this your son?" "Is this the one you say was born blind?" "How do you explain that he now can see?"

Cautiously they answered, "Yes, he is our son. And, yes, he was born blind. But we have no idea how this happened or who did it. Why don't you ask him? He's an adult who can speak for himself."

"Give glory to God!" they instructed the man. "Don't give credit to Jesus—he is a sinner."

With carefully chosen words, he told them, "I really don't know whether Jesus is a sinner or not. The only thing I know for sure is that I was blind but now I can see!"

Starting all over, they asked him again, "What exactly did he do to you? How did he actually open your eyes?"

Suddenly the mood of this impromptu trial changed. Years on the streets as a blind beggar no doubt had shaped him into a survivor who was quick with his tongue and used to abuse. He blurted out, "I've already explained all this to you, but you didn't listen. Why do you want to hear it all over again?" And then a final sarcastic barb, "You must like the story! Do you want to become his disciples too?"

Losing control and shouting insults, these Pharisees told him, "You are one of this fellow's disciples! Not us! We are disciples of Moses! We know that God spoke to Moses, but we can't even figure out where this Jesus came from."

This beggar should have been no match in a debate against these Pharisees, but he won this round in a one-minute rebuttal. "Now, that is remarkable!" he said to them. "You don't know where he comes from, yet he miraculously opened my eyes. We all know that God does not listen to sinners. God listens to godly men who do his will. This is a first. None of us has ever heard of opening the eyes of someone who was born blind. If this man weren't from God, he could never do a miracle like this."

The Pharisees switched to a personal attack. "You're no one but a lifelong sinner. Who do you think you are, talking to us like that?" And they threw him out of the synagogue.

The news traveled fast on the streets of the lower city, and it wasn't long till Jesus heard what had happened. He went looking for the man who had been inadvertently sucked into Jesus' controversy. When he found him, Jesus asked, "Do you believe that I am the Son of Man?"

Although he was obviously favorable toward Jesus, he said, "Who is he? Give me more information so I may believe in him."

Jesus told him, "You're looking right at him. He's the one talking to you right this minute!"

This was all he needed. He said, "Lord, I believe," and then he worshipped Jesus.

Again a crowd had gathered, including some of the Pharisees who had followed the man after the synagogue trial. Jesus raised his voice to be heard by everyone on the street. He said, "This is why I came to earth, so that blind people will be able to see and those who think they can see will discover they are really blind and didn't know it."

It was a metaphor the nearby Pharisees quickly determined was aimed at them. "What? Are you saying that we're blind?" they asked Jesus. Jesus said, "If you were really blind, you wouldn't be guilty of sin. But since you claim that you can see just fine, you're accountable for everything you do that is wrong."

Jesus had a sizeable audience since no one could work on the Sabbath, so this was a good opportunity for him to teach about a personal relationship with God. His diverse group of listeners included the worshipping man who was just healed, long-time disciples, a mix of friendly and hostile Pharisees, some secretly sympathetic religious leaders, and many curious onlookers who wanted to see what was going on.

Finding a good place to settle so he could be heard, Jesus started to preach a sermon that almost no one understood. "Listen to the truth! When a man climbs over the fence into the sheep pen, you know he's a thief. When a man enters through the gate, you know he is the shepherd. The guards open the gate for the shepherd, and the sheep inside immediately recognize his voice. He calls his sheep by their names, and they follow him out the gate. When he has them all out, he leads them away. They follow because his voice is familiar. They would never follow a stranger like this because his voice would be unfamiliar to them; instead they would run away in fear of a stranger's voice."

Sheep herding was a familiar part of the culture. During the winter shepherds brought their flocks into town and secured them overnight in a large community corral with a hired guard. The guard didn't really care for the sheep but kept thieves out and allowed shepherds in. Since most sheep were raised for wool, not meat, the shepherds cared for the same animals over the years and knew them well. Sheep were identified and called by name. The shepherd's voice was so familiar that a flock of fifty could respond and exit the community corral just from their shepherd's call.

When the sheep were grazing in the hills, they stayed during the night in small circular corrals made out of rocks piled into walls. The openings for entry and exit had no gates, so the shepherds slept in the openings, keeping the sheep inside and intruders outside. In a sense, the shepherds became human gates.

Explaining that this was an analogy that portrayed their relationship with God, Jesus tried again. "I teach you the truth: I am the gate for the sheep. When others came in the past and pretended to be from God, the sheep didn't recognize their voices. They were robbers. Now I am here and I am the gate; whoever enters through me will be saved. And not just saved but will happily come and go in good pastures. I'm just the opposite of a robber. The robber wants to steal and kill; I have come to give full and joyful life.

"I am the good shepherd who lays down his life for the sheep. The hired hand isn't anything like the shepherd; he doesn't own the sheep and really doesn't care what happens to them. When the hired hand is under wolf attack, he runs away and leaves the sheep unprotected. The wolf chases, scatters, and kills the unprotected flock.

"I am the good shepherd," Jesus said again. "I know my sheep and my sheep know me—just as the Father knows me and I know the Father—and I lay down my life for the sheep. All my sheep aren't right here. I have others in other flocks, and I plan to gather them as well. They'll listen to my voice calling them and come to join into one big flock with me as the shepherd. The Father loves me because I am willing to die for the sheep, come back to life, and shepherd them again. No one takes my life without my permission. I have God's permission to voluntarily sacrifice my life and then to get it back again."

Audience response was mixed. Many of the people repeated the old charge, "He is demon-possessed and completely out of his mind. Why should we listen to him?" Others could not discount the words of a man who performed miracles. "Someone who is demon-possessed doesn't sound like this," they said, shaking their heads. "Besides, can a demon open the eyes of the blind?" Once again Jesus' words were polarizing people. He did not set out to divide, but his teaching evoked very opposite opinions and contrary emotions. Some passionately believed, and others vehemently rejected what he had to say.

It was a cold December week in Jerusalem, when temperatures were typically in the forties Fahrenheit with chilling humidity as the annual rainy season began. Daylight was nearing the low point of the winter solstice, and moods would have been subdued if it were not for the excitement of Hanukkah. Jesus was in the best place for the annual eight-day festival, Jerusalem, where this feast originated.

ANTIOCHUS IV

Jews had survived terrible opposition and persecution, but none was greater than under the despotic rule of Antiochus IV Epiphanes, the king of Syria who ruled Palestine from 175 to 164 BC. Determined to eradicate the Jewish religion and culture and replace it with the culture, philosophy, and religion of the Greeks, he attacked Jerusalem in 170 BC, killing eighty thousand Jews and selling thousands more into slavery. The wealth of the temple was stolen, and the temple was converted to a center for paganism, where the chambers were used for prostitution and the high altar was dedicated to the Greek god Zeus. Pigs, considered unclean by the Jews, were offered as sacrifices where once the Jewish high priests had sacrificed lambs to God.

Antiochus made it a capital offense to possess a copy of the Hebrew Scriptures or to circumcise a baby boy. Mothers who circumcised their sons were crucified with their children hanging around their necks. Some Jews abandoned their faith under such severe persecution. Many others became martyrs when they held to their beliefs.

One of the greatest heroes of Israel arose to lead the opposition against the wicked Antiochus IV. Judas Maccabaeus and his brothers led Jewish patriots in an uprising that eventually overthrew the Syrian army in 164 BC. The Jerusalem temple was cleansed and rededicated to Yahweh. The altar was rebuilt. Robes and utensils were replaced. Survivors committed themselves to God. Judas Maccabaeus called on the people to a feast of eight days to celebrate the victory.

The plan was to light the large menorah, the candelabrum in the temple, but there wasn't enough oil to keep it burning for eight days. Then someone found a one-day supply of oil that had not been desecrated by the Syrians; it still bore the unbroken seal of the high priest. The oil was used to light the menorah. And then a miracle happened—the one-day supply of oil lasted for the entire eight days! § Jews in succeeding generations have annually celebrated the miracle every year by lighting one candle each night of Hanukkah until eight are burning. Hanukkah is the Hebrew word for dedication, so the annual celebration is also called the Feast of Dedication or the Feast of Lights.

Jesus celebrated Hanukkah that year by visiting the part of the temple called Solomon's Colonnade. Even though it was a holiday, the Jewish leaders took no time off from harassing Jesus. The opposite opinions among the Pharisees were becoming more divisive, and each side pressed Jesus for information that would bolster their views. They gathered around Jesus in the Colonnade and asked him, "How long are you going to keep us guessing? If you are the Messiah, tell us straight out."

"I did tell you, but you wouldn't believe," he said. "All the miracles I do in my Father's name speak for me, but you don't believe because you aren't my sheep. You see, I know my sheep by name. They respond to my voice and follow me. I give them eternal life so that they will never perish. I hold them tight, and no one will ever snatch them out of my hands. My Father gave them to me, and he is the greatest of all. So you can rest assured that no one can wrench them out of my Father's hands either. You see, I and the Father are one!"

Some responded to Jesus' answer with outrage, picking up rocks to stone him to death. Jesus stood his ground. Without flinching he said to them, "I've shown you a steady stream of great miracles from God. Which one of these miracles made you decide to stone me to death?"

"We're not stoning you for any of the miracles," they shouted at him. "We're going to stone you for blasphemy because you are only human but you claim to be God!" His statement that "I and the Father are one" triggered their violence against him. They knew he was not just claiming oneness of purpose with God; he was claiming to be God himself.

Jesus de-escalated the potentially violent controversy with a play on words using Old Testament literature and Hebrew theology. Quoting from Psalm 82:6, he asked his would-be assailants, "Isn't it written in your Law, 'I have said you are gods'? If the psalm-writer Asaph called them 'gods,' to whom the word of God came, and the Scripture cannot be broken, what about the Son of God sent by the Father into the world? Why would you accuse me of blasphemy because I said, 'I am God's Son'? I'll tell you what, don't believe me unless I do what my Father does. But if I do divine acts for you to see, even though you say that you don't believe me, just believe the miracles. Once you believe the miracles, maybe then you will recognize the reality behind the miracles, that the Father is in me and I am in the Father."

It was a clever argument. Their absolutely inerrant Scriptures used the word *gods* to refer to humans, so they shouldn't accuse him of blasphemy for using the same word—although he also added that he had a greater right to such self-description than anyone else. The accusers were not to be deterred by words, clever or not. They tried to separate Jesus from the crowd and physically attack him, but Jesus pulled himself out of their hands and escaped through the throng.

It hadn't taken long to come full circle to where he had been during the late summer and early fall of that year. The Pharisees hadn't changed their minds, and the cooling-off period hadn't made any permanent difference. Jesus had to fight or flee if he didn't want to end up dead by the end of the Hanukkah festival. He chose to flee—back across the Jordan River to the east bank area where John had conducted his well-known baptisms three years earlier. It was still a prominent spot where large crowds could gather but outside the immediate jurisdiction of the temple police.

Away from the volatile atmosphere of Jerusalem, the crowds gave more reflective consideration to who Jesus really was. The majority of them had been here before. Most of them were earlier disciples of John and had been baptized at this very place in the river. Changing loyalty over to Jesus had come slowly. In a tribute to their former leader, now dead, they coined a saying: "Though John never performed any miracles, everything he said about this man was true." They realized that the powerful and persuasive John had pointed them to Jesus. If John believed Jesus was the Messiah, they decided to believe themselves. A large number were added to the list of Jesus' believers.

With an even larger entourage of disciples, Jesus began his final teaching tour. He would travel once more around the countryside, then go back to Jerusalem for the last time.

CHAPTER THIRTEEN

Jesus' farewell tour covered much of the Jewish homeland outside of Jerusalem. He knew that another visit to Jerusalem would cost him his life. This journey was his last opportunity to teach, perform miracles, and prepare his followers for the movement Jesus envisioned after he was gone.

Perea was first, a pleasant region of Palestine on the eastern banks of the Jordan River. Only ten miles wide, it was a long narrow highland overlooking the river, with adequate rainfall to grow trees, cultivate olives and vines, and farm wheat. §

§ It was such attractive land that fourteen centuries earlier, as the nation of Israel migrated from Egypt to Palestine, the tribes of Gad and Reuben chose to claim it for their homeland rather than cross the Jordan under the leadership of Joshua.

The crowds were small compared to those that mobbed him in Jerusalem, but their questions were no less direct. As he taught in one of the villages, Jesus was asked if he thought only a few would enter the Messiah's kingdom.

Most Jews assumed they were safe from divine judgment because they were related to Abraham and counted among God's chosen people. Gentiles might be excluded, but Jews would be saved for God's blessing.

Jesus talked around the issue so they could figure out the answer for themselves. It wasn't difficult to tell that he was teaching an unpopular doctrine, that many Jews were lost from God's blessing and that comparatively few were going to be included in the Messiah's rule. Teaching a negative truth with a positive twist, he said that the kingdom of God was like a house with a narrow entrance. "Try hard to enter through the narrow door, because many who try to enter won't make it. Once the owner of a house gets up and closes the door, you're stuck outside pleading for him to open the door.

"You have a problem when he tells you, 'I don't know who you are or where you come from.'

"Then you'll say, 'Of course you know us! We ate and drank together, and you used to teach in our streets.'

"But the owner will reply, 'I don't know you or where you come from. Be gone, you evildoers!'

"Then watch what will happen! There will be crying and teeth grinding when you see Abraham, Isaac, Jacob, and all the other prophets in the kingdom of God, but you don't make it in. People will come from all over the world to their reserved seats at the grand opening dinner for the kingdom of God. It will be a very different lineup than you expected, with the last at the front of the line and the first at the end of the line."

This sounded like good news to Jesus' followers who were from the margins of society, but those in the religious mainstream were highly offended. As usual, there were some Pharisees in the small crowd of listeners. It was hard to tell if they were ones who disbelieved, disagreed, and wanted Jesus stopped, or if they were among those who took Jesus seriously and wanted to believe. It may have been a mixed group. In any case, they weren't in Judea or Jerusalem, where the Pharisees had greater influence. Showing interest and warmth, their small delegation approached Jesus for conversation after his teaching time. One of them warned Jesus, "Get out of here and go somewhere else. Herod wants to kill you." It was true that Herod preferred Jesus dead, but that may not have been the man's motivation. If Jesus went back across the Jordan border into the jurisdiction of the Sanhedrin, there were other threats against him besides that of Herod.

Jesus told them to give this message to Herod: "Go tell that fox that I will drive out demons and heal people today and tomorrow, and on the third day I will reach my goal. Whatever the schedule, I must keep moving today and tomorrow and the next day—because no prophet can die outside of Jerusalem!" For those who appreciated him, Jesus revealed his short-term goals of exorcising demons and healing the sick. For those who wanted him dead, he admitted that he would eventually return to Jerusalem, where he expected to die like so many earlier prophets before him.

Not every town had a synagogue, so if Jesus wanted to be in a town with a synagogue each Sabbath, it meant he had to pace his journey to arrive in the larger villages before sunset on Fridays. He was enough of a celebrity that he received many invitations to stay at people's homes. Even Pharisees wanted Jesus to visit their houses, and Jesus accepted!

Some of his disciples may have thought it was a setup, but Jesus really didn't seem to care. It could seem suspect that whenever a Pharisee invited Jesus for dinner, it was usually on a Sabbath day. They didn't seem to progress beyond whether he performed miracles on the traditional day of rest, and Jesus didn't seem to resist tripping their traps.

One Sabbath Jesus went to the home of a prominent Pharisee who also invited a number of local guests. When Jesus arrived, he was ushered to his assigned place—immediately behind a man swollen with a generalized edema (swelling from too much fluid) that was known as dropsy. The man was miserable but not terminally ill. It was the same old story—if Jesus healed the man, he would be accused of breaking the Sabbath; if Jesus didn't heal the man, he would be viewed as lacking compassion.

This time Jesus took the initiative and asked the Pharisees and religion lawyers, "Is it legal to heal on the Sabbath day?" No one answered. Once again their setup had backfired. They all sat in silence.

Jesus then put his arms around the man and healed him. Once the man was healed, Jesus immediately sent him on his way. The host and his religious cohorts had used the sick man as bait; Jesus hugged and healed him as a suffering human being. The likely thoughts of the dinner guests were predictable—that this was not an emergency;

swollen ankles and flesh never killed anyone; he could wait until Sunday instead of healing on the Sabbath. Whatever else may have been part of this patient's medical condition, Jesus cured him out of compassion.

Because they were silent when Jesus asked if it was permissible to heal on the Sabbath, the host and his friends stayed silent as the cured man walked out of the house.

Jesus had avoided the intended legal storm and started teaching. There were three lessons on humility he had for that day's gathering of guests:

The humble person cares about people. Jesus asked them, "If one of your sons or oxen falls into a well on the Sabbath day, won't you pull him out right away?

"Obviously a parent is more concerned about the plight of a son than about a legal technicality. A decent person wouldn't wait until the next day to rescue an animal in distress. Care about people and help them out when they are in trouble!"

No one responded.

The humble person lets others go ahead. Jesus had watched the guests jockey for the best seats at the meal—partly to be close to the action and mostly to capture the places of prominence. He looked around the room and explained, "When someone invites you to a wedding feast, don't take the best seat in the house, because someone more important than you may have been invited. If that's true, the host who invited both of you will come and ask you to move so the more important person can have that seat. By then you will be embarrassed and stuck with a lower-status place to sit. So try a completely different approach. When you are invited and show up at a feast, grab a lowly place to sit. Maybe then the host will see you there and insist that you move up to a more prominent place. When this happens you'll feel great because you have been honored in front of all the other guests. The teaching is this: everyone who promotes himself will be humbled, and everyone who humbles himself will be exalted."

It wasn't a wedding feast, but they all got the point.

The humble person gives without expecting anything in return. Jesus now honed in on the host of this meal. He had done what many do, invited neighbors and business associates as a way of indebting them and guaranteeing that he would be invited to their next event. So looking directly at the host, Jesus said, "When you host a meal gathering, don't use the predictable invitation list of relatives, friends, and rich neighbors just to make sure you'll be invited when they throw a party. Instead, make up an invitation list that includes the poor, lame, handicapped, and blind people. You'll get an immediate blessing even though these people can't invite you back. But don't worry, because you'll be fully repaid when the righteous are resurrected at the end of this age."

These were the kind of words that filled a room with tension. Finally one of the guests blurted out, "Blessed is the one who will eat at the feast in the kingdom of God." These words weren't original with the speaker—it was a common religious expression. He probably couldn't think of anything else to say, and his mind grabbed this phrase from Jesus' mention of the resurrection. Whatever the reason for this tension-breaking outburst, Jesus picked up on it and turned it into another teaching opportunity. He told them a parable:

"A host was preparing for a big banquet with a long guest list. When everything was ready, the host sent a servant to tell all the guests it was time to eat.

"But all the guests came up with excuses. The first one said, 'I just bought some real estate, and I need to make an inspection. Please excuse me.'

"Another invitee said, 'I just closed a deal on five yoke of oxen for my farm, and I need to give them a test run. Please excuse me.'

"Another one said, 'I just got married, so I can't come.'

"The servant reported back that all had declined. The host became really angry and ordered the servant, 'Just go and invite everyone you see on the streets, including all the poor, disabled, blind, and lame people.'

"The servant did what was ordered. Many accepted and came, but there were still plenty of empty seats in the large banquet hall.

"Then the host told the servant, 'Do whatever it takes to fill every seat. Go outside town into the countryside and make people come. Just make sure that no one on the original invitation list who gave an excuse is allowed in.' " It was an attention-getting story, not only because recruitment from the streets was unheard of, but because Jesus was referring to Gentiles as the late-arriving but also welcome guests.

This story brought a provocative ending to the dinner and the day. The guests left engaged in animated conversation as they took different paths home. Jesus' point was clear to them, that the highest priority of human life is the invitation of God to the "great banquet" of eternity in his kingdom. Those invited should let nothing slow them down or stop them from coming. God's invitation is more important than any excuse.

Crowds attracted larger crowds. § The people clamoring after Jesus needed to know the difficult side of becoming his disciples. Hushing so many people takes time, and he needed a loud voice for them all to hear. "If you want to be my disciple, it means your loyalty and love to me must make everything else look like hatred in comparison—including your father, mother, wife, children, brothers, sisters, and even your own life. Maybe you've heard this before and missed it, so I'll tell you again: if you are going to be my follower, you must be ready and willing to carry your cross every day."

That got their attention. Jesus was using hyperbole to get their attention and to make his point that their first loyalty had to be to him alone. It was relative, of course; he wasn't

§ It must not have been difficult to sense what was happening. Excitement mounted as word spread about Jesus being the long-awaited Messiah. Even those who wanted to go home didn't out of fear that they would miss out. Rumors spread that Jesus would soon make a public announcement of his messiahship, and that would begin a cascade of events including divine intervention, overthrow of the Romans, establishing God's kingdom on earth with Jesus on the throne, and the beginning of a supernatural Golden Age for Israel. No one wanted to go home a day early. Everyone wanted to be in the front row by Jesus when these history-making events happened.

expecting his followers to hate those in their families, but they should love him so much that every other relationship would seem like hate in comparison. And following him could be tough—like carrying a cross. That shocked some of them even more because crosses were ugly and despicable. Jews and Romans alike wanted no association with any cross. Jesus was telling them that loyalty to him could bring burdens that the average person instinctively avoids. He wasn't being unkind, but it was obvious that many in the crowd followed him out of impulse rather than faith. They had never thought through what the cost could be.

"Suppose one of you wants to build a tower. The first thing you'll do is sit down at a table and make a budget to see if you can afford it. If you only get as far as building the foundation and then run out of money, everyone will laugh at you for starting something you can't finish.

"Or suppose a king is about to go to war against a neighboring nation. If he only has ten thousand soldiers to fight against the other nation's twenty thousand soldiers, he'd better think long and hard before he picks the first fight. If he decides he can't win and he's a smart king, he'll send a delegation to the other king to negotiate a peace treaty as soon as possible. In the same way, figure out how much it will cost you to follow me, because any of you who do not give up everything you have cannot be my disciple."

All of this sounded threatening and overwhelming enough to make those on the fringe ready to quit and go home. Jesus' sermon was not meant to frighten them away but to make sure they understood the expectations of the man they were acclaiming as Messiah.

While some people drifted away, others, including tax collectors, pushed closer to Jesus. Hated and mistrusted by most, they had found Jesus to be accepting.

Equally steadfast were the "sinners" in the crowd. It was a broad label given to a long list of those who were not associates of the Pharisees and didn't practice the Pharisees' traditions. They even called themselves sinners, because everyone knew what it meant. Near the top of the long list were prostitutes, tax collectors, anyone who wasn't Jewish, and all those who failed to live up to the catalog of traditions promoted by the Pharisees.

Jesus welcomed and engaged these social outcasts—talking and laughing with them, touching them, and respecting them. The Pharisees and religion teachers muttered to each other in words loud enough for everyone to hear, "This man welcomes sinners and eats meals with them." The love and forgiveness of Jesus delighted the tax collectors and "sinners" but angered and alienated the religious elite.

Hearing their criticism, Jesus answered with three parables that became some of his most famous stories. The parables of the lost sheep, lost coin, and lost son are all about giving another chance to those who miserably fail.

"Imagine a shepherd with a hundred sheep who loses one of them. You know what he will do—he will leave the ninety-nine together while he hunts down the one lost sheep until he finds it. When he finds it, he will lift that sheep over his shoulder and head home as one very happy shepherd. When he arrives home, he'll gather his friends and neighbors and tell them, 'Be happy with me! I've found my lost sheep!' Well, that's the way it is in heaven when one lost sinner repents compared to ninety-nine righteous people who didn't need to repent.

"Or imagine a woman who has a prized collection of ten silver coins and discovers that one is missing. What does she do? She lights a lamp and starts looking. She sweeps every inch of her house until she finds that coin. Then she calls all her friends and neighbors over and tells them, 'Be happy with me! I found the coin I lost.' That's the way it is in heaven when the angels of God celebrate over one single sinner who repents."

Then Jesus told the parable of the prodigal son. "Once upon a time there was a man with two sons. His younger son said, 'Dad, please give me my share of the estate now rather than wait.' So the father divided up his property.

"It didn't take long for that son to cash in everything he owned and take off for a distant country. When he got there, he wasted all his money playing and partying. Once he was broke, a famine hit the country where he was living and he was in serious trouble. He got a low-paying job working on a pig farm feeding the hogs. He was so hungry that he wanted to eat the pig food, but the owner of the pig farm didn't let him.

"One day he came to his senses and realized that the servants back home had more than enough to eat while he was starving to death in a foreign land. He decided to swallow his pride, go home, admit that he had sinned against God and his father, and ask for a job.

"Before he came close to his old house, his father saw him coming and felt sorry for him. He ran from the house to his son and hugged and kissed him.

" 'Dad,' the son said, 'I've sinned against God and against you. I know I'm not worthy to be called your son.'

"Do you know what the father did? He told his house staff, 'Hurry up! Go get the best robe in the house and put it over my son's shoulders. Put a ring on his finger and new sandals on his feet. Kill a fat calf and cook it. We're going to have a welcome home party! My son was dead and now he's alive and here. He was lost and now I've found him again!' So the party began.

"As the older son came in from the fields, he heard the music and dancing and asked what was going on. One of the servants reported, 'Your kid brother came home and your father is throwing a party to celebrate!'

"The older brother lost his temper and refused to attend the party. His father came out to try to settle him down and coax him inside, but he angrily yelled, 'Hey! For years I've been working like a slave here and have done everything you've told me to do. What did it get me? You never threw a party for my friends and me. Now when this other son of yours has gone and squandered your money on prostitutes and then comes home broke, you reward him with a huge celebration!'

" 'My son,' his father replied, 'you and I are together every day. Everything I have is yours for the using. But come now, this is a time to celebrate and be happy because your brother was as good as dead, and he is alive and home again. He was lost and now he is found!' "

It was a good day for those so-called sinners. Jesus was popular and on their side. They liked his stories. But those things didn't make them his disciples.

It was a mixed crowd. It included Pharisees, social outcasts looking for friendship, sick folk hoping for healing, crowd chasers following the latest fad, and true disciples. Not just the dozen men in Jesus' inner circle, but other men and women who really believed and wanted to live out his teachings. All these various groups made Jesus' task a constant challenge. He couldn't assume that what he said yesterday was remembered by today's audience, because the crowd was always evolving. He couldn't reveal his secrets with enemies listening, since they were plotting his assassination. Yet he wanted to teach his loyal followers truths that were beyond the introductory lessons for seekers and the clever defenses against critics.

The solution to this dilemma was parables with layers of meaning. As had been true of most of Jesus' parables, they were intended to teach truth to insiders and limit the understanding of outsiders. It usually worked, although some of the parables were so hard to understand that even his most committed followers had trouble figuring out what he was talking about. That's the way it seemed when he told the parable of the shrewd manager. It was one of many lessons he taught about money.

As others listened, Jesus told his disciples, "There was a rich businessman whose accountant was accused of mismanaging his money and property. So the businessman called the accountant into his office and confronted him. 'What's going on here? I demand an audit, and you're probably going to be fired!'

"The accountant thought, *Now what am I going to do? My boss is going to fire me and I'll never get another decent job. I'm not in good enough physical shape to dig ditches and I'm too proud to go out and beg for money. Wait a minute, I have an idea! If this works, I'll be all set when I get fired—people will welcome me into their homes and take care of me without my having to work!*

"So he called in one of those who owed money to his boss and asked him how much he owed.

" 'Eight hundred gallons of olive oil,' he answered.

"The accountant told him to quickly pay back four hundred gallons, and he'd mark his account paid in full.

"Then he asked another debtor how much he owed and was told, 'A thousand bushels of wheat.'

" 'Pay eight hundred and you'll be paid up,' the accountant told him.

"When the boss found out what the accountant was doing, he commended him for his work because he was so shrewd! That's because people in this world are shrewder in dealing with one another than are the people of the light. Let me tell you, use your money to make friends for yourselves so that when you run out of cash you'll be welcomed into eternal homes.

"Those who can be trusted with little things can also be trusted with big things. Whoever is dishonest with the small stuff will also be dishonest with the big stuff. What I'm asking you is this—if you aren't trustworthy with the money you have now, how likely is it that you are going to be trustworthy with true wealth? If you haven't handled someone else's assets so far, do you think anyone is going to give you assets of your own to manage?

"No one can serve two masters, because you'll end up hating one of them and loving the other one. You cannot serve God and money." §

§ This parable was an expansion of what he earlier taught in his Sermon on the Mount.

This is a strange story subject to great misunderstanding. Some think it is one of the toughest of Jesus' parables to explain. A rich landlord turned over the management of his business to an employee who ended up doing a lousy job. Perhaps the employee thought he would get away with what he was doing because he didn't think the owner was going to check up on him. But the boss called for a full report, and the employee knew he was in deep trouble.

Knowing he would be fired, the employee started to devise a plan. He didn't have enough money to retire. He was too proud to go out and beg. He wasn't in good enough shape to get a laborer's job digging dirt. He had to come up with something else.

The manager called in the landlord's tenants. These were tenant farmers who paid their rent with a share of the crops. They were all far behind in their payments because of the manager's mismanagement. When they heard that he was in trouble, they knew that they were also in trouble.

The manager offered them a deal. He told them to pay only part of what they owed and he would mark their accounts paid in full. It was a very clever scheme. The manager's boss wouldn't be so angry with him, because the boss would have far more money than expected. The debtors would be really grateful, because they were out of debt with smaller payments. The manager's goal was to stop his boss from sending him to jail after he was fired and to make the neighbors indebted to him so they would take care of him when he didn't have anyplace else to go.

When the boss found out, he had a surprising response. He commended his employee! He didn't commend him for his mismanagement. He didn't commend him for his dishonesty. He commended him for his shrewdness. The manager had been very clever in what he did.

Jesus used this story to teach his followers about money. He didn't want them to be lousy managers. He didn't want them to be dishonest. But he did want them to be as driven toward God as the manager in the story was driven toward watching out for himself. Be smart with money, but never let money take the place of God.

The Pharisees laughed when they heard Jesus telling this story. "He is totally wrong! He doesn't make sense. No one should take financial advice from him" was their analysis. Some of the Pharisees were comparatively rich and they loved their money. The way they figured it, they kept the laws of God better than others and God blessed them with money as a reward. The poor people of society were ignorant, disobedient sinners, and that is why God withheld his blessing and kept them broke.

These particular Pharisees were rude, sneering at Jesus as he taught. He told them, "You are the ones who are so skilled at making yourselves look good to others, but God knows your hearts. What is highly valued among people is detestable in God's sight." They may have tricked others into thinking they were good, but God knew their underlying greed and detested their hypocrisy.

Jesus went on to say, "The Old Testament Law and the Prophets were preached up until John the Baptizer. Since John, the good news of the kingdom of God is being preached, and thousands are forcing their way into it." This was a rebuttal of an earlier accusation by religious teachers that Jesus had discarded the laws of God written in the Old Testament. When Jesus taught the good news that sins could be forgiven and lives could be lived righteously with God's help rather than burdensome rule-keeping, thousands of people flocked to Jesus, trying to get into the kingdom of God through him. Jesus explained that his good news didn't mean an abandonment of centuries of God's laws. To the contrary, Jesus explained, "It is easier for heaven and earth to disappear than for the tiniest stroke of a pen to drop out of the Old Testament Law." God's law endures. As an example, Jesus reiterated the law against adultery: "Any man who divorces his wife and marries another woman commits adultery, and the man who marries a divorced woman commits adultery."

This dialogue had started with money. The Pharisees thought that their prosperity proved their righteousness. Jesus wanted them to see that there was a lot more to the story of riches than first seemed obvious. He then told another parable about a rich man and a poor man–in the next life. Interestingly, this is the only time Jesus specifically named a character in one of his parables. §

§ The Latin name for the poor beggar in the parable is Lazarus (not to be confused with a friend of Jesus who lived in Bethany and was the brother of Mary and Martha), which is Eleazar in Hebrew. Some have called the rich man in this parable Dives, which isn't actually a name but is Latin for "rich man."

"There was a rich man who wore expensive purple cloth and fine linen clothes. He lived in constant luxury. At the gate of his mansion there lived a poor beggar named Eleazar, who was covered with sores that dogs came to lick. This beggar was hungry and just wanted to eat the leftovers from the rich man's dining room table.

"Eventually the poor beggar died, and the angels carried him to Abraham's side. The rich man died around the same time, and his body was buried. The rich man went to Hades, where he was tormented. He could see Abraham in the distance with Eleazar next to him. 'Father Abraham,' he called out, 'have pity on me! Send Eleazar to dip the tip of his finger in water and cool my tongue. Please—I'm in agony in this fire.'

"But Abraham replied, 'Son, remember that in your lifetime you received your good things, while Eleazar received bad things, but now he is comforted here and you are in agony. And besides all this, between us and you a great chasm has been set, so that those who want to go from here to you cannot, nor can anyone cross over from there to us.'

"He answered, 'I beg you, Father Abraham, if you can't send him to help me, please send Eleazar to my father's house, because I have five brothers who are still alive there. Let him warn them, so that they will not also come to this place of torment.'

"'They have Moses and the Prophets,' Abraham replied. 'Let them listen to them.'

"'No, Father Abraham, but if someone who died would go back to talk to them I'm sure they would repent.'

"Abraham told him, 'If they don't listen to Moses and the Prophets, they won't be convinced even if someone rises from the dead.' "

This one wasn't hard for the Pharisees or anyone else to figure out. The rich may think they are superior in this life only to discover that in the next life God favors those who are poor. The moral of the parable? They should use their money to help the poor and show they are on God's side rather than hoard their wealth and use it for their own benefit.

Trying to move beyond the repeated intrusions and get back to teaching his disciples, Jesus changed topics to talk about more than money. His time was running out, and he had so much more to tell them. He added four last lessons to this long day of teaching on how to live. They were lessons he had taught before: (1) Don't cause another to sin; (2) Repeatedly forgive; (3) Live by faith; and (4) Wholeheartedly serve God.

While his teachings often upset the religious leaders, they gave hope to the poor and outcast. They were spoken with a supernatural authority. Certainly, if Jesus was an ordinary rabbi, his instructions were open for debate. If he was more than a rabbi—if he was the Messiah and if he was actually from God—his instructions were absolute. In a small village outside Jerusalem, Jesus performed his most spectacular miracle. It was his greatest proof to date that he was from God.

CHAPTER FOURTEEN

E verything was going well. Audiences were large; converts were many. The critics were always around, but lately they were more of an irritation than an issue. Perea certainly was a quieter place than Jerusalem. Until the messenger came.

Urgent news—whether political news for the government or personal news for an individual—was delivered by messengers, running, sweaty, out of breath, pushing through a crowd like a battering ram through a gate. That day's messenger was looking for Jesus and anxious enough to interrupt him in midsentence. "Lord," he blurted, "the one you love is sick."

The messenger needed to calm down and catch his breath long enough to explain exactly who was sick. It turned out it was Lazarus of Bethany—failing fast, nearing death, not much time left. § His frantic sisters had sent the runner with the urgent plea for Jesus to come quickly.

§ Actually the sick man's name was Eleazar. It was a common Hebrew name, although this man has become better known by the Latin equivalent, Lazarus. In a region with so many languages and cultures, there was often a mix of proper names and nicknames.

Lazarus was the brother of Jesus' good friends Mary and Martha (also very common names), and Jesus had stayed in the family's home, which was at least a day's journey away in Bethany outside of Jerusalem. If Lazarus truly was in critical condition, it was unlikely that Jesus would get there in time. Besides, going to a village less than two miles outside of the capital city put Jesus right back into the danger zone of the Jerusalem leaders.

Jesus' next actions made little sense to his closest associates. First he insisted, "This sickness will not end up in death. No, it is for the glory of God and his Son." Anyone who knew Jesus for very long was well aware of his close friendship and love for Mary, Martha, and Lazarus. So it seemed incomprehensible that Jesus and his disciples stayed put for the next two days until Jesus suddenly announced, "Let's go back to Judea."

The disciples' response was unanimous: "It wasn't long ago that the Jewish leaders were trying to stone you there, and now you're going back?!" It was a practical and worthy question. But Jesus' answer stepped right over that issue.

"Every day has about twelve hours of daylight, right? If someone walks during the daylight, he doesn't stumble because he sees by earth's light. But if someone walks at night, he stumbles in the dark." The Romans had another way to say the same in Latin: *Carpe diem!* ("Seize the day!")

They probably preferred to seize the daylight there in Perea rather than take the risk of going so close to Jerusalem. But Jesus explained, "Our friend Lazarus has fallen asleep, and now it's time for me to go and wake him up."

Jesus said some things that were difficult to understand, but the disciples didn't want to sound disrespectful, so they responded, "Sleep is good. It will help him get better from whatever ails him." Jesus skirted any further euphemisms and told them, "Lazarus is dead!"

Lazarus and his death was sad news—to them and to Jesus. How Jesus knew he was dead was beyond them, but it wasn't one of those times when asking seemed like a good idea. Jesus was getting even harder to figure out, and they couldn't easily determine how he was handling this. Grief can hit different people in different ways, but it didn't seem normal when Jesus told them, "For your sake I'm glad I wasn't there in order to grow your faith. Now let's get going."

Sometimes his little group needed to take what Jesus said at face value, and sometimes they had to search for hidden meanings. Thomas concluded this was one of those hidden-meaning moments and that

Jesus wasn't really talking about Lazarus at all. Thomas remembered several references to Jesus dying in Jerusalem and somehow figured that all the talk about Lazarus was code for Jesus' own death. He told them with great authority, "Let's all go, so that we may die together with Jesus." It sounded heroic at the time, although it's hard to imagine that the majority were all that enthusiastic about going someplace to die.

By the time they arrived in Bethany, Lazarus had been dead and buried for four days. Between the time of his death and the distance Jesus had to travel when he first heard from the messenger, it was already too late for Jesus to come before his death. Bodies were washed, wrapped, and buried before sunset on the day of death.

The little village of Bethany was crowded with friends and relatives who had come from the nearby countryside and from Jerusalem to comfort Mary and Martha in their grief. The arrival of Jesus and his entourage of followers mixed the funeral with a celebrity sighting.

News of Jesus' arrival preceded him, and word soon reached the home of the grieving sisters. Martha quickly gathered her skirts and ran to meet him. Mary stayed in the house to await Jesus' arrival.

Martha's mood was a mixture of emotions—her grief was raw, but she was excited that Jesus had finally come. Still, there was lingering resentment that he had not come sooner. "Lord," she exclaimed, "if you had been here, my brother wouldn't have died. But I still believe that even now God will give you whatever you want." Not an expectation that Lazarus could be fixed, but Martha's affirmation that she still believed in Jesus' supernatural powers even though he had failed to use them to save her brother.

"Your brother will rise again," Jesus said. This was both a comforting declaration and a theological affirmation. In this belief, Jesus was aligned with the Pharisees, who taught that there was life after death, unlike the Sadducees, who taught that physical death was final. Martha thanked Jesus with her own affirmation: "I know. I truly believe my brother will rise again in the resurrection at the end of time."

Jesus told her, "I am the resurrection and the life. Whoever believes in me will live, even after he dies; and whoever lives and believes in me will never die again. Do you believe this?"

"Yes, Lord," she said, "I believe that you are the Messiah. You are the Son of God who came from heaven to earth." Her disappointment in Jesus had not reduced her faith in him.

They stood together near the grave as the crowd grew large. The appearance of Jesus again in Bethany was such a thrilling occurrence that it was enough to bring to a halt some of the professional mourners hired for the occasion.

He waited by the grave while Martha returned to the house where Lazarus had died. She entered and whispered to Mary, "He's here, and he's asking for you." Usually the guests came to the bereaved, but when Mary heard this, she quickly got up and went to him. The house was packed with company who assumed that Mary was once more headed to the gravesite to weep for her brother. They were among the few in Bethany unaware of Jesus' arrival. Seeking to be courteous and supportive, they followed Mary and Martha from the house to the grave.

As the two women neared the gravesite, the crowd parted to let them through. Mary collapsed at Jesus' feet and repeated exactly the words her sister had told Jesus earlier. "Lord, if you had been here, my brother wouldn't have died."

When Jesus saw Mary's tears and heard the collective crying of the mourners, it deeply touched his heart as well. Jesus broke the sounds of grief with a matter-of-fact question: "Where have you laid his body?"

"Come and see, Lord," several replied as they pointed toward the tomb.

The emotions of Lazarus' death must have finally hit Jesus then, and he too wept. The tears were more than sympathetic grief. Anyone could see that they were deep and genuine. "How much he must have loved Lazarus" was a comment heard from those who observed Jesus' tears. Mixed with the mourners' tears were criticisms of Jesus' late arrival and lack of intervention. "If he's good enough to give sight to the blind, he should have been able to stop his friend from dying."

As he came to the tomb, Jesus stopped, the tears visible on his cheeks. As was customary in the region, the grave was not a hole in the ground, but a cave that served as a mausoleum, with a stone door sealing the entrance.

He wiped his eyes. "Move away the stone." His voice was strong and authoritative.

Consternation filled the faces of the mourners. "But, Lord, he's been dead for four days," Mary said, "and his body will have a terrible smell by now."

Jesus asked a question that he didn't expect anyone to answer: "Didn't I tell you that if you believed, you were going to see the glory of God?"

Several of the village men, shrugging their shoulders doubtfully, pushed the stone away from the cave opening. It's hard to see into a cave, at least very far inside. Opening a tomb four days after a burial is enough to silence the nosiest crowd. Some of them had looked into opened graves before, especially after the body had decayed and the remaining bones were moved so the tomb could be reused. But it's doubtful that anyone in Bethany had ever seen a tomb opened four days after a burial. Under usual circumstances it would have been disrespectful, disgusting, spooky, and probably illegal. Somehow this was different. There were no words yet to describe whatever was going on.

Jesus lifted up his head and eyes as he prayed, "Father, thank you for listening to me as you always do. I'm praying to you out loud to help the people standing around to believe that you really did send me."

Then Jesus shouted in a voice loud enough to make people jump, "Lazarus, come out!"

Total silence.

A sound in the tomb. Could it be?

A shadow that looked like it moved just inside the doorway. Was it a reflection?

Lazarus stepped out into the sunlight, his burial wrapping requiring slow, small steps rather than a normal stride. His hands and feet had been wrapped in the traditional strips of linen, and a cloth was around his face. He looked like a ghost. *Was the dead man really alive again?*

Jesus ordered the men who had moved the stone door to unwrap the burial clothes from his body. Who would even want to touch him? But they did, and underneath the linen cloths was Lazarus—alive!

Jesus was indeed "the resurrection and the life." There were a lot of new believers in Jesus that day. Skeptics were convinced. Doubters had the evidence they were asking for. Would-be believers and hangers-on became full-fledged disciples. "Whoever believes in me will live, even after he dies." They not only believed, but they talked— it didn't take long for the news to arrive in Jerusalem.

A few were still not convinced and seized this opportunity to win favor with the chief priests and the Pharisees. An emergency meeting of the Sanhedrin was called. The purpose was to decide what to do next about Jesus. They faced some serious decisions. On the one hand, so many eyewitnesses made the miracle difficult to discredit. Politically, this particular miracle was especially divisive between the two parties of the Sanhedrin. The Pharisees had become Jesus' primary critics, but they were the ones who believed in resurrection from the dead. Jesus had provided convincing evidence that they were right. The Sadducees weren't as opposed to Jesus but now had to choose between their established no-resurrection doctrine and the news about Lazarus that was raging through the city. The debate was intense and ran late.

After urgent discussion and disagreement, both sides started asking what was being accomplished in this meeting. Then they found a common issue when one of the members argued, "Here is this man performing all these miracles. If we don't stop him, everyone is going to believe him, and then the Romans will eliminate our temple and our nation." They couldn't agree on doctrine, but they could agree that Jesus was a threat to their privilege and power. What would Caesar's response be to a Jewish Messiah? What would the Roman army do?

As they tried to find a consensus, Caiaphas, the high priest from AD 18 to 37, made an assertion that would later take on an interpretation he would never have imagined. He told the Sanhedrin, "You just don't get it! It's better to have one man die for the people than to have the entire nation of Israel perish." Even if Jesus was indeed a good man, it was better to kill him and save Israel than to save one good man and destroy the nation. When John heard about Caiaphas' statement, he later wrote, "Caiaphas did not say this by himself, but as the high priest he prophesied that Jesus would die for the Jews, and not only for the Jewish nation but also for God's children everywhere, to unite them as one."

That night all the previous plots started to come together. The decision was officially made to kill Jesus. The plan was no secret. Jesus stopped making public appearances around Jerusalem and moved to the desert village of Ephraim. He and his disciples could be safe for a while longer from the Sanhedrin and their temple police. Ephraim was remote and obscure along the northern border of Judea. It was an out-of-the-way and safe place to hole up, but Jesus soon headed out on the last leg of this farewell tour, taking his disciples back north toward their home base of Galilee. Jerusalem still was the ultimate goal, but now they traveled away from the city on the Jerusalem Road through Samaria.

For the first time in a long time, the band of twelve had Jesus to themselves. They tried to avoid public notice and minimize the crowds that had grown so large during prior travels. There was more time for teaching, questions, and remembering all the amazing events of the past three years. These last months were to be among their best together, although there had to have been a sense of looming destiny none of them even wanted to consider.

When they entered one of the Samaria-Galilee border villages, ten lepers looked like they were waiting for Jesus to arrive. Nine were Jews; one was a Samaritan. Jews and Samaritans wouldn't normally associate with one another, but this disease, the scourge of first-century society, forced the otherwise unlikely relationship.

These men kept the legal distance from Jesus, shouting out, "Jesus, Master, have pity on us!" the standard cry of all street beggars. Because they couldn't work or go home with their disease, they were used to begging from a distance. It was a gamble with little downside. If Jesus heard them, if Jesus had pity, if Jesus was willing to help them, maybe they would get some money. These ten never asked to be healed, just helped.

§ The law required an examination and clearance before anyone cured of leprosy was allowed back into society. Most priests were never asked; leprosy was a life sentence.

Jesus not only looked and listened but called back to them, "Go, show yourselves to the priests." § He hadn't healed them—yet.

That Jesus ordered them to be examined implied that they would be healed. They believed Jesus enough to start out on the journey to the priest without seeing any signs of healing. But as they went, they were healed. They looked at their arms, their legs, and at each other and then began to run. The priest examined and cleared all ten—they were free to reenter society. What excitement filled them as they left the priest!

They all headed home except one. When he had seen that he was healed, he went back to look for Jesus. Shouting praises to God, he fell at Jesus' feet and repeatedly thanked him for this miracle. He was the Samaritan.

Jesus asked him, "Weren't there ten of you? Where are the other nine? Could it be that the only one who returned to praise God was the Samaritan?" Then Jesus blessed him, saying, "Stand up and go home. Your faith has healed you." This exchange was a significant statement against ethnic prejudice. Jesus was becoming the Messiah to everyone, not only the Jews.

———— ❀ ————

Jesus' disciples had seen a lot of miracles during the years they had been with him, but they still were impressed. None was routine. They asked few questions about how Jesus did what he did, but they wondered if these miracles were indications that God's kingdom was soon coming to rule on earth. They remembered a time when some of the Pharisees had asked Jesus exactly when the kingdom would come. Jesus had answered, "The arrival of God's kingdom doesn't depend on your observations and calculations. It's not the type of thing where people can suddenly say, 'Here it is' or 'There it is,' because the kingdom of God is among you." When Jesus the King is present, he had told them, then the kingdom is present.

Jesus now overheard their conversation about God's kingdom, and he began teaching them about the future. "The time will come when you will be anxious to experience the days of the Son of Man, but you won't. People will tell you, 'There he is!' or 'Here he is!' Don't waste your time chasing after what they say. When the Son of Man comes, it will be a surprise moment like the lightning that flashes across the sky. But it won't be right away; first I must suffer in many ways, including being rejected by this generation." Spectacular divine signs were coming, they understood, but not right away. Jesus was predicting a sequence of future events that would bring him back to earth as a judge. It would be a season of amazing events leading to the direct rule of God over earth. But that was far in the future. The next great event was not God's rule on earth but Jesus' suffering and rejection.

Talking more about what to expect with his second coming to earth, Jesus told them, "The coming of the Son of Man will be a lot like the days of Noah. Life will seem pretty normal. Back then people were eating, drinking, and marrying right up to the day Noah entered the ark. Then the flood came and destroyed them all.

"It was the same in the days of Lot. Those people were eating and drinking, buying and selling, planting and building until the day Lot left Sodom. That was the day when fire and sulfur rained down from heaven and destroyed them all.

"It will be just like this on the day the Son of Man appears. On that day, if someone is roofing his house and caught by surprise, he shouldn't take time to get anything out of his house. No one working in a field should run home to get possessions. Remember Lot's wife! She looked back when she was escaping Sodom and died. Those who try to save their lives will lose them, and those prepared to lose their lives will preserve them. I tell you, on that night a couple will be in one bed, and one will be taken and the other left behind. On that day there will be two women grinding grain together outside, and one of them will be taken and the other one left alone."

There would be many late-night discussions around the campfire to sort through all that Jesus had crammed into this burst of instruction. He particularly emphasized that when God cataclysmically intervenes to judge humanity, it will take most people by surprise. They will be enjoying the cadence and routine of their everyday lives, including special events like weddings and everyday events like family mealtime. The population of the earth will be stunned, just as they were in Jesus' examples from earlier Jewish history. When God intervenes, it will be swift and decisive—triumphant for those who are ready and tragic for those who are not.

Jesus' students had more questions than they did before. Most of all, they wanted to know when and where all these prophecies would happen. He gave them a common popular proverb for an answer: "Where there is a dead body, there the vultures will gather." Like so many proverbs, this one doesn't easily translate into another culture and language. Jesus meant that when the necessary conditions are met, something inevitable will happen (for example, when an animals dies in a field or forest, vultures are sure to show up). It will be obvious when the time comes. All that Jesus predicted is inevitable, he told the twelve, but there would be generations of factors that needed to line up first.

TEACHING BY REPETITION

This teaching from Jesus that compares future events to the historic events during the lives of Lot and Noah is repeated later in Jesus' biography. The New Testament authors who recorded Jesus' life repeated similar or identical quotations from him at different times and places in his story. Some scholars think the authors were simply organizing the material in different ways. But there is another explanation.

Repetition of statements is a common practice. Politicians deliver similar or identical speeches almost every day of a campaign to different audiences in different towns on different days. Sometimes there are minor variations to adapt the speech to a particular group of listeners. Those who travel with the politicians get to know the lines, jokes, stories, and positions by memory. The same can be said of college teachers who have multiple sections of the same course. They deliver similar or identical lectures to different students in different classes.

Jesus traveled extensively throughout the land of Israel with the same basic teachings about the kingdom of God and about himself. It is obviously appropriate that he often repeated himself, and some of those repetitions came with variations. On one occasion, a specific teaching was part of a conversation. On other occasions, the same teaching was in answer to a question or part of a sermon. Jesus' longer sermons were collections of numerous teachings. For his disciples it meant that Jesus regularly reinforced their growth and understanding with repetitions on a theme.

The next day they headed south through Perea toward Judea, talking while they walked. The variety of topics and the animated conversations were so interesting that no one mentioned the significant change in direction. They were no longer going home to Galilee. Others traveling the same way were headed to Jerusalem for the annual Passover celebration. For Jesus and his friends, this would be their last journey together.

There were many roadway conversations during that last trip. Most have been forgotten, but six were so especially memorable that they were repeated and recorded.

The first one was about prayer. They often prayed together, and Jesus' disciples certainly must have had many of the same questions about prayer asked by other generations: "Does prayer really make a difference?" "If God knows everything, what is the point of praying?" "Why aren't all prayers answered with a yes?" "What if we don't say the prayers exactly right? Does that mean that God won't listen?" "Do prayers work better if they are louder, longer, more intense, or more frequent?"

Jesus used a parable to teach them that they should keep on praying and not give up when they don't get an answer from God right away. The story went like this:

"In a certain town there was a judge who didn't fear God or anyone else. And there was a widow in that same town who kept coming to him with the same petition, 'Help me to get justice against my oppressor.'

"For a long time he refused to help her, but finally he reconsidered. He told himself, 'Not because I fear God or anyone else but to get this widow off my back, I'm going to see to it that she gets justice. If I don't, she's going to wear me out with her asking.' "

Explaining his own parable, Jesus told them, "Did you hear what this unfair judge said? Well, if he'll grant justice, you can certainly expect that God will do a whole lot better when his chosen people repeatedly ask him for help. God will help them to get justice and get it soon. The question is, will believers have the patience to wait for God's final judgments when the Son of Man returns to earth, or will they give up too soon and quit believing?"

The twelve were encouraged, because there were many times when they felt like giving up. Some of their local judges were very harsh with petitioners. If an angry and arbitrary judge could be badgered into doing what was right, certainly a good God would do what is right.

If diligence and perseverance were the right way to pray, arrogance and self-righteousness were the wrong way to pray. Jesus told them another parable to explain this:

"Two men went up the road to pray at the temple in Jerusalem. The first was a Pharisee and the second was a tax collector. The Pharisee stood up and prayed about himself saying, 'God, I am most thankful not to be like other people who are robbers, evildoers, and adulterers. Thank you that I am not like that tax collector over there. I am grateful to be so good, fasting from food twice a week and tithing all the money I make.'

"The tax collector stood at a distance the same day. He wouldn't even look up to heaven when he prayed. Instead he pounded his chest and said, 'God, have mercy on me, a sinner.' "

His voice rising with emotion, Jesus added, "Let me tell you, the second one rather than the first went home from the temple justified before God. The proud person will be humbled, and the humble person will be honored by God."

The next travel conversation was about divorce. It may have come up over the divorce of King Herod Antipas, the one that led to the imprisonment and execution of John the Baptizer. But divorce and remarriage were a frequent topic in everyday conversations anyway, just as they are now.

As the group headed back toward Jerusalem, Jesus was performing more miracles and the crowds had picked up again. In the crowds were the often-present Pharisees. They now saw a convenient way to solve their problem with Jesus' popularity by dragging him into the divorce debate. If Jesus affirmed the condemnation of Herod's divorce, he might be beheaded like his cousin, and Herod would have done their job for them.

This was not an intimate conversation with the twelve as some others had been. There was a large crowd when the Pharisees asked Jesus, "Is it lawful for a man to divorce his wife for any reason at all?" This simple question was loaded with controversy. Some rabbis taught that all divorce was forbidden by God, and others taught that a man could divorce his wife simply because she prepared a meal he didn't like.

Jesus answered the question with a question, not a tactic to evade a straight answer but a standard teaching method. "What did Moses command in the Old Testament?"

The Pharisees' spokesman answered, "Moses allowed a man to initiate a certificate of divorce and then be done with her." §

§ They were referring to the Old Testament law in Deuteronomy 24:1-4 *NIV*, which states, "If a man marries a woman who becomes displeasing to him because he finds something indecent about her, and he writes her a certificate of divorce, gives it to her and sends her from his house, and if after she leaves his house she becomes the wife of another man, and her second husband dislikes her and writes her a certificate of divorce, gives it to her and sends her from his house, or if he dies, then her first husband, who divorced her, is not allowed to marry her again after she has been defiled. That would be detestable in the eyes of the Lord. Do not bring sin upon the land the Lord your God is giving you as an inheritance."

That law was written fourteen hundred years earlier, when the people of Israel were exiting the moral chaos of Egyptian culture and transitioning to a new moral code. Moses wrote this law to regulate marriage, prohibit incest, and stabilize families. In many ways the law itself had become divisive because its enforcement turned on the meaning of the words *something indecent* as the legal grounds for divorce; some rabbis said that was anything the husband didn't like while other rabbis insisted it meant sexual unfaithfulness.

Jesus knew they were focusing on the concession and missing the main point. They were so anxious to find a reason to divorce that they overlooked God's greater design for marriage. Quoting from the Old Testament story of creation in the book of Genesis, he told them, "Moses wrote this law to accommodate hard hearts. But at creation God began with a male and a female. God's design was for a man to leave his parents and permanently marry his wife so that they became one flesh. God joins a man and woman in marriage, and no one should dare to divide what God has joined."

When pressed for specific grounds for divorce, Jesus explained,

"Moses permitted you to divorce your wives because your hearts were hard. But it wasn't supposed to be this way. So let's go back to the original design. That means that if a man divorces his wife for any reason except adultery and then marries someone else, he is committing adultery."

The conversation about divorce didn't end along the Jerusalem Road. That night Jesus and his disciples stayed in the home of friends and the discussion continued. Most of them were unmarried but apparently assumed that if they did marry and it didn't work out, they could get divorces. Revealing their pessimism about marriage, they told him that if they agreed with Jesus' teaching on divorce and remarriage, they would be better off staying single.

Jesus told them again what he had said to the larger group. "Anyone who divorces his wife and then marries another woman is guilty of the sin of adultery against his wife. And the same goes for a wife. If she divorces her husband and marries another man, she commits adultery."

Jesus then added an explanation that he hadn't told the crowd outside. "Not everyone can handle what I've been teaching today; only some of those to whom I've given this truth. Some people never marry because of the way they were born. Others don't marry because of what happened to them in life § or because they chose not to be married for the sake of God's kingdom. I'm teaching God's design for marriage so that those who will listen and learn about it will also accept what I'm teaching." Directly addressing their option of celibacy, he assured them that if they didn't marry, God would help them to live moral lives while unmarried.

§ It may have surprised his disciples that Jesus spoke so forthrightly and matter-of-factly about the way some people were from birth or from what happened to them. He was referring to eunuchs, men born without normal genitals or those who were surgically emasculated. The Hebrew law (Leviticus 21:20) restricted them from offering certain sacrifices at the temple. The Jewish culture looked down on or excluded eunuchs. He even acknowledged that some were symbolic eunuchs when they became celibate and renounced marriage in answer to the call of God and his kingdom. Jesus was defining the kingdom of God as inclusive rather than exclusive.

The third conversation on the way to Jerusalem for the last time was about children. It really wasn't much of a conversation. Rather, it was one of those times when Jesus and his disciples disagreed, Jesus rebuked them, and there was no more discussion.

It started when a group of parents brought their babies and young children to the front of the crowd, asking Jesus to touch them and pray for them. To others it may have seemed cute, but the disciples thought it was disruptive and disrespectful. The number of young families multiplied. To some it may have appeared that they were crowding out many of the sick people who came to be healed and were taking so much time that Jesus couldn't teach. The disciples decided to take charge and chase the children away along with their parents.

As soon as Jesus saw what they were doing, he reprimanded his disciples and told them, "Let those little children come to me. Don't stop them! The kingdom of God belongs to youngsters like this." The disciples were genuinely shocked; they had assumed Jesus was as put out with the children's intrusions as they were. Children were typically not given preferential treatment in the culture because they held low social status. Jesus said, "I'm telling you the truth when I say that anyone who wants to receive the kingdom of God needs to become like a young child or he won't make it in."

His kingdom was made of humble ordinary people with simple childlike faith, he had told them. And teaching aside, he obviously enjoyed these children. He took them into his arms, talked with them and their parents, and prayed God's blessings on them. It was a joyful time for Jesus as he came closer to the sorrows waiting at the far end of this road to Jerusalem.

Money was the topic of the fourth teaching moment. Early the next morning a rich young man ran up to Jesus and dropped on his knees. He was so abrupt that he must have startled everyone at first, much like the father who came seeking healing for his daughter or the messenger who announced that Lazarus was dying. But no illness was involved this time; he had a spiritual question. He addressed Jesus as "Good teacher" and asked him, "What kind of good deeds do you recommend so I can get eternal life?"

Jesus asked why the man called him good, telling him, "No one is good—except God alone." Jesus was leading him to realize that people are sinners, and only God is truly good. If this young man wanted to do good, he should start with obeying the commandments of the good God, Jesus told him. "Which ones?" he asked Jesus. He had grown up in the synagogue, where he had been taught hundreds of rules.

Jesus answered, "You know them by heart: Do not murder, do not commit adultery, do not steal, do not give false testimony, do not defraud, honor your father and mother, and love your neighbor as yourself." In other words, keep the Ten Commandments.

This sounded like a good-news answer to his original question. "Teacher," he was happy to report, "I've kept these commandments since I was a little boy." But he must have known that wasn't good enough or he wouldn't have run to Jesus early in the morning to find out something further. "What more do I need to do?" he asked.

Jesus later told some of his disciples that he loved this young visitor. He was a genuine seeker, an appealing person who really was trying to do the right thing. That made it all the more difficult to look him in the eye and tell him, "You're still not there yet. Something is missing. Sell everything you own, give the proceeds to the poor, and you'll have your treasure in heaven. Then come, follow me."

The young man said nothing. His face fell and a wave of sadness ran though him. He was very rich and couldn't imagine trading in his wealth as Jesus had described. As he slowly walked away, Jesus spoke with a sadness of his own, "The truth is that it can be very hard for a rich man to enter the kingdom of heaven. Actually, it's easier for a camel to slide through the eye of a needle than for a rich man to make it into the kingdom of God." §

§ This was an exaggeration, of course, a figure of speech. Camels were the largest animals around, and needle holes were as small as anything they usually saw. Like this sad rich man, others who have money and possessions struggle with making them less than all-important.

His disciples were flabbergasted. The popular notion was that wealth was evidence of God's blessing and riches were assurance of eternal life. If this fellow couldn't make it to God, "Who then can be saved?" they asked.

It was a rhetorical question, but Jesus answered it anyway. "This may not be humanly possible, but it's different with God's help; all things are possible with God."

Peter was taking in every word. "We've left everything to follow you! Will we get anything in the end?" he asked Jesus. Indeed, Peter had walked away from a secure fishing business and his home and family to follow Jesus. He had given up everything.

Jesus was sensitive to Peter's question and grateful for his sacrifice. Jesus told him, "I'll tell you the truth. At that time when God fixes everything that is messed up in this world, the Son of Man will sit on his throne of glory, and you will sit on one of a dozen other thrones. You'll be one of the judges of Israel! And not just you! Everyone who has left home, wife, husband, brothers, sisters, father, mother, children, and businesses or who has suffered for my sake will receive a hundred times as much as sacrificed and will inherit eternal life as well! Just remember that many who are first now will be last then, and many who are last now will be first then."

God's goodness was the theme of the fifth conversation along the Jerusalem Road, maybe continuing on from the wealthy young man's question. Jesus told a parable that upset some listeners then and has upset others since that time. The question concerned those who joined Jesus later. How much less of a reward would go to them?

"The kingdom of heaven is like a landowner," Jesus began the parable, "who began hiring help early in the morning. He promised to pay them one denarius for the day's work and then sent them into his vineyard to get started.

"At about nine o'clock the landowner went back to town and saw some unemployed workers standing around the marketplace with nothing to do. He told them, 'Come work in my vineyard, and I'll pay you a fair wage.' So they joined the rest of the crew.

"He went back around noon and again around three o'clock and did the same thing. At about five o'clock he went looking a fifth time and found some more workers standing around doing nothing. He asked them, 'Why are you still hanging out in the marketplace? Why aren't you working?'

" 'We're not working because no one has hired us,' they answered.

"He said to them, 'Well, I'll hire you. There's not much daylight left, so get over to my vineyard and get started.'

"That night he told his foreman, 'Call the workers and pay them their wages, beginning with the last ones hired and moving in order to the first.'

"The workers who were hired at five came and each was paid a denarius. When the crew that started early in the morning saw this they were thrilled and expected an extra big payment. But each one of them also received a denarius. They complained to the landowner who hired them, 'These guys worked for only one hour, and you're paying them the same as we get for working all day in the heat? You've made them equal with us!'

"The landowner looked at their spokesman and said, 'Listen, my friend. I'm paying you a fair wage. You agreed in advance that your pay was one denarius for the day, and that's exactly what you're getting. Take your denarius and go home. If I want to pay the other workers a denarius, that's my right. It's my money, and I have the right to pay whatever I choose. Are you envious because I'm generous?' "

While Jesus' story may have upset the sense of fairness in his listeners, its purpose was to explain the character and behavior of God. God is the ultimate ruler, who is sovereign and can do anything he wants. The rewards God gives are good and are primarily determined not by human work but divine generosity. Jesus wanted his students to identify with the crew that started at five o'clock and appreciate God's overpayment of wages. Unfortunately, some of his listeners missed the point of the parable and identified with the crew that started at nine and felt cheated because others received more.

This was another parable that was worthy of a discussion that went late into the night. Long after Jesus fell asleep, his disciples were still debating the concepts of justice and generosity.

The sixth conversation was about Jesus' death and resurrection. As they came closer to Jerusalem, a mixed sense of amazement and fear started to set in. Everyone knew the Sanhedrin had an arrest warrant out for Jesus. The Messiah was sent from God. They had thought he was going to overthrow the Romans and establish God's kingdom on earth and that a new Golden Age was about to begin with Jesus as the leader. So why did some of the Jewish leaders want to kill him? How was Jesus going to miraculously turn their opposition into a spectacular victory?

While confident of the outcome, there were inevitable doubts. What if the warrant worked? What if Jesus was arrested? What if he ended up in jail, even executed like John the Baptizer? No, that could never happen, they assured one another.

The more they talked about all this, the farther ahead on the road was Jesus. They had to catch up in order to ask him what he thought was going to happen. He took them aside and gave them an answer, but it wasn't what they wanted to hear.

"We are going up to Jerusalem," he told them. "When we get there, I am going to be betrayed to the chief priests and teachers of the law. They will condemn me to death and will hand me over to the Gentiles for execution. The Gentiles will mock me, spit on me, flog me, and kill me. Three days later I will rise back to life." This last explanation was very clear, but the first part was so unbelievable they simply could not capture the whole of what he was saying.

The seventh discussion turned out to be the question of who was the greatest among them. Some of these conversations had been limited to the twelve disciples. A few included crowds of local strangers. Some were shared with a larger group of Jesus' followers who were traveling with him to the Passover. The number changed from day to day as newcomers joined and some became tired and dropped out and went home.

One of the fellow travelers was Mrs. Zebedee, the mother of James and John. She was a widow from an upper-middle-class family that owned homes in both Galilee, where their fishing business was based, and in Jerusalem. She probably traveled often on the Jerusalem Road between her two residences. As a faithful believer in Jesus, she followed him from Galilee to the end of his life in Jerusalem. Not only did she personally believe in Jesus, but two of her sons, James and John bar Zebedee, were part of Jesus' inner circle of disciples.

Traveling with the crowd, she was convinced that Jesus probably was the Messiah and was coming close to being crowned king of Israel. Thinking how good it would be for her sons to hold high positions in King Jesus' coming government, she decided to approach him about it.

At what she thought was the right moment, Mrs. Zebedee went up to Jesus alongside John and James. She knelt down and asked Jesus to grant a favor.

"What is it you want?" Jesus asked.

"Please promise that one of my sons will sit at your right and the other at your left in your kingdom," she asked as convincingly as she could. As if this weren't audacious enough, John and James chimed in with their own request. They said, "Teacher, we're going to ask you for a favor and would really like for you to say yes."

"And what do you two want me to do for you?"

Echoing their mother's request, they said, "Let one of us sit at your right and the other at your left when you're crowned king." They would leave it up to Jesus to determine who would become his number one man and who would become number two!

Jesus was amazingly patient and kind in response to these requests. At least Mrs. Zebedee wasn't asking for herself, and he could understand that this mother wanted her sons close to Jesus. But James and John should have known better.

"You have no idea what you're asking for," Jesus said softly. "Do you really think that you would be able to drink the cup I'm going to drink? Could you handle the baptism I've got coming?" He was thinking about crucifixion.

"We can," they answered. They were thinking about coronation.

Not wanting to hurt them or frighten them, Jesus gave an affirmation as he denied their request. "You *will* drink the cup I drink and be baptized with the baptism I am baptized with, but it's not up to me to decide who sits where. These places have already been reserved by God the Father." They had no idea what was ahead for them or how difficult it would be. Jesus simply left the future job assignments for God the Father to decide.

When the other ten heard about this conversation, they were far less gracious and generous. They became indignant with James and John. It's not hard to imagine their barrage of questions. "Who do you two think you are, anyway? What right do you have to be our superiors? How dare you ask for such prominent positions? We're never going to trust you two again!"

The anger and conflict were real, so Jesus called them together and said, "You know that Gentile leaders are domineering and push their authority on others. But you're not to be like that. So I'm going to tell you again and hope that this time it sinks in: if you want to be great, you have to become a servant; if you want to be number one you must start out as a slave. Look at me—I'm the Son of Man, but I didn't come to earth to be served but to serve and to offer my life as a ransom to save others." It was not a new message. They had heard it before. But they had forgotten. At least James and John had forgotten.

It was the end of that day's conversation about who was the greatest but not the last time they would struggle with their own personal ambitions.

———— ❊ ————

They had come a long way over the past few weeks, from Galilee to Judea. The sixty miles may not have seemed far, but it took a long time. Jesus walked with crowds numbering in the thousands, and he stopped at many villages, lingering for lengthy teaching and conversation.

The goal was to reach Jerusalem in time for the Passover, but there was time for a diversion to Jericho. As far as is known, Jesus had never been there before and wanted to visit the famous city. §

§ There is a treacherous road from Jerusalem into Jericho, winding through arid mountainous terrain populated with bands of robbers who preyed on lone travelers and small caravans. The larger caravans carrying merchandise on this major trade route were well armed and less likely to be attacked. Jesus' group was large enough to be left alone.

The first sight of Jericho was spectacular. It was a prosperous oasis in a below-sea-level desert setting. The actual city has had several different locations over the centuries but none more magnificent than the one Jesus came to see. Herod the Great and his successors built a large winter palace in Jericho with magnificent ornamental gardens. Besides investing money in the city, the kings made money from Jericho's palm and balsam groves. Because it was a hub on trade routes between three continents, taxes on caravans were also a lucrative source of revenue.

§ The blind beggars were an interesting group. Dependent on sounds and smells instead of sight, they learned to beg in different trade languages. Most of them probably could tell from the sounds whether the caravans specialized in spices, slaves, gems, or some other commodity from distant countries. The potential alms from each caravan were predictable by country of origin, language of merchants, commodity traded, and size of caravan. Learning to beg in multiple languages and styles could significantly increase income.

Where there was wealth there was also poverty. Strategically positioned between the old ruined city and the new city of Jericho was a gathering of every type of beggar. § They could get more alms per day in Jericho than in the more populous Jerusalem fifteen miles away.

As Jesus moved beyond the old city, there was a large crowd following him. Those with noisy demands often made it difficult for the rest to hear. It didn't help when they reached the row of beggars and they started shouting for alms. One of them couldn't tell what kind of caravan was passing; the sounds weren't familiar. He asked those with sight what was going on. "Jesus of Nazareth is passing by," they told him. His heart jumped with hope. Stories of Jesus had traveled with many of the caravans that passed through Jericho, so he knew much about the rabbi from Galilee who taught truth and performed miracles. He had heard that Jesus made blind men able to see. What if Jesus would heal him? He shouted in Aramaic, "Jesus, Son of David, have mercy on me! Jesus, Son of David, have mercy on me!" Those with Jesus tried to hush him. A few bluntly told him to shut up rather than just throwing a few coins to silence his shouts.

It wasn't the plea for mercy or the volume of his shouting that distressed those with Jesus. It was the blind man's title for Jesus: "Son of David." This was a well-known messianic title. The blind man was imploring Jesus for mercy on the basis of Jesus being the Messiah. In politically diverse and volatile Jericho, such shouts could be asking for trouble. The Romans weren't going to risk competition with a religious leader who had crowds proclaiming him to be their political leader—certainly not in financially profitable Jericho.

This blind man, Bar Timaeus, the son of Timaeus, didn't care about the worriers in the crowd or the politics of the Roman army. This was his one chance to gain his eyesight, and he wasn't going to be silenced by anyone else's agenda. "Jesus, Son of David, have mercy on me! Jesus, Son of David, have mercy on me!" Another blind beggar made it a duet. "Jesus, Son of David, have mercy on me!"

They didn't see when Jesus stopped nor with the crowd noise did they hear Jesus say, "Call him. Bring him over to me." Several men close to Jesus went back and told Bar Timaeus, "Cheer up! He's calling you."

Bar Timaeus threw off his cloak, jumped to his feet, and stumbled toward Jesus, his blind friend not far behind. Jesus asked, "What do you want me to do for you?" Bar Timaeus started to answer before Jesus finished the question: "Rabbi, I want to see!" His friend certainly agreed. "Lord, we want our sight!"

Compassionately touching their blind eyes, Jesus said, "Receive your sight. Your faith has healed you." Immediately both men could see. And the first one they saw was Jesus.

Not only were they no longer blind beggars, but they instantly chose to become Jesus' followers.

As Jesus and the crowd entered new Jericho it was obvious that the biggest and best house was the winter palace of the Herods. Zacchaeus also had a home in the city but nothing close to the Herod house. He was well known in Jericho because he was the chief tax collector, a potentially lucrative position although it came with the usual measure of disrespect that a tax collector so often suffered. What he probably resented most were the frequent insults and jokes about his short stature.

When Zacchaeus heard that Jesus was passing through Jericho, he wanted to see him for himself. To enter a crowd had certain risks for Zacchaeus. After all, it really wasn't a large city and he could be easily recognized. Thinking all this through and planning ahead, he anticipated Jesus' route and walked ahead to a part of the road that went past a large sycamore tree. It was the perfect place for him to see without being seen; with so many branches and lush leaves, sycamores are easy to climb. No one would ever know.

As the crowd around Jesus came near the tree, he could see and hear as if he were as close as one of Jesus' disciples. His plan worked perfectly—until Jesus stopped. He looked up and said, "Zacchaeus, come down here right now. I want to stay at your house today." It was enough of a surprise to make him nearly fall out of the tree. He would not be the only one surprised that day. Jesus was deliberately choosing to go to the home of a man who was ritually unclean because he associated with Gentiles.

Jesus and Zacchaeus walked to his house together, which automatically gave him respect that no amount of money could buy. A transformation of the man was quickly taking place for all to see.

The crowd began to mutter, "He has gone to be the houseguest of a 'sinner.' " They couldn't hear what Jesus and Zacchaeus were talking about. "Look, Lord," Zacchaeus was telling Jesus, "I will give half of my assets to the poor! I'll do it right here and now. And anyone I've cheated will be repaid four hundred percent."

"Zacchaeus, salvation has come to you in your house today. Whatever you've been before, today you are a son of Abraham, the man of faith. I am the Son of Man, and I came to seek and to save people like you who are lost."

Regardless of any past abuses this tax collector may have committed, Jesus was pleased with his attitude and generosity and counted him as a son of Abraham. As the "Son of Man," Jesus' purpose was to find and save people like Zacchaeus.

By the time Jesus left the house, his popularity in Jericho had dipped—at least among those who resented contact with tax collectors. Eventually they would see the changes in their chief tax collector, but on that day it must have appeared that Jesus had compromised his allegiance to the poor in favor of a collector of Roman taxes.

But Jesus was still enough of a celebrity to gather additional people as he moved through Jericho. After a relatively short visit, he took the same road he had entered town on, the road back toward Jerusalem.

Jesus paused to teach the crowd, including the once-blind beggars, on the outskirts of the oasis before departing toward Jerusalem. He told a parable that was now so familiar to the twelve disciples that they could quote it almost word for word. § He used it often, with variations in each telling and application.

Jesus told them, "Once upon a time there was a man with royal blood. He took a long trip to a far country in order to be appointed king of his homeland. The day he left he sum-

§ The particular variation on this parable pertained to a piece of Jericho history. In 4 BC when King Herod the Great died, he left a will dividing his kingdom among his three sons: Herod Antipas, Herod Philip, and Archelaus. Because Herod ruled a sub-kingdom of the Roman Empire, his will had to be ratified by Caesar himself. Archelaus had inherited the province of Judea, including Jerusalem. He traveled

moned three of his servants and gave them ten minas. 'Invest this money while I'm gone, and I'll check with you when I return,' he told them.

"Because his subjects hated him, they sent a delegation to follow. 'We don't want this man to be our king,' the delegates said.

"He won. He was crowned king and returned home. When he arrived, the new king called his servants to find out how they handled his money while he was gone. The first one reported, 'Your Majesty, I invested your mina, and it has grown to ten minas.'

"'Well done, my good servant!' the king replied. 'Because you have been trustworthy managing so little so well, I'm putting you in charge of ten of my cities.'

"The second came and said, 'Your Majesty, your mina has earned five more.'

"The king answered, 'You take charge of five cities.'

"Then the third servant came and said, 'Your Majesty, here is your original mina. § I have kept it safely wrapped up in a piece of cloth. I was afraid of you and that I might disappoint you, because I know you are a hard master who always makes a profit even when you didn't make an investment.'

"His king replied, 'I'm going to deal with you exactly the way you just described me, you wicked incompetent servant. You knew that I am a hard master who always makes a profit even when I didn't make an investment? Then why didn't you at least get some basic interest on my mina and give me some profit when I returned?'

to Rome for Caesar's approval, but most of the Jews didn't want him to be their king, so they sent a delegation to Rome to contest the will and oppose the appointment of Archelaus. The protest failed. Caesar rejected the desire of the people and awarded the rule of Judea to Archelaus. All of this was familiar to the people who heard this parable. The purpose of the parable was not to teach about the politics of the Herod family, however. It was to teach about the Son of Man coming from heaven to earth to save those who are lost.

§ A mina was equal to about three months' wages for the average worker. The basic Greek coin was the silver drachma. One hundred drachmas equaled one mina, and there were six thousand drachmas to the talent. For most people the ten minas in Jesus' parable would be considered a lot of money.

"Then he said to his guards, 'Take his mina away from him and give it to the first servant, who has ten minas.'

" 'But, Your Majesty,' they said, 'he already has ten!'

"The king replied, 'Here's the way I work: everyone who has gets more; anyone who has nothing loses what he has. And as far as those enemies who opposed my coronation are concerned, seize them and kill them while I watch.' "

Bar Timaeus and his once-blind friend were intrigued by the parable but didn't understand its meaning. At first they thought it was an endorsement of Herodian rule over Judea. Then they figured it was more about money management. Finally they went to a few of Jesus' disciples and asked what Jesus' point was. They no doubt didn't ask Jesus because he seemed busy and tired.

The disciples were sympathetic, saying that it often took them a long time to figure out the meaning of Jesus' stories. Sometimes they didn't understand even after Jesus explained what he meant. They had learned not to press all the details.

Truth be told, not even Jesus' longest-term disciples figured out what this parable meant until about a year later. In the parable the king is Jesus. He planned to die and return to heaven. He would be away for a long time, during which his followers would be trusted to manage his resources on earth. When he returned to earth he would ask for an accounting and then would generously reward those who had been faithful. The point? Jesus was going away and wanted his disciples to be trustworthy in his absence.

While his disciples were discussing all this, Jesus slipped out of their roadside camp and started along the caravan route. Next stop: Bethany, less than two miles outside of Jerusalem.

CHAPTER FIFTEEN

T he roads were jammed that Friday, the eighth of Nisan (March 30), AD 30, with Jews on their way to Passover, only one week away. Devout men from Jericho considered it a privilege to walk merely fifteen miles to celebrate in Jerusalem. §

Jerusalem was usually a small city, at least compared to Rome—year-round residents numbered in the thousands. When the Jewish historian Josephus reported the expanded Passover population, he estimated it exploded to about three million. That seems like an impossible hyperbole. One hundred thousand might be more like it. But who knows? There were too many to count.

§ Officially every Jewish male was required to go to Jerusalem three times a year (Feast of Passover, Feast of Weeks, and Feast of Tabernacles), but that was impossible for those who had to travel from as far away as Alexandria in Egypt or from Rome itself. Some came only once in a lifetime, if at all. The men from Jericho could make it in a day when foot traffic wasn't too heavy.

Jesus must have gotten an early start out of Jericho on Friday, because the travel distance allowed on the Sabbath was no more than a "Sabbath day's journey" of half a mile. He wouldn't want to be delayed along the desert roadside with a throng of pilgrims and no synagogue nearby on Saturday. If he camped not far from Bethany that Friday night, he could arrive in the village Saturday morning and take part in Sabbath services.

Without his usual large following, it was easier to go unrecognized among the other travelers on the Jericho Road and hear them talking about him along the way. They were looking for Jesus, and he was right there.

Even more were looking for him around the temple in Jerusalem. "What do you think? Isn't he coming to the Feast at all?" On the one hand, some thought he would come because all male Jews were required to do so and Jesus' habit was to keep the Law. On the other hand, they knew there was a warrant out for his arrest, and others assumed he would stay away for safety.

The warrant extended beyond Jesus. The chief priests and Pharisees had given orders under the authority of the Sanhedrin that anyone who saw Jesus or knew how to find him was required to report this information.

That Saturday a large crowd—perhaps thousands—streamed out of Jerusalem toward Bethany, technically breaking the travel limit. Most of them were pilgrims who first heard about Lazarus when they got into town in preparation for the Passover, just days away. They wanted to see Lazarus for themselves, and this created a mob scene in tiny Bethany. When word reached Jerusalem that Jesus was in Bethany, it compounded the motivation for the pilgrims to make the trip—some to see Lazarus, some to see Jesus, some to see both. The chief priests were frightened and angry by the swell of movement toward Bethany, so much so that they initiated plans to kill Lazarus as well. The chief priests felt more and more threatened by the growing numbers who were believing in Jesus because of the Lazarus miracle.

While in Bethany, Jesus stayed at the home of Simon, § a relative of Mary, Martha, and Lazarus. Simon's home was large enough for the Saturday-night dinner planned to honor Jesus and Lazarus.

Anticipating Jesus' return to Bethany before the Passover in Jerusalem, Martha had planned the gathering at the home of Simon the Leper. She served the meal to the guests as they reclined

§ Simon may have had an interesting and miraculous story of his own, although far short of being raised from death. He apparently contracted leprosy and thus would have been forced to leave his home and family. Because the name Simon was so common, he was nicknamed Simon the Leper. That he was living in his home in Bethany indicates he must have been cured of the disease, perhaps in another of Jesus' miracles. Even though the disease was gone, the nickname stuck.

around the courtyard dining table. During the meal, Mary came behind Jesus and opened an alabaster jar filled with a litra of very expensive spikenard perfume. § The aroma wafted across the table within seconds.

§ *Litra* is a Greek word for a measurement equaling about a pint. Spikenard was extracted from an aromatic Himalayan plant of the valerian family and cost a fortune. The litra was worth a year's wages. Some families sacrificed for years to own this or similar commodities and carefully hid them in secret places to protect the items from robbers. The purpose was said to be preparation for death and burial because the nard was used for external embalming. However, a supply of nard also served as a family's life savings. In Mary's case, this may have been most of her life savings.

When she first opened the jar, Mary poured some of the nard on Jesus' head. This was a gracious and hospitable custom to honor the most important guest. Everyone certainly was impressed with her thoughtfulness and generosity, even though her pouring seemed excessive. But what she did next caused gasps and consternation around the table.

She knelt at the end of the lounge chair and poured out the nard on his feet. Then she reached behind to push back her head covering and unfasten her hair. Her long, dark hair

§ This incident closely mirrors the incident at the home of Simon the Pharisee, where the prostitute poured her perfume on Jesus' feet.

fell in front of her, and she used it as a towel to dry Jesus' feet. §

So many social rules were broken in less than a minute that the entire room was left speechless. First of all, respected hosts and hostesses anointed heads, but only the lowliest of servants and slaves washed and anointed feet. Second, adult women never allowed their long hair to be seen in public. Hair was deemed a matter of pride and intimacy—to be shown only to her husband and immediate family members. Third, she had just used up a life savings' worth of perfume.

Judas broke the silence with a stern rebuke. "Why didn't she sell this perfume in the market and give the money to poor people?" he demanded. "It was worth a year's wages." Others joined in, repeating the indictment almost word for word. "Why this waste?" they asked. "This perfume could have been sold at a high price and the money given to the poor." Mary's carefully planned expression of love had been given a totally unexpected twist. She didn't respond, but one could believe that if she had, she would have expressed surprise and hurt.

Judas' criticism compounded with the others was overwhelmingly outweighed by Jesus' defense. "Leave her alone," he told them. "Why are you bothering her? She has done a beautiful thing for me. It's good to help the poor, and there will be plenty more opportunities to do so. But you won't have me around much longer. Mary has blessed me while she is able to do so. She has poured perfume on my body to prepare for when I am dead and buried. The wonderful truth is that everywhere my gospel is preached in the world, Mary's story from today will be told, and people will remember her."

All those times when Mary had listened to Jesus talking about his upcoming death, she must have heard and understood better than anyone else. Not only did she listen and believe what he said, she decided to do something no one else thought about doing. She gave her most valuable asset as an expression of love for her teacher and as a declaration that she took his predicted death seriously.

After his Saturday night stay at Simon's house, Jesus awakened at sunrise with plans to go into Jerusalem. Everything so far in his life was pointing toward this morning. All the secret-keeping was over. All the restrictions on telling about miracles were lifted. All the delays waiting for the right time were past. Passover was less than five full days away. Jesus was going public as the true Messiah, his coming-out to the nation of Israel. This very Sunday morning, he would face the arrest warrant and death threats of the chief priests. It was the beginning of the first day of the last week of his life.

Between Bethany and Jerusalem is the Mount of Olives, a favorite retreat for Jesus when visiting either place. As he walked west, people followed with growing excitement. The line of pilgrims coming from Jerusalem to see Lazarus was reversed as they heard the news and joined the crowd led by Jesus.

Bethany was small, but Bethphage was much smaller, hardly a village at all and located on the side of the Mount of Olives. Just outside Bethany, Jesus ordered two of his disciples to run ahead. "Go to that village over there. Right inside town you'll see a donkey tied up, one that's young and has never been ridden. Untie her and her colt, and bring them both here to me. If anyone asks what you're doing just say the Lord needs them, and he'll say it's okay. Tell him you'll return them later."

It worked exactly as Jesus had indicated. The two men entered Bethphage and walked down the street to a house where a donkey and colt were tied outside. When they untied the colt, leaving the donkey, some people standing around asked, "What are you doing, untying that colt?" When they repeated what Jesus had told them to say, the questioners said, "Oh, all right, take both if you want!"

When they led the colt to Jesus, they saddled her with their own cloaks and Jesus mounted. The crowd took over from there. Some pealed off their outerwear, laying the clothing on the dirt road as a carpet for the colt. Hundreds more did the same. People ripped branches off palm trees, either laying them down as part of the welcome carpet or waving them over their heads as if they were in a parade for a triumphant king returning from war.

Someone in the back of the crowd yelled, "Hosanna! Blessed is he who comes in the name of the Lord!" Some nearby echoed, "Hosanna! Blessed is the coming kingdom of our father David!" Several more shouted, "Hosanna in the highest!" Then the crowd went wild with excitement. "Hosanna! Blessed is the King of Israel!" § The people had turned this journey into a coronation parade.

§ The word *hosanna* technically meant "save now," although it was used as an expression of praise and acclamation. The rest of their shouts were quotes from the Old Testament descriptive of the Messiah.

As they came down the road off the Mount of Olives toward the Eastern Gate, the shouts became louder and louder. Those who had committed to be Jesus' followers praised God with the loudest voices of all: "Blessed is the king who comes in God's name! Peace in heaven! Glory in the highest!"

Of course his enemies among the Pharisees were beside themselves with anger, fuming at this powerful new display of support, but they couldn't quell the passion and enthusiasm of the people. So they directed Jesus to stop the crowd, saying, "Teacher, tell your disciples to stop this demonstration immediately!" Jesus answered, "You know, if they stop, the stones will start shouting instead."

Everyone was in high spirits except the Pharisees and Jesus. Not that he wasn't pleased with the praise, but when he looked at the city of Jerusalem, his heart was deeply moved. He saw the beautiful city gate, the strong wall, the white marble of the temple, and the smoke of a thousand cook fires. And he wept. With tears flowing, he spoke words that only a few close by could hear. "If you only knew what would bring peace to this city, but you just can't see it. It won't be long until your enemies will circle and siege you. They'll smash you and your children on the ground. They will completely dismantle the city stone by stone. All this because you didn't recognize when God came your way!"

§ There were mass executions. Every building was destroyed, including the temple. Only three pillars were left standing in the entire city. Those who were not killed were sold into slavery. Titus returned to Rome as a conqueror, holding up the golden candelabrum from the temple. He built the Arch of Titus as a landmark for tourists to visit, even into the twenty-first century, marking the destruction of Jerusalem.

Jesus saw beyond the joy of this Sunday morning to a terrible day in AD 70 when the Roman army under Titus would conquer and devastate this beautiful city. § That was why Jesus wept while the crowds shouted and sang.

For the religious leaders who were hoping and planning to arrest Jesus, this was their worst nightmare come true. The Jews in droves were turning to Jesus, and the situation was getting totally out of control.

For Jesus' closest disciples it was a time of great confusion. They couldn't reconcile his continual predictions of suffering and death with the peoples' acclamation of his leadership and Messiahship.

For Jesus this was all about fulfillment of Old Testament prophecy. Zechariah, the sixth-century-BC Jewish prophet, had given a prediction about the Messiah known by heart to many in Jesus' generation: " 'Do not be afraid, O Daughter of Zion; see, your king is coming, seated on a donkey's colt.' " Jesus knew the power of both Scripture and symbols. Kings coming for war rode horses; kings coming for peace rode donkeys. And merely riding into the city on a donkey was itself a public announcement that he was claiming to be the King of Israel.

Once inside the city gates, the crowd of thousands ballooned beyond count. Much of the city's population was either there or heard about the royal procession. The Pharisees, disparaging the whole scene, said, "Look at what is happening! He's winning; we're losing. The whole world is chasing after him!"

An antiphonal chant erupted with half of the people shouting, "Who is this?" and the other half shouting back, "This is Prophet Jesus of Nazareth in Galilee."

The parade snaked through the city streets and into the temple courtyard, where the blind and lame came to Jesus for healing. He talked to them over the din of the crowd, touching them and healing them.

Along with their parents, children were caught up in the mood. They also shouted, "Hosanna to the Son of David!"

Jesus was triumphantly marching straight into the home territory of the chief priests and his other enemies. Their anger and disdain and fear boiled over, but there was little they could do at the moment. Some pointed accusing fingers at him, charging that it was disgustingly inappropriate the way children had been drawn into the emotional exuberance. Several asked Jesus, "Do you *hear* what these children are saying?" Jesus answered with a quote from the poetry of Psalm 8:2: "From the lips of children and infants God has ordained praise."

The celebration lasted until sunset, when Jesus and his twelve disciples slipped away from the temple, out the gate, and returned to

Bethany, where they again spent the night.

Perhaps Jesus skipped breakfast on Monday morning, rousing his disciples to head back toward the city—they could always find food along the way. Just outside Bethany, Jesus said, "I'm hungry. Let's see if we can eat some figs off that tree over there."

They walked over to the tree and looked for some fruit for breakfast. But all of them knew figs were out of season and there wouldn't be anything on it to eat. Jesus' real purpose wasn't breakfast but an object lesson for his disciples. §

§ In Hebrew literature the fig tree was used as a symbol for the nation of Israel.

He wanted them to know that as far as he was concerned, Israel was like a tree covered with good-looking leaves, but it was fruitless. Israel had plenty of rules and rituals that looked religious, but the fruit of genuine godliness was lacking. When they arrived at the tree, Jesus spoke to it: "May no one ever eat your fruit again!" The disciples heard what he said, and a few of them caught the meaning— long-term judgment on the superficiality of religion among the majority of their nation.

It was still early when they went across the Kidron Valley on the east side of the city, climbed up the stone ramp, and passed through the Beautiful Gate. Its high doors of Corinthian bronze opened directly onto Mount Zion, where the temple was located. §

§ Zion is also a shortened name for the whole city, and Mount Zion is often called the Temple Mount. Today it refers to a section of Jerusalem just south of the Old City.

Most of the people at the temple were merchants setting up for business in the Court of the Gentiles on the south side of the temple proper. As Jesus walked from the Beautiful Gate across Solomon's Porch, he could hear the animals bleating and pigeons cooing as well as the merchants talking and arguing. As he turned the corner, he was outraged with a sight he had faced before. But on that day he burst out with violent righteous indignation. The temple looked more like a commercial bazaar than a place to worship God.

No one tried to stop him. The merchants said nothing. The chief priests, temple theologians, and members of the Sanhedrin who were up that early saw Jesus' outburst and just stood there. But they became all the more enraged toward killing him.

Some of the merchants and crowd had no idea who Jesus was or what he was doing, but someone among his group of followers immediately remembered a line from one of the old Jewish psalms written by King David: "Zeal for your house consumes me." These men liked what they saw—Jesus was committed, courageous, and confrontational in support of God's temple. §

If anyone else had done what Jesus did, they probably would have been arrested by the temple police and severely beaten. But Jesus had a spiritual authority and righteous indignation that defied any attempts to subdue him. And they feared his supernatural powers. He was too popular with the masses to risk a confrontation—his side would outnumber the authorities and merchants if a brawl broke out. So they all just let him clean out the temple merchants.

The noise of fleeing merchants was enough to make the crowd grow even faster. Among those arriving were Greeks who had come for Passover. As Gentiles they were allowed into the outer terrace on the south side of the temple but could come no farther. The inner area was slightly elevated above this Court of the Gentiles with a fencelike barrier and signs in Greek and Latin threatening probable death to any Gentiles who crossed the line.

Like everyone else in Jerusalem that Passover season, the Greek visitors had heard all about Jesus and wanted to experience his teaching for themselves. But knowing that Gentiles had to be very careful in a fanatically religious Jewish crowd, they decided to check first. When asking around concerning who controlled access to Jesus, they heard about John, Simon, Nathanael, Levi, and Philip.

§ New Testament author John reports that Jesus chased the merchants out of the temple early in his public life, while authors Matthew, Mark, and Luke report the temple confrontation during the final week of his life. Most modern scholars conclude that it was one event and that John places it earlier to symbolically show Jesus' authority. Other scholars conclude that Jesus cleaned out the merchants two times, two or three years apart.

Why did Jesus kick out the merchants?

Every male Jew was required to pay a half-shekel temple tax once each year. A half shekel was roughly equivalent to two days' wages for a worker. In those days there was no single standard currency. A mix of coins from Rome, Greece, Egypt, Syria, and other places was used. However, the leaders of the temple would accept only Jewish coins—those without "graven images" on them. So money had to be changed before any tax was paid or offering was given.

The Passover Festival was the most likely time to visit and the usual time to pay the temple tax. So each year money-exchange booths were set up for the pilgrims. Some were in villages, some were in and around Jerusalem, and many actually moved onto the temple grounds and into the temple courtyard. It was a reasonable and necessary service.

A problem arose when exorbitant rates were charged. Some moneychangers had fees ranging from sixteen to thirty-three percent. Not only were these rates high, they were especially burdensome for the many poor people of Israel. They came to worship God. They could barely afford the half-shekel, and then they had to pay an expensive broker's fee in addition. Dishonest moneychangers were becoming rich on the backs of the poor. But most of them provided a necessary service at a fair profit.

Another important element of the Jewish religion was animal sacrifices. Devout Jews needed to offer one sacrifice or another just about every time they came to worship at the temple. People living in Jerusalem typically didn't have animals to bring, and those living outside were limited by how far they could walk and bring an animal for sacrifice. So booths were set up to sell the sacrificial pigeons, sheep, and other animals. Outside the temple, the animals were comparatively inexpensive—typically the equivalent of less than two days' wages. Temple leaders appointed inspectors to make sure the animals were without spot or blemish (no cuts, diseases, deformities, or broken bones). The inspectors could be tough on the animals brought from the outside and reject them as unacceptable for sacrifice. Meanwhile, booths inside the temple sold sacrificial animals that were preapproved. The problem was with those merchants who made a greedy markup. It could mean that a pair of doves costing less than half a shekel outside the temple grounds cost as much as six shekels inside—another cruel burden on the poor people who came to worship God.

Reacting against these abuses of the poor worshippers and flagrant profiteering, Jesus started dumping over the moneychangers' tables, kicking over benches containing doves in cages, and pulling over the cloth-covered booths. With every violent action, he shouted Scripture quotes from the prophets Isaiah and Jeremiah: "God says, 'My house will be called a house of prayer for all nations.' You have turned it into a robbers' den."

Passion for the poor and contempt for their unjust treatment were not Jesus' only motivation. In actual practice, most of the moneychangers and merchants in the temple probably made minimal profit. The greater problem was the way their tables, benches, and booths crowded out worshippers.

In earlier generations the temple was not so restrictive. In the first century, however, the temple was designed with the Court of the Gentiles, the Court of Women, and the Court of Israel—each more restrictive than the one before. Jewish women were prohibited from entering the Court of Israel. Gentile men and women were restricted from the Court of Women and the Court of Israel; they were allowed only in the Court of Gentiles. Apparently the merchants consumed so much space in the Court of Gentiles that they crowded out many of the worshippers from the only space where they were allowed. Jesus made space for those who wanted to worship God, insisting that the temple was for all nations.

They quickly recognized that most, except Philip with a Greek name, had Jewish names. Without knowing how a Jewish disciple of Jesus shared a name with the father of Alexander the Great, their famous Philip of Macedon, they figured he might be friendlier to Greeks than the rest. When they finally found Philip, they told him, "We would like to see Jesus." Philip didn't know how to respond and didn't want to be responsible, so he told them to stay put and wait while he checked with Andrew. Andrew didn't want to make the decision either, so they both approached Jesus and asked him what to do. Jesus didn't give them a direct answer, but he also didn't indicate any problem with this. They told the Greeks to come closer and listen as Jesus talked about what was going to happen that week.

"The time has finally come for the Son of Man to be glorified," Jesus was saying as they approached. "The truth is that a seed never grows into anything more unless it is planted in the ground and dies. But when this happens, it sprouts and multiplies into many seeds. This same principle applies to people. The person who loves this present life is going to lose it, but the one who loves eternal life so much that this present life is hated by comparison will live forever. Anyone who wants to follow me as my disciple must stick with me like a servant with a master. My Father will specially bless every disciple who serves me."

The "time" Jesus was talking about was later that week when he would die. Referring to his own death and the results it would bring, he made the case that the path to meaningful eternal life was trusting and serving him. Then his mood turned reflective. His voice dropped, almost as if talking to himself, although those close by, including the Greeks, heard what he said. "I have a troubled heart," he acknowledged. "What should I say? Should I pray for God the Father to rescue me out of what I am facing? No. Of course not. This is the whole reason I'm here. Instead I'm going to pray for my Father to make himself look really good through everything that happens to me this week." Jesus' questions didn't reduce his resolve to go through with the reason he came to earth. Whatever happened, he was determined to glorify God.

Then they all clearly heard the voice thunder out of heaven. "I have glorified my name before, and I will glorify my name again." A few said it was an angel who spoke, but the rest said it was God himself.

Those who heard it were quaking with wonder, but Jesus was not disturbed. He explained to them, "This voice you just heard was for your benefit, not mine. The time has come for judgment on the world and driving out Prince Satan. I'm going to be lifted up, and when that happens everyone will be drawn to me." This was the week for an all-out war against the devil, the chief of evil in the world, and the battle was going to be won when Jesus was lifted up from earth. It was not then obvious to his listeners that he was referring to being lifted up on a cross to die. They responded with honest curiosity. "We were taught that when the Messiah comes he will stay forever, so what are you talking about when you say, 'lifted up'? Who is the 'Son of Man,' anyway?"

Jesus urged them to listen more carefully and benefit from his teaching while they still could before he died. "You're not going to have 'the light of the world' around much longer. You'd better take full advantage of my presence with you before darkness comes. The person who walks in the dark gets lost. Trust in the light and take full advantage of the light right now. That's the way to become one of the 'sons of light.' "

Jesus had become a master at slipping out of crowds when he chose to end his teaching sessions. He had said all he was going to say for now, so he went into hiding inside the city of Jerusalem. A logical place for him to go was John's family residence in Jerusalem, where there was privacy and safety, at least for the moment.

He wondered aloud what it would take to convince more to believe. He had healed the sick, fed the thousands, and even raised the dead, but that wasn't spectacular enough to convince some of them. His critics always offered some explanation or found some way to turn the truth into a lie, miracles from God into phenomena from the devil. Jesus knew the answer to his own questions—the prophet Isaiah had said it well: "Lord God, who believes our message? Who has been touched by the hand of God?"

Isaiah had looked seven hundred years into the future to see Jesus' glory and greatness when he wrote, "Their eyes have been blinded and their hearts turned cold so they can't see, can't understand, and can't respond. Otherwise they would be healed by God." Jesus was facing the same kind of spiritual unresponsiveness as faced by Isaiah generations earlier.

§ There certainly were plenty of believers. Not all the top religious leaders were like Annas and Caiaphas and the majority of the Sanhedrin. Nicodemus, a good example, was a member of the Sanhedrin and an advocate for Jesus. Another was a wealthy man named Joseph of Arimathea.

Jesus wasn't talking about everybody. § There were secret believers who were intimidated by the powerful outspoken Pharisees, and these followers were afraid of the threats to excommunicate everyone who openly believed in Jesus. Others on the outer edges of the circles around Jesus didn't want to give up the praise and power of their positions in order to openly follow him.

His disciples listened as Jesus opened his heart, his thoughts, and his feelings to them. It wasn't a good time to ask questions. They were seeing a different side of their teacher than the bold, angry reformer who threw the merchants out of the temple that morning. Jesus' voice became passionate, and he said, "When someone believes in me, he doesn't believe only in me; he also believes in God who sent me. Looking at me is like looking at God. I came to earth as a light so those who believe won't live in darkness.

"I don't judge those who hear me and don't do what I say," Jesus continued. "I didn't come to judge but to save. Those who don't believe will be judged, all right; they'll eventually be judged by my words that they ignored. After all, my words don't just come from me. God the Father told me what to say. What God says leads to eternal life, and I'm only passing his words along."

If Jesus' critics had heard this, they would have been all the more adamant that Jesus was either delusional or heretical—or both. He insisted he was sent from heaven by God and that believing in God and believing in Jesus were the same thing. The only way to the light of truth and eternal life is Jesus.

Then they went back to their safe house in Bethany for another night. This was to be their pattern for the next few days. Jesus taught at the temple during daylight hours, and they lodged in Bethany during the night.

Tuesday morning they awakened in Bethany, and the thirteen retraced Monday's journey. As they left Bethany, the same fig tree was sighted, only this day it was completely dead from the roots up. Peter saw it first and said, "Rabbi, look! That's the fig tree you talked to yesterday, and it's dead today!" It was months ahead of the fig harvest, but the lack of early buds meant there would be no harvest from that particular tree. Jesus' judgment on the tree was analogous to divine judgment on unbelievers in Israel and the coming judgment forty years later on the temple.

Peter and the rest were impressed that Jesus could simply condemn a tree and the next day it was withered as if it had died years before. They didn't care about the tree. They just wanted to know how Jesus did this.

"It's all about faith," Jesus taught them. "Have faith in God! Let me tell you how faith works. If anyone says to this mountain, 'Go, jump into the sea,' and really believes deep in his heart that it will happen, God will dump that mountain into the sea. I'm telling you, ask in prayer, really believe, and you've got it. And, by the way, while you're standing there praying, forgive whoever you've had a problem with; that way God in heaven will forgive your sins."

They realized Jesus wasn't talking about moving an actual mountain into the Mediterranean Sea. He was using a common figure of speech. The rabbis referred to the seemingly impossible difficulties in people's lives as mountains. Jesus wanted his followers to pray with faith—not just for what they wanted, but for what was consistent with what God wanted and behavior in line with what God asked, such as forgiving others.

As they rounded the Mount of Olives, the city of Jerusalem came into sight for the third time in three days. They passed through the east gate as a group and again climbed the stairs into the temple courtyard. Today Jesus set up class on the east side along Solomon's Porch overlooking the Valley of Kidron and the Mount of Olives. The people were learning Jesus' routine, and a large gathering of pilgrims was waiting for him when he arrived. Before his teaching could begin, Jesus was confronted by a delegation from the three Jewish leadership groups of the city: chief priests, teachers of the law, and elders.

The chief priests were a small group, but the fact that there was more than one chief priest (or high priest) was an anomaly in Jewish law and tradition. The high priest normally held a lifetime appointment. However, the Romans took away the authority for high priest selection from the people and gave it to their governor. They even forced the high priest to store his robes and liturgical vestments in the Fortress of Antonia, where Roman soldiers were barracked adjacent to the temple. It was one more reminder of who was in charge. As living chief priests were deposed and new chief priests were appointed by the Romans, their number changed from a religious monarchy of one to a religious oligarchy of several. Sometimes the people unofficially recognized the continuing authority of the former chief priest even after the Romans had deposed him.

The teachers of the law were the officially trained theologians. They were similar to seminary or religion professors in modern cultures.

Elders were the governing leaders of the Jewish religious community. In other cultures they would parallel the board of directors in a business or the city council in a town.

Together these three groups composed the governing aristocracy of religious Jerusalem, although ultimate criminal, civil, and military authority very much belonged to the Romans. The three groups were all represented in the Sanhedrin, which served as the combined legislature and Supreme Court of Judaism.

When the representatives of the chief priests, teachers of the law, and elders approached Jesus, it was to ask another trick question: "Where did you get your authority to do what you do?" If they could get Jesus to publicly commit a major offense, they could arrest and try him without the usual witnesses. The question was a setup to get him arrested no matter how he answered. If Jesus said his authority came from God, they would accuse him of blasphemy, arrest him, and haul him off to trial. If Jesus said he didn't have the authority to clear businesses out of the temple and take over the religious teaching, they would accuse him of trespassing and illegal teaching, arrest him, and haul him off to trial. There would not need to be any witnesses because his accusers would have heard Jesus' statement themselves.

When Jesus answered their questions with a question of his own, it was more than a clever debate tactic. This question-question dialogue was a standard teaching/learning method used by many rabbis out on Solomon's Porch. A clever question not only showed that the person speaking understood the original question but was smart enough to escalate the discussion to a more significant and sophisticated level.

With a large crowd listening, Jesus said, "I will ask you one question. You answer my question and then I'll answer yours. Was John's baptism from God or men? What do you say?"

The delegation didn't know how to respond. John the Baptizer had been honored as a popular and powerful prophet from God and now as a martyr and hero since King Herod had executed him. Thousands of people had heard John, believed him, and been baptized by him. Many in the crowd that Tuesday morning had been baptized by John and described themselves as his disciples. Most important, John had publicly declared that Jesus was the Lamb of God. Jesus' simple question put the delegation in a terrible bind. They withdrew for a private caucus and said to each other, "If we say it was from God, he'll ask why we didn't believe and get baptized ourselves. But if we say from men, the crowd will turn against us out of loyalty to John the Baptizer."

They wanted Jesus stuck no matter how he answered, and now they were stuck no matter how they answered. So all they could come up with was, "We don't know." Very humiliating since they were the educated leaders who *should* know.

Jesus continued the debate. "If you won't answer my question, then I'm not going to answer your question." Not that Jesus was unwilling to tell—he had explained the answer often. These critics weren't seeking information and answers. They had deliberately chosen to disbelieve Jesus and were out to destroy him. Jesus was willing to tell the truth, but he wasn't going to aid his enemies. Continuing his teaching for the day, Jesus involved the listeners by asking, "What do you think?"

He began to tell them a series of parables that explained God's attitudes and actions concerning the present generation of Israel. The parables were squarely aimed at the delegation and all the chief priests, teachers of the law, and elders they represented.

"Once upon a time there was a man with two sons. He asked the first to work in his vineyard, but he refused. Then the son changed his mind and went to work. The father asked his second son to work in his vineyard and he said yes but never showed up. Which son did what the father wanted?"

The audience answered in unison, "The first!"

Jesus said to the religious leaders, "You may be surprised to know the truth that tax collectors and prostitutes are ahead of you in the line to God's kingdom. John came to show you the way to righteous living, but you wouldn't believe him—but the tax collectors and prostitutes believed! Even when you saw what was happening, you refused to change your minds and believe him."

The parable was clear. Jesus didn't always use parables to obscure his meaning from his detractors but sometimes to make issues patently clear to them. The religious leaders were like the bad son, and the outcasts of society were like the good son.

"Listen up!" he told everyone. "I have another parable for you to hear." His disciples had heard this one many times before, but they never tired of either the story or the audience reaction.

"There once was a man who planted a vineyard on his land," Jesus told them. "He built a security wall with a lookout tower around the vineyard and installed a winepress inside the wall. Then he rented the vineyard to some tenants with the understanding that they would pay a percentage of the crop for their rent. At harvest time he sent one of his men to collect, but they grabbed and beat him before throwing him out with no payment. The owner decided to give them a second chance by sending a second rent collector. The tenants hit him over the head and humiliated him. Offering a third chance, the owner sent a third representative, whom they killed. Believe it or not, he kept sending more collectors, and they were all beaten or murdered.

"Offering a last chance to the tenants, the owner sent his own son, whom he loved with all his heart. He was sure that the tenants would treat his son with respect. But instead they conspired to kill the son to block him from inheriting the vineyard so they could get it for themselves. They actually killed the owner's son!

"What do you think the owner will do? He'll come himself to kill all the tenants and give the vineyard to others instead."

There were a lot of people listening to this parable, and eventually most of them shouted back at Jesus, "May this never happen!" They knew he was talking about the leaders of Israel repeatedly rejecting God's prophets until God was ready to give up on them and move his special blessing to others.

" 'May this never happen,' you say? Well, then," Jesus asked, "what do you think is the meaning of the words you sing at the temple?" He then quoted from the lyric poetry of Psalm 118:

> "The stone the builders rejected
> has become the capstone;
> the Lord has done this,
> and it is marvelous in our eyes."

In terms so blunt that the religious leaders couldn't miss the meaning, Jesus added, "It will happen! The kingdom of God will be taken away from you and given to others who will do what God wants them to do. Whoever stumbles on this stone gets broken in pieces; whoever the stone falls on gets smashed." Several of them turned to each other with expressions of incredulity and said, "He's talking about us!"

The leaders would have called the temple police to arrest him then and there except most of the crowd adored him as a prophet of God. The leaders couldn't risk starting a riot and calling down the wrath of the Romans. Disgusted, they left, although they didn't go too far away. There were three stories of chambers that ringed the north, east, and south sides of the temple square. They had their choice of convenient places to convene and discuss what to do next.

§ Later Christians understood this parable to say that God expanded the kingdom of heaven to the church, especially when Jerusalem and the temple were destroyed in AD 70. The second round of invitees included Jews and Gentiles alike, although some weren't true disciples of Jesus, and these phonies were removed from the church.

Even though the religious leaders were gone, Jesus told one more parable they should have heard. It was similar to the first two and was another that the disciples had heard before. This one portrayed the leaders of Israel as guests invited to God's banquet. §

This is the way Jesus told it:

"The kingdom of heaven is like a king who threw a wedding banquet for his son. He sent his servants to those who had been invited to the banquet to tell them it was time to start, but they refused to come.

"Then he sent a second team of servants and told them, 'Make sure they know it's time to eat. My oxen and fattened cattle have been butchered and are ready for the grill. Come and take your reserved seat at the banquet table.'

"The people ignored the second invitation just like the first. They headed for their farm fields or their businesses in town. Others grabbed the king's messengers and abused and killed them. The king was so furious that he sent his army to slaughter the murderers and burn down their city in retaliation.

"The next day the king told his servants to recruit anyone they could find for the wedding banquet. The servants brought in all kinds of good and bad people to fill every seat.

"When the king arrived, he saw a man who didn't bother to dress up for the wedding. 'How did you get in dressed like that?' the king asked to the man's stunned embarrassment.

"Then the king called the guards to tie him up and throw him out into the dark night, where there is crying and teeth grinding.

"Many are invited, but few are chosen," Jesus concluded.

Meanwhile the Pharisees were hatching another plan to destroy Jesus. Meeting nearby, they proposed an alliance few would have predicted. Although the Herodians and Pharisees were usually enemies, they conspired now in a common cause—they needed each other. The Herodians were collaborators with the Roman government and favored the Roman occupation because it sustained the dynasty of the Herod family and kept the rest of them in comfortable success. The Pharisees resented the Romans and wanted them out of Israel, especially Judea and Jerusalem. As far as many of the Pharisees were concerned, it would be just fine if every Roman were either deported or executed and not allowed back in Judea for eternity. In spite of their differences, they found a way to cooperate in a conspiracy against Jesus. It was a clever plan, but they needed some fresh faces. Jesus and the crowds had become familiar with the usual antagonists.

The Pharisees recruited a team of their disciples plus some Herodians to show up in the crowd around Jesus. When Jesus was taking questions, one of them said with seeming innocence, "Teacher, we know you are a man of integrity and truthfully teach the way of God. You are always fair and never corrupted by pressure from special interest groups. So will you give to us your unbiased opinion? Is it right to pay taxes to Caesar or not?"

Jesus quickly read his intention and said, "You are such hypocrites! It's another trap, isn't it? Let me see the kind of coin you use to pay your taxes." One of the questioners pulled out a silver Roman denarius that he handed to Jesus. Jesus held it up and asked, "Whose face is portrayed on this coin? And whose inscription?"

"Caesar's," everyone answered.

Then he said to them, "Give to Caesar what is Caesar's, and give to God what is God's."

Even his enemies were amazed by the wisdom of his answer. Coins bore Caesar's image; people bear God's image. Give coins to Caesar and give yourself to God. There wasn't much left to say, so the spies left the crowd, reporting to their senders what had happened.

This was turning out to be a long Tuesday with one conflict or confrontation after another. So far Jesus had won every round, though the number of antagonists seemed no smaller. The Sadducees were next, and they were convinced they had honed a careful theological argument that no one who believed in resurrection from death could answer.

§ It was recorded in Deuteronomy 25 and was called the Law of Levirate Marriage: "If brothers are living together and one of them dies without a son, his widow must not marry outside the family. Her husband's brother shall take her and marry her and fulfill the duty of a brother-in-law to her. The first son she bears shall carry on the name of the dead brother so that his name will not be blotted out from Israel" (verses 5-7 NIV).

They were lawyers, and their argument turned on an Old Testament law that required the brother of a deceased husband to marry his widowed sister-in-law and father a child who would be credited to the deceased. §

They asked Jesus a hypothetical question referring to this law: "Teacher, the Law from Moses says that if a husband dies childless, his brother is required to marry his widow and father children in his name. Suppose there were seven brothers. The oldest married and died without children. So his next brother married the widow and died without children. And the next brother married her and died without children. Eventually she went through seven brothers and died childless. Here's the question: when everyone is raised from the dead who will she be married to?" §

§ It was an argument based on ridiculing the idea of life after death. They believed that when a person died, that one was dead and that was it. It sounded ludicrous that a woman would have to spend forever with seven legitimate husbands—who would she sleep with at night?—so there must be no resurrection, they figured, hoping to catch Jesus out on a limb.

Jesus started by exposing their ignorance. "The problem here is that you don't know the Scriptures, and you underestimate the power of God." That was a harsh blow, because they prided themselves on their detailed knowledge of the

Pentateuch and professed faith in God's power. §

Jesus continued, "In this life people get married to each other. But in the future, those who are resurrected from the dead won't get married and won't ever die. In this way they will be like the angels. They will be God's children of the resurrection.

§ The Pentateuch, also called the Law of Moses, is the first five books of the Old Testament. Authorship is attributed to Moses. The books are Genesis, Exodus, Leviticus, Numbers, and Deuteronomy.

"You have made up your minds there is no resurrection, and you're wrong about that. Remember the story about Moses and the burning bush where God spoke to him? It proves there will be a resurrection, because Moses called the Lord 'the God of Abraham, Isaac, and Jacob'—not that he *was* their God but that he *is* their God. Since he is the God of the living and they had died, they must live again."

It was a good enough answer to make even those who asked the leading question smile, applaud, and tell Jesus, "Well said, teacher! Well said!"

The explanation of this legal argument turns on two points: (1) People marry in this life to have children, but not in the next life, so the question has a defective premise and doesn't have anything to do with resurrection; and (2) When God talked to Moses through a burning bush in the desert, he referred to himself as the God of Abraham, the God of Isaac, and the God of Jacob, all of whom had already died. However, God talked about them in the present tense as being alive. Therefore, there must be life after death. Abraham, Isaac, and Jacob are all awaiting resurrection.

Jesus had adapted his teaching to fit his audience. Another time and place would have called for a different argument. For these Sadducees it demonstrated Jesus' broad understanding of their philosophy, his comprehensive knowledge of Hebrew Scripture, and his quick wit and rhetorical skills.

The Pharisees were next in line to question him. These Pharisees were genuine seekers who were aware of the stance of their leaders against Jesus, but they were personally open and sympathetic. They were impressed with how he had answered the Sadducees. It wasn't a trick when their spokesman, a leading religious lawyer, asked, "Teacher, which is the most important commandment of all?" Jesus answered in kind.

"The most important one is this: 'Hear, O Israel, the Lord our God, the Lord is one. Love the Lord your God with all your heart and with all your soul and with all your mind and with all your strength.' The second is this: 'Love your neighbor as yourself.' There is no commandment greater than these."

"Good answer, teacher," the Pharisee replied. "You're absolutely right when you say that there is one God and only one God. To love God with heart, mind, and strength and to love your neighbor is more important than offerings and sacrifices at the temple."

Jesus heard this Pharisee's words and sensed his heart as he told him, "You're coming close to the kingdom of God." This particular Pharisee was the last in line that Tuesday during the open-question time on Solomon's Porch. Now it was Jesus' turn to ask a question.

Not far from Jesus, a group of Pharisees were gathered in conversation, probably discussing their failed plots and Jesus' successes that day. No doubt some of them were newly rattled by the way Jesus had just responded to the expert who asked which is the most important commandment. They feared that some of their own were defecting to follow Jesus. They wanted to make every effort to close ranks before that happened.

"Pharisees," Jesus called out, "will you answer a question for me?" They were caught off guard, preferring to be on the offensive, but nodded their heads in agreement.

"What are your thoughts about the Messiah? Whose son is he?" Jesus asked. It was such an undemanding question that half a dozen could answer at the same time, not even considering that they were walking into a theological trap. "The son of David," they replied. Everyone knew the Messiah was to be a descendant of their famous king from a millennium earlier.

"Really?" Jesus asked. "How is it then that David, speaking words inspired by the Spirit of God, calls him Lord in Psalm 110?§ You remember, don't you, what David said? 'The Lord says to my Lord: "Sit at my right hand until I put your enemies under your feet." ' Explain why David would call the Messiah his Lord if the Messiah is David's son."

§ They didn't actually refer to psalms by number. The numbering of chapters and verses in both the Old Testament and the New Testament was a much later editorial addition to the Bible.

No one answered. Jesus looked at them and they stared back. Finally the Pharisees looked at each other helplessly and walked away in defeat. Jesus was showing that the Messiah is actually superior to David even though he came to earth years later as a descendant of David. It was a teaching the Pharisees were unwilling to consider. They agreed that the Messiah was to be a male descendant of David, but they were unwilling to acknowledge the Messiah as superior. And further, they were unwilling to admit that Jesus was the Messiah by any definition.

Jesus was done with the questions and answers for that day. He had every reason to be fed up with the self-righteous religious leaders who were doing more damage than good to the people he loved and taught. Jesus launched into a speech that covered a litany of direct attacks against the majority of the Pharisees. With a strong voice only a decibel below a shout, he preached a sermon to a jam-packed crowd on Solomon's Porch.

"These religion lawyers and Pharisees hold Moses' seat of authority in Israel, so you must do what they say. Just don't do what they do, because they don't practice what they preach. They put heavy loads on others' shoulders but will never carry anything themselves.

§ The head and hand boxes referred to are phylacteries.

"Everything they do is to show off: They make their head and hand boxes with scraps of Scripture extra big and the law-reminder tassels on their garments extra long;§ they love the place of honor at banquets and the most important seats in the synagogues; they acquire widows' houses and for a show make lengthy prayers. Such men will be severely punished!

"They love to be recognized in the marketplaces and called *rabbi*. Don't call anyone *rabbi*. You are all brothers with only one Master, who is God. Likewise with calling men *father*. God in heaven is your father. And *teacher*—your real teacher is the Messiah. The greatest one will be the servant. Whoever promotes himself will be humbled and whoever humbles himself will be promoted by God.

"Grief to you, teachers of the law and Pharisees! You are such hypocrites. You shut people out of the kingdom of heaven. Do you know something? You're not going to get in yourselves, and you block others from getting in!

"Grief to you, blind guides! You say such ridiculous things, like 'if someone swears by the temple, it's meaningless, but if the same person swears by the gold on top of the temple, the oath is binding.' How utterly foolish! Do you really think that the gold is somehow greater than the temple? Then you have this other ridiculous teaching that 'if someone swears by the temple altar, it's meaningless; but it counts if someone swears by what is laid on the altar.' You are so blind. Which is more valuable, the altar or what's on it? If someone swears by the altar, everything on it is automatically included. And anyone who swears by the temple includes whoever is in it. And the person that swears by heaven swears by God who is in heaven.

"Grief to you, teachers of the law and Pharisees. You are such hypocrites! You give ten percent of your garden spices—mint, dill, and cumin. But you haven't kept the more important matters of the law—justice, mercy, and faithfulness. You should have practiced the latter without neglecting the former. You blind guides! You strain out a gnat but then turn around and swallow a camel!

"Grief to you, teachers of the law and Pharisees. You are such hypocrites! You carefully overclean the outside of the cup and dish but leave the inside full of greed and self service. You blind Pharisees! What you need to do is focus your attention on cleaning the inside of the cup and dish and quit worrying about what it looks like to everyone else.

"Grief to you, teachers of the law and Pharisees. You are such hypocrites! You are like whitewashed tombs painted to look nice but are full of dead skin and bones on the inside. You make yourselves look so righteous on the outside when you are rotten with hypocrisy and evil on the inside.

"Grief to you, teachers of the law and Pharisees. You are such hypocrites! You work hard to build elaborate tombs for the prophets and decorate graves to honor righteous people who have died. You love to say, 'If we had lived back then, we would have treated all the prophets of God with honor. We would never have attacked and killed them.' The truth is that when you talk like that you are merely affirming that you are descendants of those who mistreated the prophets, and if you lived then you would have done what they did. You do exactly what you say you don't do. You're just finishing what your ancestors started.

"You are a pack of poisonous snakes! Do you really think you're going to escape being condemned to hell? What happens when I send you prophets and wise teachers? You kill and crucify. You beat them up in your synagogues. You run them out of town. Do you want to know what is going to happen to you? You will be held accountable for their blood, starting with Abel at the beginning of history and coming recently to Zechariah son of Berekiah, whom you murdered right near here between the temple and the altar. From A to Z, it all comes down on you!"

His speech complete, Jesus turned his back on the temple crowd and walked to the end of the portico, where he could see out to the rest of Jerusalem. He spoke words he had said before, although this time it was as if he were bidding farewell to the city: "O Jerusalem, Jerusalem, you who kill the prophets and stone those God sends to you. Over and over I've just wanted to gather you in my arms like a hen gathers her chicks under her wings. But you always run away. Look at your house; it is left desolate. I must tell you that you're not going to see me again after this week, not until you say, 'Blessed is he who comes in the name of the Lord.' " Referring to the temple as their house, he anticipated its destruction. These woeful words were sad and bleak, although they ended with hope and promise—"Blessed is he who comes in the name of the Lord."

§ In the Court of Women were receptacles where worshippers deposited their offerings to underwrite the expenses of the temple. There were thirteen containers, all shaped like large trumpets with the narrow end up. Each container was designated to receive money for a different function in the temple—wood for burning sacrifices, incense for the altar, upkeep on the temple, and others.

Teaching and preaching were tiring, and Jesus looked for a place to sit. He left the large area of Solomon's Porch, part of the open courtyard surrounding the temple itself, and entered the Court of Women. Jewish men were allowed entrance to the women's area, but this was as far into the temple as females were allowed to go. §

Opposite the offering chests along the outside perimeter of this court were benches where Jesus sat and watched the crowd. A steady stream of donors were making contributions. It wasn't difficult to see or hear the approximate amounts of their offerings, and it was obvious some were quite large. Following some rich people making significant contributions, a poor widow walked up and put two leptas in the container. §

Her gift was enough to bring a smile to Jesus' lips. Calling the attention of his disciples, he nodded toward her and said to them, "Let me tell you, this poor widow has put more into the treasury than all the others. They all gave out of their wealth; she gave out of her poverty. She gave everything she had to live on!"

§ A lepta was a Jewish coin in an economy that mostly used Roman and Greek money. They were small, thin, and made of copper. The value was tiny.

Near the end of a day with more than the usual share of controversies, this was an experience that totally delighted a weary Jesus.

CHAPTER SIXTEEN

T urning back toward the east wall of Jerusalem, Jesus' disciples looked at the temple buildings and noted admiringly, "This place is magnificent! The stones are massive."

It was indeed a stunning sight. After forty-nine years of construction, the temple still wasn't completed (AD 30) and wouldn't be completed for another thirty-four years.

The temple followed the design of Solomon's temple built nearly a thousand years earlier and destroyed by the Babylonians in 587 BC. It was constructed of cream-colored stone decorated with gold—80 feet wide and 180 feet high, and a high main doorway that was 36 feet wide by 60 feet high.

The men with Jesus were right. It was truly magnificent. And it was even more impressive for the followers of Jesus who were mostly from rural Galilee and had not seen it that often, if at all.

But Jesus asked them, "Do you see all these things? The truth is, not one stone here will be left on another; every one will be brought down." He gave no further explanation, and they must have wondered what he meant.

They climbed to the other side of the valley and sat down on the Mount of Olives, where they had an even better view of the city and the temple. Peter, James, John, and Andrew approached Jesus and asked if they could have a private conversation with him. They wanted to know more about his predicted destruction of Jerusalem. "Tell us," they asked, "when this will happen and what will signal your coming and the end of this age."

THE TEMPLE IN JERUSALEM

The temple area was 1,478 feet from north to south by 985 feet from east to west. Built on top of rock, some parts of the site had been flattened, but most of it was filled with rubble from the many destructions of the city. A wall of large stone blocks about three feet high and sixteen feet long surrounded everything. Porticoes with columns and colonnades circled the outer courts. It was about 450 feet from the top of the southeast corner to the floor of the Kidron Valley below. Inside the walls was the rectangular box-shaped temple itself surrounded by large courtyards. The slightly elevated temple was accessed by ramps that led up from the courtyard level.

Historian Josephus describes the temple as having an entire facade covered with gold plates. In the sun the reflection was nearly blinding, and on a clear day its brilliance could be seen for miles. The upper parts of the structure were pure white, probably marble, adding to its radiance. Once a year the priests whitewashed this upper section. Gold spikes lined the roof. Twelve steps led up to the entrance into the temple vestibule. Carved oak beams made up the lintel of the portal. Like the facade, the inner walls of the vestibule also were gilded. The vestibule rose to the full height of the inner portions of the temple, but an extra twenty-six feet in width on each side formed two rooms that housed sacrificial implements.

They asked two very good questions that could not be quickly answered. They probably thought the end of the temple and the end of history would come at about the same time. Jesus wasn't ready to fully reveal that the temple would be destroyed in just forty years or that Jesus' return to earth and the culmination of history would be after an interlude of thousands of years. He answered both questions with a long lesson predicting many future events. Some of it they had heard before. Some was new. This was the first time they had heard Jesus put so much of it together.

He started out by warning them about false claims by deceivers who claimed to be other messiahs or maybe even would claim to be

Jesus. "Keep your eyes open so you don't get tricked. There will come a whole string of counterfeits using my name and claiming, 'I am the Christ.' Some will actually believe them. You will hear news stories about wars or rumors that there are wars coming, but I don't want you to be alarmed. There will be lots of stories like this, but they don't mark the end. Nations will fight nations and kingdoms will fight kingdoms. There will be earthquakes, famines, and plagues in different places; there will be frightening events and terrifying things happening in the sky. This is not the end. At most, this is the beginning of the end."

He was giving them insider information that wasn't appropriate for public teaching. "Expect false prophets who will recruit followers. Evil will increase. The love of many devout people will start cooling off, although those who stay strong to the end will be saved. At the same time all these events are happening, my gospel of God's kingdom will be preached around the world as a witness to every nation. Then the end will come. As far as you personally are concerned, you'll be assaulted and persecuted for preaching my message. Powerful men will haul you in front of authorities from synagogues to prisons and governors to kings, all because you are associated with me. Something very good will come out of your troubles; you will have ample opportunity to tell these people in authority about me.

"I don't want you to worry in advance about how you will take care of yourselves when you are going through all this. When the time comes, I'll tell you what to say so that you speak wise words that no adversary will be able to refute. How hard will this get? Even your parents, brothers, relatives, and friends may turn against you to the point of trying to kill you. Everybody will hate you because of me. You'll get divine protection so you won't even lose your hair. By hanging in there, you will gain life."

Alluding to the prophet Daniel's prediction of a terrible desolation, Jesus told them more about the impending destruction of their holy city. "When you see Jerusalem besieged by foreign armies, you'll know that its desolation won't be long. Everyone should stay out of the city of Jerusalem when this happens. Just head for the hills. This will be the punishment predicted by the prophet. It will be an awful time, especially for those who are vulnerable, like pregnant women and nursing mothers. Get down on your knees and pray that when it's time for you to flee, it's not winter or a Sabbath day. Let me tell you that it will be worse than any time in previous history. And worse than anything in future history, for that matter. If God didn't intervene and hurry up this devastation, no one would live through it; but out of concern for his chosen people God will shorten the process. Distress will be everywhere. Wrath will flow out against people. Some will die in battle and others will be prisoners of war. Jerusalem will be conquered and trampled by Gentiles who will keep the destruction going until their time is up.

"Remember my advance warning. If someone says they have the Messiah or says, 'There he is!' don't listen or believe them. There will be many false messiahs; even some who perform miracles to deceive God's people, if that's even possible.

"If you hear a news report that the Messiah is out in the desert, don't go there looking. If someone offers inside information that he's hiding in some house, don't believe it. When I really come it will be very visible, like lightning that streaks from one side of the sky all the way to the other. That's the way it will be when the Son of Man comes. You know the old saying, 'Wherever there is a carcass, there the vultures will gather.' "

Looking far into the future and employing apocalyptic imagery, Jesus was answering their second question when he said, "There will be visible signs in the sun, moon, and stars. Here on earth, countries will be destabilized by the storms and turmoil of the sea. Grown men will pass out because they are so terrified over what is happening in the sky. The Son of Man will visibly appear in the sky, and every country on earth will moan and groan. They will see the Son of Man coming from heaven to earth with power and glory. Angels will play loud trumpets. God's special people will be gathered from everywhere."

It all sounded ominous and frightening, but that wasn't reflected in Jesus' voice. Although describing future events more dramatic than anything in previous history, he sounded matter-of-fact and even hopeful. "When all this gets started," he said, "stand tall and look around, because it means that God is very close to redeeming you once and for all."

"Tell us exactly when all these amazing things are going to happen," they implored Jesus.

"Well," he laughed, "it's not quite that simple! Let me teach you a lesson from the fig tree. Watch its changes, and you can tell the coming changes of season—not the exact date when the weather will change, but you certainly know what's coming.

"Tender twigs and budding leaves mean that summer is near. The truth is that when all this happens, the current generation will live to see it all wrapped up. Even though someday heaven and earth will be gone, my words will never be gone.

"Nobody knows exactly when all my prophecies will come true—not the angels in heaven, not even the Son; just the Father. Check back on the way it was when Noah was around, because that's the way it will be when the Son of Man comes. At the time of the big flood, people were doing most of the usual activities of life: eating, drinking, getting married, and everything else that most people do. At least that's the way it was until the flood caught them by surprise and they were swept away. That's the way it will be when the Son of Man comes. Out of two working in a field, one will be taken and one will be left. Two women grinding at a mill will be reduced to one because the other is taken.

"All of this is to say be on guard! Be alert! Be careful, or your hearts will be overwhelmed with the problems of life and you will end up partying, getting drunk, and worrying all the time. Then these predicted events will catch you by total surprise. Keep your eyes open. Pray that you'll not get caught up in the middle of the worst of what will happen. Pray that you'll make it through and someday stand before the Son of Man. Please understand that I'm predicting global, not local events. This is going to be everywhere on earth.

"You can't know when it's all going to come together. It's rather like a man who goes away, leaving his servants to take care of everything. He thinks he has everything covered with a checklist and assignments, right down to who guards which door. But his house is burglarized anyway. If he knew when the burglar was going to show up, he would have been better prepared. It's the same with the Son of Man. You don't know when he's coming, so stay on high alert all the time."

Jesus was impressing on them the importance of patience and diligence during the period between his departure from earth and his return to earth. Knowing that repeated stories and teachings have deeper impact, he brought his point home several times in several ways.

"Pretend you are among the servants left to guard the house. Stay constantly on guard because you don't know when the burglar is coming. It could be any time. Whatever you do, don't fall asleep on guard duty. Keep your eyes peeled.

"Or think of it this way," he said, and he started another parable. "Who is the household manager who is assigned to feeding the servants while the boss is away? If he's smart, he'll be doing a good job when the boss comes home. If he does a good job, the boss will put him in charge of the entire estate and business. On the other hand, if the servant assigned management responsibilities is sluggish and irresponsible, he'll tell himself, 'With the boss gone, I can beat up the other servants, eat whatever I want, and party with fellow drunkards.' He'll be surprised when the boss shows up, gives him a chewing out, and sentences him to the prison where all hypocrites end up, a place where people sob and grind their teeth."

Next, Jesus told them a wedding parable. It made the same point one more time, using a Jewish courtship tradition where friends of the bride waited up during the night for the "surprise" visit of the groom, who came to get her. "The kingdom of heaven is like ten bridesmaids," Jesus said, "who took their lamps and went to meet the groom. Five were foolish and five were wise. The foolish ones took their lamps but forgot to take any lamp oil. The wise bridesmaids took lamps and plenty of lamp oil. The groom didn't come till really late, and they became sleepy waiting.

"At midnight someone shouted, 'He's here! Let's go welcome him!'

"The bridesmaids were startled awake and quickly tried to light their lamps. Having run out of oil, the foolish ones asked if they could borrow some from the wise ones. But the wise bridesmaids refused because they had only enough for themselves. 'Go buy your own,' they told them.

"The foolish bridesmaids went shopping and were gone when the groom arrived. The wise ones were ready and waiting and went with him to the wedding dinner. The party started and the door was locked.

"When the foolish bridesmaids finally showed up and tried to get in, they were denied."

"Do you catch the parable's meaning?" Jesus asked Peter, James, John, and Andrew. "When I'm gone, you and all my disciples must keep watch, because you never know when I'm coming back to get you."

They certainly thought they caught the meaning. But they had asked for a timeline, and Jesus was hammering them with a call to faithfulness.

Jesus had another parable he wanted them to hear on the same point. They had heard a version of it before, but he wanted them to hear it again.

"This next parable," Jesus started, "is about a man going on a trip, who called a meeting of his household staff and entrusted his estate to them until he returned. To servant number one he gave five talents,§ to servant number two

§ As stated before, a talent was a measure of money—a lot of money! However, the word has a different meaning in English, referring to natural or God-given abilities.

Although not intended by Jesus or his first biographers, the parable has taken on a different application by readers of the English Bible as they have imagined receiving various abilities for which they are held accountable to God.

he gave two talents, and to servant number three he gave one talent. The amounts were based on each servant's ability to handle money. While the boss was gone, servants one and two both doubled the money entrusted to them. Servant three put the single talent entrusted to him in a box that he buried outside where no one could find it.

"The boss was away longer than expected but finally returned home and asked for a report on his money. Servant one handed back ten talents, and servant two returned four talents. The boss responded with a smile and warm praise. 'Good job, both of you! You've done exactly what I wanted you to do, so I'm going to promote you to greater responsibility. Come and celebrate with me. You've made me a happy man.'

"Servant three came to give his report. He said, 'My master, I've watched you over the years and seen that you are very demanding. You harvest more than you sow and collect crops where you never planted a single seed. I was so scared I would lose your money that I just buried it for the whole time you were gone. Here, I've brought the talent back to you. Look at it, it's the same money. You can check it out if you want.'

"The boss called him wicked and lazy and told the servant that if he knew his boss so well, he should have at least put the money in a bank and earned some interest during all this time.

"Then the boss surprised everyone by ordering servant three to turn his one talent over to servant one. Even though he had less, it all went to the servant with the most.

"Finally, the boss fired servant three and had him thrown out of the house even though it was dark outside. The servant cried and ground his teeth."

These were intriguing stories, but his disciples didn't always understand the meaning of his parables and wanted him to just tell them what the future would be like when he returned to earth.

Jesus responded by saying, "When the Son of Man spectacularly returns to earth with angels from heaven, he will sit on his glorious heavenly throne. People from all over the world will line up in front of him, and he will sort them out the way a shepherd sorts sheep from goats—sheep on the right and goats on the left.

"Then the King will tell those on his right who are blessed by God my Father, 'Come and take your inheritance, the kingdom that has been ready and waiting for you since the beginning of time. I was hungry and you fed me. I was thirsty and you gave me a beverage. I was homeless and you invited me to your home. I needed clothes and you bought some for me. I was sick and you became my nurse. I was in prison and you came to see me.'

"The righteous people on the right will ask, 'Your Majesty, we don't remember seeing you hungry or thirsty! We don't remember giving you food or something to drink. We don't remember any of these things you say we did for you. When did all this happen?'

"The King will tell them, 'You did these things for me when you did them for the most unimportant of my brothers.'

" 'And as for those of you on the left,' the King added, 'you are cursed, so get out of here and into the eternal fire ignited for the devil and his demons. Do you want to know why? Because when I was hungry, thirsty, homeless, needed clothes, sick, and in prison, you did absolutely nothing to help me.'

"Those on the left will answer, 'Your Majesty, we never saw you with these kinds of needs and didn't help you!'

" 'Oh yes, you did see me,' the King will tell them. 'You saw lots of unimportant people with great needs and did nothing at all to help. That was me you didn't help!'

"There was nothing more to say. The righteous on the right went to eternal life and the ones on the left went to eternal death."

The sun was now setting before them, and Jesus was a day nearer to death. The other eight disciples had been in various conversations nearby while Jesus was talking to Peter, James, John, and Andrew. When all thirteen of them were gathered together again, it was just the start of another day for them (Jewish days were usually counted from sunset to sunset), but for Jesus the end of Tuesday was another day closer to the cross. Jesus said, "As you know, the Feast of Unleavened Bread and Passover are two days from now—that's when the Son of Man will be turned in to be crucified."

The reference to his crucifixion should have shocked them, but it didn't seem to raise any alarms. They had heard him talk like this before, and he hadn't been crucified so far. Maybe it was just another one of his parables or figures of speech.

It was dark when they walked back to stay overnight in Bethany, but the path off the mountain was well worn. Then when they reached the road between Jerusalem and Bethany, a blind man could have found his way because there were so many people traveling on it.

Wednesday was Jesus' day off. What was a quiet day for Jesus and most of his friends was a busy day for the Sanhedrin in Jerusalem. An unofficial meeting of the chief priests and elders was held in the palace of Caiaphas. He lived in the palace as a perquisite of his position he held from AD 18 to 36 when Vitellius, the governor of Syria, deposed him. It was a large, expensive home that he knew well even before he became high priest, because his wife's father, Annas, was the previous high priest. In fact, the house was large enough for Annas and the rest of his family to retain residence there even after his son-in-law replaced him.

§ By this time in Jewish history, the once distinct Passover and Feast of Unleavened Bread had merged into an eight-day event always beginning on the fourteenth day of Nisan, the first month in the Jewish calendar (March or April in modern calendars).

The day was spent plotting to kill Jesus. They decided it had to be done before the start of the feasts and that meant soon. §

In plotting Jesus' execution, the Jewish leaders wanted to minimize conflict with the Passover events as much as possible. They weren't driven by a religious concern but by a political worry. "We'd better not kill him during the Feast or we may have a riot on our hands," was their consensus of opinion.

Another problem they had to solve was how to find him. Though easy enough when he was teaching a large crowd in the temple, that was too dangerous lest the people turn against them. To find him secluded in this city of thousands was almost impossible without insider information and help. Arresting Jesus was not going to be as easy as it first appeared. There just didn't seem to be any good way to get him into their custody without risking a riot.

Then the chief priests heard what seemed like the best news in a long time. One of Jesus' closest followers wanted to help them arrest him.

It is hard to determine exactly what motivated Judas. He may have been deeply disappointed about the coronation parade the previous Sunday. It had not led to a pact between Jesus and the religious leaders that would catapult Jesus to the throne of Israel. He may have thought Jesus needed a little impetus to use his supernatural powers for political purposes, and an arrest by the Sanhedrin would force his hand. Whatever he was thinking, his feelings opened the door for Satan himself to get into Judas' head and push him to make an offer to the chief priests and elders. "How much are you willing to pay me if I turn him over to you?" he asked at the palace.

A representative of the Sanhedrin counted out thirty silver coins and carefully placed them in a cloth bag that he handed to Judas. It was a deal. Judas promised to find a way to hand Jesus over to them in a secluded place before the deadline in less than thirty-six hours. Did he really think this would end up with an actual crucifixion? Probably not.

It was all turning into a horror beyond the imagination for the other eleven who had spent the past forty-two months so close to Jesus. One of their own was going to betray him to enemies who wanted him dead.

CHAPTER SEVENTEEN

T hursday morning dawned with some consternation among the disciples. It was the first day of the annual festival, but no arrangements had been made for celebrating the Passover—or so the twelve assumed. "Where do you want to eat the Passover? We need to get started," they noted to Jesus. After all, it was no small task to find a venue in a very crowded city and assemble all the necessary food and acceptable utensils and be ready on time.

Jesus said, "Peter and John, you are my choice! Go and make preparations for the thirteen of us to eat the Passover in Jerusalem."

"Yes, Master," they agreed, "but where did you have in mind for us to go and prepare? Today is the day, you know," they reminded him.

Jesus matter-of-factly told them, "Go into Jerusalem, and as you enter the city you'll see a man carrying a jar of water who will be looking to meet you." Because women usually carried water, it would not be difficult to identify a man carrying one of the large jars.

"When you find this man, just follow him right into whatever house he enters," Jesus instructed. "Once inside, say to the owner of the house, 'The Teacher wants to know where is the guest room to eat the Passover with my disciples.' He will take you to a large upstairs dining room. Start getting everything ready."

Realizing that Jesus had foreseen this already, they went into the city, saw the man with the water jar on his head, followed him into a house, met the owner, and were directed into a spacious upstairs dining hall.

All thirteen men who gathered in the upper room of that Jerusalem house knew every detail of the Passover celebration by heart from a lifetime of annual rituals. In some ways it could not have been more routine, and in other ways it could not have been more significant. Jesus had plans for this Passover meal that would make it one of the most memorable nights of their lives.

PASSOVER

The history of the Passover was at the very center of Jewish faith and tradition. It is an annual ritual reenactment of one of God's greatest miracles for his people. For 430 years, the ancestors of the nation of Israel had lived in the Egyptian East Delta. What started out as a friendly alliance with the Egyptians became cruel enslavement of the Jews. They were overworked, beaten, humiliated, and murdered. The people cried out to God for help, and he sent Moses to become their spokesperson and leader to freedom. He was an eighty-year-old Jew by birth who had been raised in the royal court as an adopted son of Pharaoh's daughter. Moses knew the language, culture, and legal processes of the Egyptian government.

When Moses asked the emperor to release the Jewish population of more than a million, the emperor refused. Repeated requests were all denied. Finally, God sent an escalating series of plagues on the Egyptians, always exempting the Jews from the pestilence. First the Nile River turned blood red. Next there were frogs, followed by a plague of gnats. Each plague made life more miserable and was followed by a renewed request from Moses to Pharaoh, "Let my people go!" Every request was denied.

At the tenth and final plague, God ordered the angel of death to sweep across Egypt and take the life of every firstborn in the kingdom. There was a terrible epidemic of death that night, and the Egyptians grieved, from the lowest peasant to Pharaoh himself. Only the Jews were exempt. God had warned them about what was going to happen and instructed them to kill a lamb and spread its blood on the doorpost of each home. When the angel of death came, he would pass over the houses with the blood posted, sparing the Jewish firstborns. Also, they were to pack up and get ready to leave Egypt forever. This meant eating a farewell meal of meat from the sacrificed lambs and hastily baking bread without leaven—some to eat and the rest to take along on their journey.

God ordered an annual reenactment of the original event. After the Passover, the Feast of Unleavened Bread was observed for seven days, from the fifteenth to the twenty-first of Nisan. The Passover was one day, and the Feast of Unleavened Bread took a week. Since these events were back-to-back, they added up to an eight-day festival. Although originally separate, by the first century the two were sometimes referred to as a single event. During those eight days, unleavened bread was the only kind of bread eaten and menial work was postponed until after the feast. The first and last days of the weeklong Feast of Unleavened Bread were classified as holy convocations when special sacrifices were offered at the temple.

Once everything was set up and the sun had set, the ritual began. First there was a candlelight search for any leaven in the house, and all leaven found had to be removed. Then they gathered around a low table. Carefully positioned symbolic elements included the roasted lamb, unleavened bread, bitter herbs, a variety of other condiments, and four cups of wine. Carefully stipulated hand washing was meticulously followed. The story of the first Passover in Egypt was recounted, usually between a father and son if it was a family gathering. They sang together part of the Hallel from the Psalms (Psalms 113-118).

When everything was set, they all reclined on the floor around the meal, and Jesus told them, "I really wanted to eat this Passover together with you before my suffering began. This will be my last meal until the Passover is fulfilled in the kingdom of God."

It all seemed picture perfect, but perfection was pierced with human emotions and personalities. Small talk around the table turned into a controversy. Hearing Jesus use the word *kingdom* started them thinking once again about which ones of them would be the greatest in the government of King Jesus. An argument broke out as several of the disciples positioned themselves for superiority.

Jesus brought them back together with a gentle rebuke: "Kings enjoy using their power to tell others what to do. They like to call themselves flattering names to show off how good they are. Don't be like them! The greatest one should think and act like the youngest in a family; the boss here should think and act like a servant. Who is greatest—the dinner guest or the waiter? It's the dinner guest. But I'm here to serve. You men have stuck with me so far in my tough times. As King, I confer my kingdom on you just as God the Father conferred his kingdom on me. Someday you'll eat at my dining table in my kingdom; someday you'll sit on thrones judging your native nation of Israel."

This was familiar territory for Jesus and for his disciples. He had spoken to this issue in the past, but it didn't seem to stay with them.

So many things must have been whirling through Jesus' mind. They were reclining together around a meal that would take hours. He was coming close to leaving this world and going back to heaven with God the Father. Time was running out, and he wanted to teach these disciples whom he loved so many more lessons; he especially wanted to teach them to stop fighting about superiority and how to be humble servants of others. He looked across at Judas and knew that the devil already had convinced Judas to betray him. Jesus had an object lesson that was better taught after Judas was gone, but he didn't wait for that.

Jesus rose from the floor and took off his outer clothes, picked up a towel, and tied it around his waist. At first the others didn't pay much attention as he poured water into a bowl and came up behind them. John was first. The two of them had a particularly close bond. Jesus knelt down and washed John's feet with the water from the bowl. In a wealthier house with servants, it would have been their job to wash the feet of guests.

Once they were clean, Jesus took the towel and gently dried John's feet. The room had fallen silent. He moved around the circle, washing the feet of Thomas, James, Judas, and Nathanael. No one knew what to say. When he came to Peter, Peter broke the silence.

"Lord, are you planning to wash my feet?"

"This may not make sense to you now, but it will later," Jesus told him.

"No," he told Jesus, "I would never let you wash my feet!"

"If I don't wash your feet, we're through."

"Okay, all right," Peter responded, "if that's the way it is, Lord, then don't just wash my feet, but wash my hands and head as well!" Peter had a tendency of going to extremes.

"Think of it this way, Peter," Jesus told him. "If you take a bath in the morning, your body is clean; only your feet need to be washed." The custom was to bathe at home before going to someone's home for dinner and then to wash one's feet again at the host's house upon arrival. However, Jesus obviously had moved from social customs to talking about spiritual issues when, referring to Judas, he added, "You all are clean, but not every one of you."

When he had finished the foot-washing, he put on his outer clothes and returned to his place. "Do you understand what I have done for you?" he asked them. "You call me *Teacher* and *Lord*, as you should, because that's who I am. Since I, your Teacher and Lord, have washed your feet, you should regularly wash each other's feet. The truth is that no servant is greater than his superior and no messenger is greater than the sender. Now that you've heard my explanation of these things, you will be blessed if you do what I have told you."

The other eleven didn't immediately understand what Jesus said next, but Judas must have caught it right away. Jesus told them, "Let me say something that doesn't include everyone here. I know whom I've chosen. What I'm saying is to fulfill the prophecy of Scripture that 'the one who shares my bread has lifted up his heel to hurt me.'

"I'm going to tell you what is going to happen so that when it happens you will believe who I am. The truth is, those who accept my representatives accept me, and whoever accepts me also accepts the God who sent me."

As the meal progressed there was less conversation than usual.

They tried to focus on the Passover story, but they knew that more was happening than was being spoken. Jesus' manner was subdued, quiet. The whole mood of the room was serious.

He broke one of the periods of silence and said, "One of you is going to betray me." No one responded. Jesus then said, "The hand of the betrayer is on the table right now. I'm going to go where God sends me, but there will be great grief for the one who betrays me. He'd be better off if he'd never been born."

They stared at one another, wondering what all this meant and what to say. Whispered conversations began among pairs and triplets around the circle. The sadness of Jesus was contagious as they tried to figure out who the traitor must be. Ironically, they had started the meal debating who was superior. Now they were each wondering who was the betrayer. They started to inquire, "Jesus, please say that I'm not the one." Jesus didn't answer. Then Thomas said, "Certainly it isn't me, Lord." Although each one asked, their questions were interspersed with eating and sparse conversations.

John was reclining next to Jesus. Jesus particularly loved him, and they shared the closest relationship of any in the group. Nearby was Peter, who gestured to John and quietly told him to ask Jesus who the betrayer was. When he thought it was the right moment and no one else could hear, John leaned in close to Jesus and whispered, "Lord, who is it?"

Jesus whispered back to John, "I'm going to dip this piece of bread in that dish and then hand it to the betrayer."

When Jesus dipped a piece of bread, he gave it to Judas Iscariot. The others couldn't see it happen, but as soon as Judas took the bread, Satan entered into him. Judas accepted the piece of bread and said, "Surely not I, Rabbi?"

"Yes, Judas," he answered. "It is you."

Others were talking when this exchange took place, so not everyone caught all that was said. As soon as Jesus had answered him, Judas got up to leave. Jesus said, "Get on with it." In the confusion of the moment, the other men thought Jesus was sending him on an errand to buy something or donate to the poor, since Judas was in charge of the group's money. It was dark out by the time he left.

It was different with Judas gone. The mood was still serious but less oppressive. Referring to himself as the Son of Man and using the word *glorify* to mean "making to look good," Jesus told them, "The Son of Man is glorified and God is glorified in the Son of Man. Not just later but right now."

Once again pensive and reflective, Jesus was talking more and more like a man who could see death around the corner. "You are like my children, and it is nearly time to say good-bye. You're going to look for me but not find me. Where I'm going you can't follow.

"Remember my new commandment for you to live by: love each other! Just as I have loved you, love each other. The main way others will know that you are my disciples is your love for each other."

Peter asked Jesus the obvious question, "Lord, where are you going?"

Jesus was less than specific in his answer: "You really can't go there, at least not now."

"But, Jesus, where are you going?"

"All right," Jesus told them, "you want me to be more direct? Let me tell you what is going to happen tonight. Every one of you is going to fall apart because of me. It's like the prediction of the prophet Zechariah, 'I will strike the shepherd, and all the sheep will be scattered.' But understand this—after I'm back to life I'll be in Galilee before you can get there."

Peter ignored Jesus' statement that he was going back to Galilee and focused instead on the prediction about everyone's loyalty. He insisted, "Jesus, even if every other follower deserts you, I won't! For sure!"

Using his birth name instead of his nickname, Jesus said to Peter, "Simon, Simon, Satan wants to separate us like chaff is separated from wheat. But, Simon, I have prayed that your faith won't collapse. When you finally come back, use your experience in failure to strengthen others."

Peter became even more insistent. Didn't Jesus catch on to the depth of his loyalty? "Lord, I am ready to go all the way with you, even if it means prison or death."

"Simon, you have no idea how hard this night is going to become," Jesus warned him.

"Lord, what do you mean that I can't follow you right now?" Peter wanted to know. "I'm ready to die for you."

"Listen to what I'm saying," Jesus answered. "Before you hear the rooster's wake-up crowing, you'll deny knowing me three times!"

"Oh, no!" Peter protested. "I would die first!" The rest of Jesus' disciples earnestly agreed with Peter and reaffirmed their love and loyalty all the way to death.

Still trying to communicate the horrors ahead, Jesus said, "Do you remember when I sent seventy-two of you out across Judea without extra supplies? Did you need anything?"

"Nothing!" they answered. "God supplied everything we needed through those along the way."

"Well, that was an easier time," Jesus explained. "Tonight and after tonight it will be very different. This time you should take everything you might need—purse, bag, even a sword. The scriptures are referring to me when they say, 'And he was numbered with the transgressors.' I'm telling you that this prediction is going to be fulfilled in me. The fulfillment is happening already and soon will be finished."

His disciples said, "Look, Lord, we have two swords."

They completely misread what he was telling them. He was warning them how hard it was going to be, using as examples things like purses, bags, and swords—the kind of supplies travelers packed for a trip. They were merely illustrations. He could have listed money, food, and transportation instead.

It was obvious they simply were not going to grasp everything that night. Jesus said, "That is enough for now," and dropped the subject.

Returning to the Passover traditions, Jesus distributed the second cup of wine to them, prayed thanksgiving to God, and told them, "Take this and divide it between you. This is the last time I'm going to drink this wine before God's kingdom comes."

Passover order

The Passover order went like this:

1. Opening events—a prayer of blessing; first cup of wine; herbs served.
2. Words of the Passover liturgy and story recited; second cup of wine drunk; part of the Hallel sung.
3. The meal—a prayer of blessing; the unleavened bread and lamb served and eaten with bitter herbs; the third cup of wine drunk.
4. More of the Hallel psalms sung; the fourth cup of wine drunk.

After the disciples drank the second cup of wine and were still eating the roasted lamb, Jesus picked up some of the crackerlike unleavened bread, thanked God, broke it into pieces, distributed it to the eleven men, and said, "This is my body given for you; do this to remember me."

Then he picked up the third cup of wine and again offered a prayer of thanksgiving. He distributed the wine to the men and told them, "Drink from the cup, all of you. This cup is the new covenant in my blood which is poured out for many for the forgiveness of sins."

Anticipating that this was the first of many times like it, Jesus told them, "Whenever you do this, remember me because I won't be here with you. I'm not going to drink of this fruit of the vine from now until that day when you and I can drink anew in my Father's kingdom. But whenever you eat this bread and drink this cup between now and then, you are announcing my death until I come back to earth."

JEWISH PASSOVER BECOMES
CHRISTIAN COMMUNION

This Passover meal was Jesus' last supper with his disciples before
he died and the beginning of a whole new meaning for Passover. The
disciples would reenact that night many times over. They would teach
other Christians to do the same and pass a new tradition down to
future generations. The name Passover would slip from prominence
among Jesus' followers and be replaced with new descriptions like
the Lord's Supper, Eucharist, and Holy Communion.

For the most part, the Passover was complete, but they lingered
to talk. Jesus knew his time was running out and there was so much
more to tell them.

Tuesday night, on the Mount of Olives, he had taught them about
the future in terms of their nation of Israel. Now he wanted to teach
them about their own future, for themselves and the new disciples
living during the years between his present life on earth and his later
return to earth. He started at the end, talking about heaven.

Jesus said, "Do not let what is happening upset you. You trust
God and you can trust me. My Father's house is big enough for every-
body. If there was anything to worry about, I would have told you.
I'm headed home to my Father's house to get it ready for you, and
then I'm coming to get you so I can bring you back home with me.
You know where I'm going."

Maybe the others knew where this place was, but Thomas didn't
and asked, "Lord, maybe we're supposed to know where you're going,
but we really don't. So how are we supposed to find the way to get
there?"

Jesus answered, "I am the way, and the truth, and the life. No one
gets to the Father unless he comes by way of me. If you knew me well
enough, you would know the Father for yourselves. Actually, from now
on you *do* know the Father because you've seen him through me."

Thomas still didn't understand, but Philip interrupted before he had a chance to say anything. "Lord, show us the Father, and that will be everything we will ever need," Philip avowed.

Jesus said, "Don't you know me, Philip, even after all these years we've been together? Anyone who has seen me has seen the Father. How can you ask me to show you the Father? By now, don't you believe that I'm in the Father and the Father is in me? I'm not just telling you my own opinion. The Father is doing his work in and through me. You need to fully believe that I am in the Father and the Father is in me; after all, you've seen the proof in my miracles. The truth is that anyone who truly believes in me will do the kinds of things I've been doing. In fact, my followers are going to do even more than I've been doing once I've gone back to live with the Father in heaven. Just ask for my help—pray in my name—and I'll do what you ask in a way that will enhance the reputation of God the Father."

If those Pharisees who were his adversaries had heard this, they would have been convinced they had their final proof of his blasphemy: Jesus claimed to be God and to have divine powers to answer human prayers. But they weren't there, and Jesus was free to be candid with his loyal followers. "If you love me as you say you do, you're going to do what I've told you."

And then he taught them about the Holy Spirit. §

Jesus explained, "When I ask the Father, he will send you another to stay with you forever. He will be your friend, counselor, and advocate. He is the true Holy Spirit. The rest of the world won't have him because they can't see him, know him, or accept him. But you're different— you'll see him; he'll come to live with you and

§ This is a teaching that later was explained in the Christian doctrine of the Trinity (there is one God who eternally exists in three distinct persons called the Father, the Son, and the Spirit).

in you. So you don't need to worry that I'm abandoning you like orphans. I'll still be with you through the Spirit. Others won't see me anymore but you will. I'll be alive and my life will give you life. You'll experience all this when the time comes; you'll know from experience that I am in the Father, you're in me, and I'm in you through the Spirit. When I say *you*, I'm talking about everyone who hears and does what I say. I'm talking about everyone who loves me and accepts love from the Father and me. Those are the people who will see and experience me."

Then Thaddaeus asked, "But, Lord, why do you intend to show yourself just to us and not to everybody in the world?" §

§ Thaddaeus was a nickname. His more formal name was Judas the son of James, not to be confused with Judas from the village of Kerioth who had left that evening after Jesus exposed him as the traitor. It is not hard to see why he would prefer to be called Thaddaeus rather than Judas.

Jesus replied to Thaddaeus, "God's truth is this: anyone who really loves me is going to do what I teach. My Father will love him. My Father and I will come and make our home with anyone who loves and obeys us. But it won't be like this for those who don't love me and ignore what I've taught. What I'm telling you doesn't come just from me—these are words from the Father."

Jesus further explained, "I've taught you a lot of important things during our time together. When your new friend, the Holy Spirit, comes to you from the Father, he will remind you about what I've taught and teach you a whole lot more. I'm leaving you with peace and promise—peace that exceeds anything this world has to offer. So you don't need to worry, have a heavy heart, or be afraid." Indeed, faithful followers were promised special treatment—a supernatural peace not available anywhere else.

"You remember what I said before about going away and then coming back? If you love me the way you say you do, you need to be glad for me that I'm going to the Father, who is greatest of all. The reason I've told you all this in advance is so you'll wholeheartedly believe when all my predictions happen. I'm almost done telling you all these things. Time is just about up. The devil is on his way to fight me, although he's not going to win. Everything that is going to happen over the next few days will teach the world that I totally love the Father and do whatever he wants me to do."

It was getting late. Jesus was ready to leave their host's house.

"Come on; let's get out of here," he said and started to get up. The others didn't move. They didn't understand all he said that night, but they did hear him announce that this was nearly the end of their time together. They wanted to hold on to him as long as possible. Jesus looked around at their faces and then settled back down and continued teaching them.

Using his love of metaphors and other word pictures, Jesus tapped into one of the richest analogies of the Jewish people—the vine. In their frequent travels, Jesus and his followers had walked past and through many vineyards with their vines, branches, grapes, gardeners, and winepresses. In Hebrew literature, the vine was one of the most frequent symbols for the nation of Israel.

"Picture a vineyard. I'm the vine in this vineyard. My Father is the gardener. As my Father works the vineyard, he cuts off fruitless branches and prunes fruitful branches to make them more productive." Jesus had just proposed himself to be the vine instead of Israel.

"Now think of yourselves as part of this vineyard," he continued. "You're in good shape because of my teaching. You're going to live in me, and I'm going to live in you. It has to be that way because branches can't survive, much less be fruitful, unless they stay connected to the vine. I'm the vine in this vineyard, and you're the branches. Stay connected to me and you'll produce clusters of grapes; disconnect and you won't produce one single grape. In fact, anyone who detaches from me will end up like a branch that shrivels up and gets burned on the scrap heap. But as long as you stay connected to me and do what I say, there is nothing to worry about. Ask for whatever you want, and I'll see that you get it. My Father looks good when you are disciples of mine who are like branches full of hundreds of grapes.

"The Father loves me with all his heart, and I love you the same way. Stay right in the middle of my love for you. If you do what I've been telling you, you'll stay in the middle just as I have done what the Father has said and have stayed in the middle of his love. I'm telling you this because I want you to have happy joyful lives. That's what makes me happy and joyful!"

Jesus paused to look with love around his little group. "If you can't remember every detail of all I've taught, be sure to remember my main command: love each other just as I have loved you. There is no love greater than the love that is willing to die for a friend. You are my friends who do what I ask you to do. Sometimes you've been called my servants, but I don't want to use that term because servants don't know what their master is doing. You are my friends! I've told you everything the Father told me. I chose you—you didn't choose me! I chose you and assigned you to grow basketfuls of fruit that will last. Bear fruit and the Father will give you whatever you request in my name. Just don't forget my main command: love each other!"

But a loyal relationship with Jesus meant more than fruit and love. It came with a cost, he warned them. "If you are hated by the world, remember that the world hated me before it hated you. You'll be hated because you're not on the world's team. The world would love you if you were on its team. But you're on my team instead, and that's why you are hated. Just keep remembering how the world hated me first, and you shouldn't expect to get better treatment than I received. Servants don't get treated better than their masters! If I was persecuted, you'll be persecuted. If they obeyed what I taught, they'll obey what you teach. If you wear my name, you'll get the same treatment I did because they don't know the Father. If I hadn't come to earth in the first place, they wouldn't have reacted in such a guilty way. But I did come, and they don't have any excuse for their ignorance because I've told them the truth. When it comes to hating me, they're hating the Father who sent me. Actually, they're just fulfilling one more old prophecy from a long time ago: 'They hated me for no good reason.' "

All this was a lot to absorb after the emotional Passover, but there would be later opportunities to fit together and understand more of Jesus' teachings. He told them, "All this will make more sense when your new friend, the Holy Spirit of truth, comes to you. Remember? I'm going to send him to you from the Father. He will verify and clarify everything I've been saying, and then it will be your job to tell others all that I've taught you these past three and a half years."

Even with the presence and help of the Spirit, Jesus' followers would be tempted to defect. Pressure and persecution were now concentrated on Jesus, but when he was no longer around, it would be focused on his followers. Jesus' concern for them was evident as he said, "I'm telling you all this now so you won't defect later. You need to be ready for serious abuse. Our enemies will excommunicate you from your synagogue. It will get so bad that anyone who murders you will think he is doing God a favor. Their bad behavior is all rooted in ignorance of the Father and me. This advance warning will help you out when the actual time comes. I didn't tell you sooner because I was always with you, but now that I'm leaving you need to know."

This was one of those times when it was better to listen than to ask questions. Although some times it was hard for the men to keep silent, especially Peter. Jesus said, "I keep telling you that I'm going back to the Father, and none of you asks me where I'm going!" Didn't Jesus remember? Less than an hour earlier Peter had directly asked Jesus, "Lord, where are you going?" Jesus hadn't given a very satisfying answer in response. Was he now accusing them of never asking?

Actually, Jesus had understood Peter's question as an expression of regret that he was leaving rather than an interest in his destination. Once Jesus dealt with how they were going to make it without him, they could have repeated the question with a greater interest in his destination than in his departure. Anyway, he stuck with the topic of his leaving and explained, "You're grieving because of everything I've told you, but it's actually good for you that I'm leaving. The only way you're going to get the Holy Spirit as your live-in friend is for me to leave. When I leave and he comes, his job will be to convince the people of this world all about the truths of sin, righteousness, and judgment. Sin, because they don't believe in me; righteousness, because I'm going back to the Father and will be out of sight; judgment, because Satan is convicted and condemned."

They were weighed down with information and exhortation. While wanting to take in every word Jesus spoke, it would take them a long time to process all he was saying to them. Jesus knew what was happening and said, "I have so much more to tell you, but you're already overloaded. It can wait until the Spirit comes, and he'll teach you the rest of what you need to learn. He won't just tell you his own opinion either; he'll tell you what the Father wants you to hear about the future. The Spirit will glorify and make me look good by taking my resources and giving them to you. Everything that the Father has is mine, and I'm teamed up with the Spirit, who is going to pass what I have along to you."

Realizing that the minutes were counting down and he had a schedule to keep, Jesus told them, "It won't be long now and you won't see me, at least for a little while."

Some of his disciples whispered to one another, "What does he mean by all this?" "How long is 'a little while'?" "I just don't understand what he is saying."

Jesus heard their murmurs and questions and said, "Let me try one more time. What will happen is this. You are going to cry with grief while the rest of the world around you rejoices and parties. But just wait. Your grief will turn into joy. What you are about to experience is like a woman whose pain in childbirth turns into joy when her baby is born. You'll go through pain, but you'll be happy when I see you again. In fact, it will be such a great joy that it will last the rest of your lives. And when you experience this new joy, today's questions won't matter anymore. That's when you will pray and the Father will give you whatever you ask for in my name. Just ask and receive—that will top off your newfound joy!

"I know that it bothers you when I use figures of speech to explain things, but it won't be long until everything will be plain and make sense to you. You'll ask and get straight answers. I love you, and the Father loves you as much as I do because you are believers. I'm talking about God the Father whom I left when I came to earth, but I'm soon going to see him when I return to heaven."

"Thank you, Jesus!" they said. "We appreciate it when you skip the figures of speech and use plain direct language. It makes it even more obvious that you know everything! You can answer questions before they are asked. This helps us believe that you came from God."

"You believe at last!" Jesus exclaimed. "I'm glad you believe now when you're all together; but soon you'll be split up and go to your homes. I'll be alone without you. But I won't be really alone because the Father will stay with me.

"My dear friends, I've told you everything that I've said tonight so that you can have peace in a troubled world. Be courageous, because I have overcome the world."

The lesson was over. There was one last thing to do before leaving that upstairs room. Jesus wanted to pray. It was a most extraordinary prayer.

THE OTHER LORD'S PRAYER

Probably the best known prayer of Jesus is the one popularly called "the Lord's Prayer," starting out, "Our Father who is in heaven." Ironically, it has been misnamed; it was not primarily a prayer of Jesus but a sample prayer for his followers. It was a template for others to follow and amend to fit their own situation and needs.

The true Lord's Prayer was the one he prayed that night after the Passover meal. It wasn't for others to mimic; this was a deep, intimate communication between the soul of Jesus and God his Father. The prayer is a fascinating mixture of the immediate and the future. Jesus prays as a man on the eve of his death, but he also prays as if he were already back in heaven and talking to God on behalf of his present and future followers on earth. Sometimes called the "High Priestly Prayer of Jesus," he prays as the priest representing his disciples to the high throne of God. Part of the wonder of this prayer is that it was so openly shared for others to hear.

Unlike modern western cultures that have followed the European tradition of bowing heads and kneeling before a sovereign monarch, Jesus prayed in a Jewish prayer posture—standing with his eyes open and his head lifted up toward heaven.

Jesus prayed, "Father, the time has finally come. Glorify your Son, so that I may glorify you. You granted me authority over the entire human race so that I can give eternal life to all you have given to me. I'm ready to give this eternal life to people so that they may know you, the only true God, and know me, Jesus the Messiah, whom you sent.

"I've brought you glory here on earth by doing the work you asked me to do. Now, Father, I pray that you will glorify me in your presence with the glory I used to have before the beginning of this world.

"I have revealed you to the list of people you gave me. These were your people on the list, and they have obeyed your message. They now know that everything I have comes from you. I told them your message and they accepted it. They believed me when I told them you sent me. Now I am praying for them. Not for everyone in the world, but just for those on your list. Father, we're in this together. Everything that is yours is mine and everything that is mine is yours. They have followed me and made me look good through their faith. Now it's time for me to depart this world, leave them behind, and come home to you. Holy Father, please protect them in my absence by the power of your name. Make them one as we are one. Keep them safe as I have kept them safe. Only one has been lost, and he is the one destined to destruction as predicted in the Scriptures.

"I'm headed home, but I want to pray these things before I leave so they will get a head start on joy. They are facing hatred and persecution because of our message. They don't belong in this world, but I'm not praying to bring them home with me; I'm praying for you to help and care for them as long as they stay behind. They don't belong to this world any more than I do. Make them holy by your truth here on earth as your word is holy in heaven. As you sent me as your ambassador to this world, send them as ambassadors with credentials from heaven. For their sakes I am holy so that they may be holy.

"Father, I am praying beyond your short list to a much longer list. May more names of believers be added in the years to come. May they too be one as you and I are one. May they be so connected to us that the world will believe their message that you sent me. May they be blessed with our kind of unity—I in them and you in me. May the world see their unity, hear the gospel message through them, and see how much you love them, just as you love me.

"Father, I deeply desire that everyone on the list you gave me will come to our heaven and see me in my glory at home, the glory you gave me before the world was created.

"My righteous Father, even though this world doesn't know you as I know you, they have gotten to know me and heard me tell them about your sending me here. I've told them about you and will keep telling them as long as I'm here, all so they will know how much you love me and them and so that I can be forever connected to them."

After his prayer was complete, his uplifted arms came down. It was silent for a few moments, and then Jesus began to sing another verse of the Hallel. The others joined with him, singing, "The Lord is my strength and my song."

When they finished the hymn, Jesus led the way down the outside stairs, through the streets of Jerusalem, and out the eastern gate. They crossed the Kidron Valley in the light of a full moon and went up the Mount of Olives to Jesus' favorite place of retreat, the Garden of Gethsemane.

The rest of the night was so awful he almost died.

CHAPTER EIGHTEEN

G ethsemane was a comfortable and familiar place, holding a myriad of good memories. Jesus and his disciples had been there so often that every tree and path must have been familiar. When they had been there during daylight hours, Jerusalem gleamed like a celestial city with all its whitewashed houses and the magnificent temple on the western horizon. At night the city could appear almost mystical with the flickering of oil lanterns in the windows. It was especially beautiful at sunset with the smoke from cooking fires turning the sun's rays into a rainbow of oranges, yellows, and reds.

But this was not a night for joy. Those old trees for which Mount Olivet was named would witness anguish and tyranny before the night was over. That Thursday night would become a moral preview of the physical destruction of the garden and all the olive trees in AD 70 when the soldiers of Titus would cut down every one of them.

"Sit here while I go over there and pray," Jesus told his disciples as he pointed toward his place of prayer in an abandoned oil press. § They had spent several hours together there on Tuesday afternoon. "Pray that you won't cave in to temptation."

"Peter," Jesus said, "you and the Zebedee brothers come with me." The four of them walked the path to the oil press. During the short walk, a dark cloud of sorrow and trouble fell over Jesus like a sudden storm on Galilee's lake.

§ Gethsemane means "oil press," and that is where the garden got its name. Olives were gathered in baskets and transported to a shallow rock cistern and then crushed with a large upright millstone.

Jesus said, "My soul is so sad that I feel like I'm going to die!" Of course this was absolutely frightening to his friends—he was dying before their eyes, but it was not like other deaths they had seen. It was almost as if he were being crushed to death by a massive but unseen spiritual mountain. Forcing himself to go on, he told the three to stay there and stay alert.

§ Abba was the Aramaic name that children called their fathers, similar to Daddy. It was an unusual and particularly intimate term for Jesus to use. Interestingly, the term carried over into the Greek-language worship of early Christians.

Jesus went a short distance and collapsed onto his knees in a position for prayer. He painfully said to God, "Abba, Father, you can do absolutely anything. § Take this cup of suffering and death away from me. Yet it's not what I want, but what you want."

Supernatural forces were colliding. Jesus dreaded the horrific death coming the next day. He knew that God was his Father and had ultimate divine powers. The anticipation of the cup of death was already taking him down. How could he endure all that was coming? He pleaded with his Father for a way out. Others had received miracles to meet their needs, and now he prayed for a miracle to meet his need.

Jesus must have known the answer—no—before he asked. God's will was for him to die on Friday, and Jesus, the Son of God, was committed to doing the will of his Father. The agony of all this was horribly wrenching, and the divine response was to send an angel—not an angel to call off the suffering, but an angel to give him strength. With the renewed physical and spiritual strength the angel provided, Jesus prayed even more earnestly and passionately. Sweat dripped off him like drops of blood pouring to the ground.

Jesus stood up and went back to his disciples, yearning for the company and support of his dearest friends. Despite all their misunderstanding of him and his message, along with too many moments of selfishness, they were the ones who were closest to him, and he loved them deeply. He wanted their help. Instead of finding them praying for him, he found them sleeping. One further blow to a man who was already down and dying. Jesus looked at Peter with sadness as he asked them all, "Are you asleep? Could you not keep your eyes open for just an hour?" No one answered—maybe just one woke up enough to hear him say, "Stay awake and pray so that you will not slip into temptation. The spirit may be willing, but the body is weak."

Jesus went back to his place of prayer, his heart heavy with grief. The ground was still damp from tears and sweat. He knelt a second time and prayed the same request: "My Father, if you still say I have to drink this cup of agony, I'll do what you want." It was a statement with an implied question. And the answer was still no. This wasn't going to be called off.

Seeking their support, he returned again to his friends. They had been there for him in the past. They had as recently as their supper together declared their love loud and long. Judas the betrayer was gone, and the loyal eleven remained. But his closest were asleep again. Jesus turned around and returned to pray. Same prayer. Same answer.

Jesus returned to his disciples and commented, "Are you still sleeping?" But there was no condemnation in his voice. Their rest was over. The garden was about to become a battlefield. "Wake up. It's almost time. They're coming for me," he announced. "Get up! Let's go! Here comes the man who is going to betray me."

As the words rolled off Jesus' tongue, Judas appeared on the path. He had been to this place often and rightly guessed Jesus would go to Gethsemane after the Passover dinner.

As the betrayer entered the grove of olive trees, it was clear in the moonlight that he hadn't come alone. He was accompanied by a delegation of officials representing the chief priests, religion teachers, elders, and Pharisees, and they were backed up by most of a Roman cohort of soldiers. § They were armed with torches, lanterns, swords, clubs, and other weapons, none of which seemed necessary in the light of the full moon and their intent to arrest the unarmed Jesus.

Knowing what to expect, Jesus did not resist. He stepped forward and asked the posse, "Whom

§ A "cohort" was normally six hundred men, although it was hard to tell if it was actually that many because the area was small and crowded. The expression may have been used in a general sense to communicate a sizable group of soldiers.

do you want?"

"Jesus of Nazareth," replied the leader of the Sanhedrin delegation.

"I am."

When he identified himself, the arresters stepped back, and many of them fell to the ground in awe. §

§ There was something about the manner in which he said, "I am" that was like the same words from God to Moses in the desert. Moses had asked God's name and was told, "My name is I Am."

When no one else came to get him, Jesus asked again, "Whom do you want?"

Same answer. "We've come for Jesus of Nazareth."

"I told you that I am Jesus of Nazareth. If you are looking for me, then let these men go." He pointed to the eleven, not including Judas.

Judas was standing with the Sanhedrin representatives and the soldiers. Jesus didn't want to drag his followers into jail with him; he wanted to fulfill his promise to God that he wouldn't lose any of the followers God had entrusted to his care.

The mob may have thought it possible that a loyal follower was playing the part of Jesus and they could mistakenly arrest a stand-in. Even though Jesus admitted who he was, they wanted confirmation from Judas. They had a prearranged signal. "The one I kiss is the man; arrest him," Judas had told them as they left the city and headed toward the Mount of Olives. It was an easier promise than when actually standing in front of Jesus.

Judas said, "Greetings, Rabbi."

"Friend, do what you came to do," Jesus responded.

Judas quickly kissed Jesus, who said, "Judas, are you really going to betray the Son of Man with a kiss?"

It all suddenly became clear to the eleven. As the soldiers stepped forward to seize and arrest Jesus, his disciples shouted, "Jesus, should we fight with our swords?" Peter's dagger was already drawn, and he lunged at Malchus, cutting off the right ear of the high priest's servant.

It all happened quickly. Jesus shouted his own command, "Stop right now! Put your sword away, Simon! Those who fight with a sword die by a sword. Don't you know that I could ask my Father to send twelve legions of angels to defend me? But how then would the Scripture's predictions be fulfilled? Do you think I should escape the cup that the Father has given me to drink?" Then Jesus performed his last miracle before death—he put back the soldier's ear and healed him.

Jesus turned to those arresting him, almost as if he were in charge of the proceedings. "Does it look to you like I'm commanding a rebel army so you needed to bring your weapons to arrest me? I've been publicly teaching at the temple every day, and you didn't arrest me there. So what's going on here? Evil darkness is taking over! The predictions of the prophets are coming true!"

While Jesus spoke to his enemies, fear took over, and all eleven of his disciples abandoned him and ran away. There was even an onlooker named Mark, § a distant follower of Jesus, watching from behind one of the olive trees. When he saw the disciples take off, he started to run away too. A soldier grabbed him by his clothes, but he tore away so the clothes ripped off and the soldier was left holding his robe. Mark wasn't wearing anything underneath and ran away naked.

With Jesus now in their custody, the soldiers took him back across the Kidron Valley and into the city, where they delivered him to the courtyard of Annas for the first of a series of trials. The first of these trials was held in Jewish courts. §

§ This peculiar piece of the story comes from the writing of Mark, and although he never actually says who ran away naked, many have assumed that an incident like this would best be remembered by the person to whom it happened. And it would make sense for Mark not to mention his own name. Unlike in Greek culture, the Jews were very modest and abhorred nakedness in front of others. It would be common to wear a loincloth as an undergarment, and that may be what Mark meant, rather than completely unclothed.

§ In addition to the Mosaic Law in the Pentateuch, there were many oral traditions passed down and accumulated through the generations, dealing with details of civil and religious life. There is uncertainty about the detailed trial rules in first-century Jerusalem. Later records describe the practice of Jewish law and trials, but they were written after the first century. Assuming that these descriptions apply also to first-century practices, the trial procedures here are probable.

§ The Sanhedrin was considered the Supreme Court of Jews, not only in the land of Israel but for Jews living anywhere in the world. The Sanhedrin consisted of seventy men. It included priests, scribes, and elders who met very specific qualifications: (1) full-blooded Jew (that is, both parents were Jews), (2) extensive knowledge of Jewish law, (3) multilingual (so they could hear cases in different languages, because translation was forbidden), (4) solid reputation, and (5) no personal interest in the case (or they had to recuse themselves).

Jesus was accused of offenses carrying the death penalty. This made the judicial process much simpler, narrowing the scope and volume of the laws. Only the Sanhedrin could hear capital cases. §

The soldiers brought Jesus to Annas, who had been retired from the office of high priest for fifteen years. The Romans had replaced him with his son-in-law Caiaphas as the current high priest, although many Jews still considered Annas their legitimate spiritual leader. Annas was never far from power because his successors included five of his sons plus Caiaphas.

Jesus' first trial was during the night in spite of the law against legal proceedings after dark. It started with Annas interrogating Jesus about his disciples and his teachings. Protecting them from similar charges, Jesus didn't tell their names, although he was candid about his teaching. "I have spoken openly to the world," Jesus said. "I regularly taught in synagogues or at the temple, the places where all Jews go to assemble. I didn't speak in secret. There is no need for you to question me. Just ask all those who heard me teach. They certainly know what I said."

TRIAL RULES ACCORDING TO THE TALMUD

Anyone accused of a capital offense was legally protected from self-incrimination and could not be asked questions in his trial.

Witnesses were required to give complete testimony. Unlike modern western judicial systems where the testimony of one witness may build on the testimony of another witness, the Jewish witness had to give his complete testimony of the whole crime. Those who testified were to be eyewitnesses and had to corroborate that any other witnesses had also seen the crime.

Two witnesses were always required in capital cases, and their testimonies had to agree in every detail. The witnesses were to be examined separately to be sure they were not collaborating. In one famous Jewish case, Susanna was falsely indicted for adultery. She was acquitted because the witnesses reported two different types of trees under which the alleged crime was committed. If witnesses were found to have perjured themselves, they received the same punishment that would have been given to the original defendant if convicted (which is what happened in the case of Susanna).

The overall effect of these laws meant that it was virtually impossible to convict anyone of a capital crime, and legal capital punishment was virtually nonexistent. Jewish law overwhelmingly benefited the accused. Defendants were truly considered innocent until proven guilty.

All capital trials were required to be conducted between the morning sacrifice at the temple and the evening sacrifice at the temple, which meant they were always to be during daylight hours. That communicated that the proceedings were in clear view of God and the people.

Judges served as defenders, always seeking acquittal when possible. Conviction required a majority with at least a two-vote margin (a 35-34 vote could not convict, for example; it would have to be 35-33 to convict). In one of the most unusual protections of the law, a unanimous vote for conviction was invalid. It was believed that a unanimous vote was a sign of possible prejudice or mob mentality; the assumption was that no case was likely to be so one-sided that there wouldn't be a single sympathetic judge on the court.

Cases were to be heard all at once. Recesses or continuances were forbidden once the trial had begun, except that a guilty verdict and sentence could not be handed down on the same day. There always had to be a night in between so that judges could reconsider, pray, seek new evidence, and possibly change a verdict. Capital cases always took at least two days.

Assuming these principles were in place during Jesus' time, all of this shows that Jesus was not tried under a primitive or unsophisticated judicial system. Of course, no system is perfect, and it is not the laws that ultimately guarantee justice; it is the people who have hearts and heads for justice and use good laws properly.

A court official standing nearby slapped his face and angrily asked, "Is this the way you answer the high priest?"

He had no right to strike Jesus unless he had done something wrong. With amazing poise, Jesus turned to him and said, "If I said the wrong thing, please testify to my mistake. But if I told the truth, why did you just hit me?"

It was apparent that Jesus knew the law and intended to invoke it. That was no doubt a surprise to Annas, who had never personally met or heard Jesus before. He may have assumed that he was an illiterate, ignorant, and unsophisticated itinerant rabble-rouser from Galilee who would be overwhelmed by his superiors in the big city. Whatever Annas' assessment, he decided to pass the defendant on to Caiaphas and let him handle the popular rabbi himself.

The temple police took Jesus to the home of the high priest, where Caiaphas was in a late meeting with former chief priests as well as the elders and teachers of the law and several other temple officials. Although most of the membership of the Sanhedrin was present, it wasn't a legal meeting because they weren't in their courtroom. When Jesus was brought in, they were in the midst of a discussion on how to recruit false evidence to use in trial against him so he would be convicted and executed. It was turning out to be more difficult than they expected; they were meeting with little success. There were plenty of witnesses willing to commit perjury, but they weren't very credible.

At almost the same time Jesus was brought in, a new group of potential witnesses arrived. One of them testified, "I heard the defendant say he could destroy God's temple and then rebuild it within three days." Others testified that they had heard Jesus say, "I will tear down this man-made temple, and in three days I'll build another one without human help." Close, but not close enough. The more they were pressed on the details of their testimony, the more discrepancies showed up.

Frustrated by the lineup of unbelievable witnesses, Caiaphas was left with no option but to directly question Jesus. Leaping to his feet, he demanded, "Are you not going to respond? What do you say about this testimony that these witnesses are bringing against you?"—as if the testimony had been credible. Jesus knew the law. He knew he wasn't required to answer. So he said nothing.

Caiaphas knew that almost every pious Jew would respond to an invocation of the name of God even if it meant self-incrimination. He instructed Jesus, "I charge you under oath by the living God to declare to us if you are the Messiah, the Son of God."

The ploy seemingly worked. "Yes, I am," Jesus answered. "Someday every one of you will see me, the Son of Man, sitting at the right hand of Almighty God and then coming to earth on the clouds of heaven."

The high priest tore his clothes in a dramatic gesture of shock and dismay, wailing, "Blasphemy! He has blasphemed against God! We don't need witnesses! You've all heard this blasphemy for yourselves. What do you think? What do you say?"

"Guilty!" they all shouted. "He deserves death!" The unanimity should have been a cause for a retrial, but no one pressed that point of law so late at night. Jesus' admission that he was both the Messiah and the future ruler alongside God was a claim no mere mortal could rightly make. They concluded that their charge of blasphemy against God was now confirmed.

The pretense of a legitimate trial further degenerated as members of the Sanhedrin started to spit in Jesus' face. Because he was still tied up, he couldn't even brush off their saliva or deflect their fists when they punched him. The trial turned to further anarchy as several of the guards put a blindfold over his eyes and made sport of him. They spun him around, beat him, and mockingly demanded, "Prophesy! Who hit you?" They were out of control, and their insults multiplied. Jesus just took the degrading humiliation without saying anything.

John and Peter had followed the arrest party at a distance. There was enough light from the moon and the group was sufficiently large and loud that it wasn't difficult to keep in sight. When they reached the residence of the high priest, John, whose family had a home in Jerusalem and knew the high priest, easily got through the gate into the courtyard, but Peter had to wait outside. A few minutes later John talked to the girl who was watching the gate and convinced her to let Peter come in. It all went very smoothly until the girl saw Peter's face in the moonlight and asked him, "Aren't you one of his disciples?"

Peter quickly and firmly said, "No, I am not!" His first impulse probably was that lying was the only way he would get in.

The night was clear and cold, as was typical at this altitude in this season. When the guards started a fire in the middle of the courtyard, many gathered around to get warm—servants, guards, officials, and Peter. Peter was largely unnoticed until a servant girl who worked for the high priest stopped and stared at him. Finally she thought she remembered how she knew him. "You're one of his disciples, aren't you? Yes, you are! You were with Jesus of Galilee!"

Peter's reaction was quick. "I don't know what you're talking about."

"Yes you do! You are a disciple of that Nazarene, Jesus," she insisted.

More emphatically he spoke so everyone nearby could hear, "Woman, I don't know him. I don't even know what you're talking about. How many times do I need to tell you? I am not one of that man's disciples!" As he talked he moved backward toward the gate.

Another girl saw him and announced, "He's one of them! Look at him. This fellow was part of the group with Jesus of Nazareth." Others agreed, "She's right. You're one of them, and you know it."

Surrounded by those identifying him as a disciple of Jesus, Peter again denied affiliation with Jesus, this time swearing with an oath as he said, "Listen! I don't know the man! I don't know the man! How many times do I need to tell you?"

When everything calmed down, it appeared that the worst was over for Peter. He stayed near the gate where he could watch but could more easily run away if there were problems. After about an hour, several people standing nearby started saying to one another, "I think I recognize that man over there. I heard him talk with a Galilean accent. Certainly he is one of those who came to Jerusalem with Jesus." One of them decided to talk directly to him. "There's no doubt about it. Your accent gives you away." Peter called down a string of curses on himself and totally denied knowing Jesus. § "I don't know this man you're talking about," he exclaimed. "I don't know anything about this at all."

The clincher came when one of the high priest's servants walked up. He wasn't just any servant; he was a relative of Malchus, whose ear had been cut off by Peter a few hours earlier in the Garden of Gethsemane. Hearing what was being said, he got right in Peter's face and confronted him. "I recognize you. I saw you over in the olive grove with Jesus when he was arrested. You know I did!"

As Peter opened his mouth for another ineffectual denial, a rooster began to crow. Jesus, bound and between soldiers, had been brought into sight on the far side of the courtyard beyond the fire. As the rooster crowed, Jesus' eyes caught Peter's and Peter remembered what Jesus had said earlier, "Before the rooster crows, you will deny knowing me three times." §

§ Peter's curses weren't profanity or vulgarity, but he was swearing by various things that he didn't know Jesus. It was a type of behavior Jesus had addressed in the Sermon on the Mount when he said, "Some people are pretty creative in the oaths they take, swearing by heaven as God's throne or earth as God's footstool or Jerusalem as the city of God. Others say, 'I swear by my own head that I'll do what I promise,' as if we can even control which hairs grow in black or white! Simplify your promises. Don't swear by anything. Just say yes that you are going to do something and then do it. Just say no, you're not going to do something and then don't do it. Don't let Satan twist your words into fake promises that you don't really intend to keep."

§ Peter denied Jesus repeatedly—entering the courtyard, in the courtyard, and leaving the courtyard. Depending on how the denials are counted, it was at least three times.

What emotions did Peter feel? Ashamed? Afraid? Disappointed? Angry with himself? Peter ran from the courtyard and wept bitterly.

As the eastern sky lightened and sunrise neared, the high priest called for an official meeting of the Sanhedrin. Skipping most of the legalities that should have governed this procedure, Caiaphas spoke for the Sanhedrin and directed Jesus, "If you are the Messiah, say so."

Jesus answered, "If I tell you the truth, you won't believe me. Besides, if I asked you a question you wouldn't answer me. So let me answer like this: from now on the Son of Man will be seated at Almighty God's right hand."

Jesus' answer wasn't quite direct enough for their purposes, so they rephrased the question and asked him, "Are you saying that you are the Son of God?"

"You are right when you say that I am."

"Why do we need any more? We have all heard what he said!" they exclaimed to one another. There wasn't even a need to vote. He was obviously guilty. He claimed to be the Son of God.

SHORTENING THE PROCEEDINGS

Because the sun was now up, this meeting would meet that requirement of the law. Not everyone was present but almost all were. The usual practice was to sit in a semicircle with the accused facing the court. Having made up their minds long before, the members of the Sanhedrin dispensed with many of the usual legal constraints. Normally in capital cases they would hear at least two witnesses, and members of the court would render their opinions. Anyone who spoke for acquittal was forbidden to later argue for conviction; anyone who spoke for conviction could change his mind and later speak for acquittal. Then there would be a roll-call vote starting with the youngest and going to the oldest.

They were supposed to state the formal accusation against the defendant, but everyone seemed to know they were accusing him of the capital offense of blasphemy. There is no record that the indictment was read.

So it was settled. Or was it? While the Sanhedrin under Jewish law once had the authority to execute, they were now subject to

Roman law, and only the governor could authorize capital punishment. Apparently they thought the governor would do it. He had ordered other executions as a political expedient to keep the Sanhedrin happy, so he would probably sign off on killing Jesus.

Jesus was tied up once again and held for transfer to the court of Pilate, the Roman governor of Judea.

While the entire Sanhedrin prepared to march from the residence of the high priest over to the palace of the Roman governor, Judas heard what was happening and was overcome with remorse. He returned to the chief priests and elders to give back the thirty silver coins he had been paid to identify Jesus for arrest. "I have sinned," he told them. "I have betrayed an innocent man."

"That's your problem, not ours," they said. "What's it to us? Whatever you did is your responsibility. Besides, it's too late now anyway."

Frustrated and depressed, Judas threw the coins on the temple floor and left to commit suicide in a forlorn place near where the Kidron and Hinnom Valleys meet in the south of Jerusalem. § He hanged himself and his body fell to the rocks below with an impact that ripped him open so that his intestines and other internal organs burst out. Those who found him spread the story around Jerusalem for weeks, and the people nicknamed the field where he died *Akeldama*, "the Field of Blood."

§ The record of Judas' death describes the results, not the process. His death was violent and bloody. The best explanation is that he put a rope around a high tree above a rocky field, closed the noose around his neck, and jumped. The rope snapped his neck and then the rope broke.

Having received the money back from Judas, the chief priests weren't sure what to do with it. One of them insisted, "It is against the law to put this blood money into the treasury." When they heard the stories rumored around Jerusalem about where and how Judas died, they decided to purchase the Akeldama land and turn it into a cemetery for indigent foreigners who died in Jerusalem. At the time they didn't realize that their pragmatic decision fulfilled a five-hundred-year-old prophecy by Zechariah: "They took the thirty silver coins, the price set on him by the people of Israel, and they used them to buy the potter's field, as the Lord commanded me."

The Sanhedrin, with the help of temple guards, transported Jesus from Caiaphas' house in the upper city to Pilate's house north of the temple at the Fortress of Antonia. Although it was not a long distance, the journey through crowded city streets was not easy.

Somewhere en route the charges against Jesus were changed. The Jewish leaders knew that a blasphemy conviction before the Sanhedrin was meaningless under Roman law and that the governor was unlikely to order an execution for a local religious sin. They needed charges that had standing in a Roman court.

The other challenge the religious leaders faced dealt with ritual purity. Entering a Gentile residence made a Jew ritually impure and temporarily disqualified from temple worship for the Passover and Feast of Unleavened Bread. Sensitive to their needs, Pilate agreed to come outside to talk with the members of the Sanhedrin rather than have them enter his court. It was one of many unusual concessions a Roman governor had to make to keep the peace in one of the empire's most difficult to control provinces.

§ Roman law was efficient. Some historians have observed that western culture took religion from the Jews, literature from the Greeks, and law from the Romans. The typical Roman trial was divided into four parts: indictment, examination, defense, and verdict.

Pilate's most important appearance in history began on Friday, April 6, AD 30, when he first met Jesus. It was still early, not long after dawn, which was a typical starting time of Roman trials. When everyone had assembled outside the palace, Pilate asked, "What charges are you bringing against this man?" § Pilate knew and followed the law, first asking for a statement of the charges.

The Sanhedrin were caught by surprise because they had hoped he would just sign the execution order without formal proceedings. The best response they could come up with was, "If this man wasn't a criminal, we wouldn't have brought him to you."

That wasn't an adequate answer for Pilate, so he tried to dismiss them, saying, "Take him away and judge him by your own law."

He should have known they would not go away so easily. Their objection was predictable: "But he's accused of a capital offense, and we don't have the right to execute." As Jesus stood there listening to this verbal exchange, he knew all this was happening to fulfill his prediction that he would die by crucifixion, the Roman method of capital punishment.

Several members of the Sanhedrin who knew Roman law eventually told Pilate what they knew he legally needed to hear: "Our investigation indicates that this man is guilty of subversion of our nation. He speaks against paying taxes to Caesar and claims to be the Messiah. He says he is a king." It was an accusation laden with irony because they hardly thought of the Roman Empire as "our nation," they hated paying Roman taxes, and they acknowledged Tiberius Caesar as their king with great reluctance.

PONTIUS PILATE

Pontius Pilate came to Palestine in AD 26, and his job wasn't easy. A seasoned soldier, he had received his appointment as procurator through marriage to the emperor's granddaughter.

On his first trip to Jerusalem, he marched into the city carrying Roman military standards topped with metal images of the emperor, who claimed to be a god. The Jews were outraged by this display of graven images in their holy city. They protested to no avail, even following Pilate home to his residence up north in Caesarea on the Mediterranean coast. They hounded him for five days until he erupted in anger. Pilate invited the protesters to meet him in the amphitheater in Caesarea, where he surrounded them with soldiers and ordered them to submit or die. The valiant and patriotic Jews bared their necks and invited the soldiers to kill them. Not even Pilate was ruthless enough for this kind of wholesale slaughter, so he relented and stopped using the standards in military processionals.

His next major confrontation with the Jews was over a much-needed aqueduct to bring more water into Jerusalem. In order to finance the construction project, he took money from the temple treasury. The people were furious and rioted against this outrage. Pilate responded by disguising some of his soldiers as Jews and sending them into the crowd. On a prearranged signal, the soldiers drew their hidden weapons, clubbing and stabbing many to death. The Jewish leaders threatened to report him to the emperor for his unjust violence.

A third confrontation that marked his rocky governorship was similar to the first. His soldiers had votive shields with the name Tiberius Caesar written on them. Pilate ordered that these ceremonial shields be hung in the Palace of Herod on the west side of Jerusalem's upper city. Because these shields were dedicated to recognition of the emperor as divine, the people asked Pilate to remove them. He refused. This time a delegation of leading Jewish citizens appealed to Tiberius, who overruled Pilate and ordered the shields removed.

The final undoing of Pilate came after his historic encounter with Jesus. In AD 35 Pilate was unnecessarily vicious in quelling a minor uprising in Samaria. Because Samaria had been traditionally loyal to the emperor, the Roman legate to Syria intervened. He reported what happened to Tiberius, and the emperor ordered Pilate back to Rome. While Pilate was traveling from Palestine to Rome, the emperor died and Pilate disappeared from the historical record. Tradition reports that he committed suicide.

Having received an indictment of sorts in compliance with Roman law, Pilate turned around and went back inside the praetorium, ordering that Jesus be brought in for examination. The Jews wouldn't enter, so the accusers were all outside.

Pilate was seated. Jesus stood. "Are you the king of the Jews?" Pilate asked.

"Yes," answered Jesus, "just as you say. Is this your conclusion or did you hear it from others?" His question was not a diversion. Jesus was asking if Pilate was inquiring from a Jewish point of view, in which case the answer would be, "Yes, I am the king of the Jews," or from a Roman point of view, in which case the answer would be, "No, Caesar is king of the Romans."

"Am I a Jew?" Pilate scowled. Many Romans held as much disdain for Jews as many Jews held for Romans. "Your religious leaders and people arrested you and brought you here. What did you do?" Pilate was sticking with Roman law in this trial.

"My kingdom isn't an earthly kingdom. If it were, my servants would have raised arms to defend me against arrest. My kingdom comes from someplace else," Jesus explained.

It was an answer that gave Pilate a quiet sigh of relief. Jesus wasn't planning to muster an army to fight the Romans. He claimed to lead some kind of otherworldly realm. "You are a king, then!" Pilate said.

Jesus was unlike any other accused criminal Pilate had tried. Jesus' defense wasn't really a defense at all. It seemed as if he were the judge and Pilate were the defendant. Jesus answered him, "Yes, I am a king. In fact, I came to earth in order to be born a king, one who tells the truth. Everyone who believes in truth listens to what I say."

"What is truth?" Pilate asked as if he were a Greek philosopher dialoguing near the acropolis in Athens. But he didn't wait for Jesus to answer. He had decided his verdict and was ready to move on to the next items on his agenda for that Friday.

Pilate stood up and walked out to the waiting Sanhedrin and company. "I have examined the defendant and find no legal basis for the charges against him!"

His accusers weren't going to accept a quick dismissal of the charges. They knew from past experience that enough pressure could change Pilate's mind. One after another and then many at once, they shouted a litany of accusations at Jesus. Still standing near enough to each other for conversation, Pilate turned back to Jesus and asked him, "Don't you hear the charges they are bringing against you?" Jesus gave no reply. Pilate was amazed at the powerful presence and sense of authority exuding from a prisoner under such pressure.

The accusations kept coming so quickly and simultaneously that it was impossible to distinguish what they were saying. Someone with an unusually loud and powerful voice shouted, "He incites crowds all over the province of Judea. He started teaching in Galilee and worked his way down here."

Suddenly Pilate saw a politically convenient way to escape this growing conflict. "He's from Galilee?! Why didn't someone say so? If he's a Galilean, he's under the jurisdiction of Herod, not me. Take him to Herod! He's in Jerusalem for the Feast and will be glad to meet this Jesus."

So, on the order of Pilate, a unit of Roman soldiers transferred Jesus across the city from the praetorium on the northeast side of town to the Palace of Herod on the west side of town.

Herod was indeed delighted. He had wanted to meet Jesus for the last few years and was especially hopeful Jesus would perform some miracles for him to see. The king was full of questions, and they flowed out of his mouth. At first he may have assumed that Jesus was slow to answer because the questions were so clever and demanding, but then he realized that Jesus was deliberately silent. The room wasn't quiet, though. The chief priests and teachers of the law from the Sanhedrin had come inside this time and were bombarding Jesus with accusations. He answered none of them.

In the courts of Annas and Caiaphas, the accusation was religious blasphemy. In the court of Pilate, the accusation was political treason. In the court of Herod Antipas, there was no clearly defined indictment. It didn't seem to matter. Herod didn't appear to take this confrontation very seriously. He treated his meeting with Jesus as if it were for his entertainment. When Jesus didn't answer, those present mocked him and made fun of him. One of Herod's soldiers draped Jesus in an elegant robe and Herod sent Jesus—still wearing this impressive robe—back to Pilate without ever rendering a verdict. Ironically, Herod and Pilate became friends because of this contact, whereas before this they were avowed enemies.

Pilate didn't want Jesus back. Why would he want anything to do with someone who might trigger a riot or rebellion? Jerusalem was always ready to explode, and Pilate must have hoped to pour water on these incendiary flames rather than fan them into a wildfire. But he wasn't having much success and had to come up with another strategy to get past Jesus.

An infrequent practice of some Roman governors was to placate the people once a year by granting a pardon to one popular prisoner on death row. It was an easy ploy because the released man could always be rearrested and recharged if the governor really wanted him executed. With Jesus on the docket and Barabbas in a holding cell, this seemed like a good time to offer the crowd a choice. Barabbas was a well-known insurrectionist convicted of murder during a recent uprising, and he was awaiting execution.

Anticipating the offer, many had gathered in a new crowd outside the praetorium asking for a prisoner pardon and release. Pilate told the chief priests and leaders who were back at his palace, "You brought me this man accused of inciting insurrection among the people. I have examined him in your presence and have found no basis for your charges against him. Neither has Herod, who sent him back here. Look at the defendant. You can see for yourselves that he has done nothing deserving of death. I'm going to punish him and release him." To subsequent generations and cultures, this would make no sense. Why would someone found innocent be punished? §

§ It appears that Pilate knew exactly what he was doing. Legally, he found Jesus not guilty and planned to release him. Politically, he may have assumed that a beating would satisfy the crowd and shut Jesus down for a while. It could be a good all-around compromise to bring closure to this whole event.

The Sanhedrin wanted more blood than Pilate was offering. They were looking for execution, not compromise.

Falling back on the prisoner release idea, Pilate may have assumed that the popularity of Jesus would win him more votes for release than the politically controversial Barabbas could ever garner. So Pilate raised his voice over the heads of the religious leaders and asked the assembled crowd, "Which one do you want me to release to you: Barabbas or Jesus 'the Messiah'?"

While people in the crowd discussed the proposal, he sat down in his judge's chair and received a written message from his wife. Her note told him, "Don't have anything to do with this Jesus. He is an innocent man. I have been suffering all day over a dream I had about him." Pilate took her dreams seriously. While he was sitting and contemplating her message, the chief priests and elders spread out and began to work the crowd. Many of these people were aligned with them already. It didn't take long to persuade enough of them to choose Barabbas over Jesus. Pilate stood up again and asked the crowd, "Which of the two do you want me to release to you?" They shouted back in a united voice, "Barabbas! Barabbas! Away with Jesus! Release Barabbas to us!"

Pilate asked the people, "What about Jesus? Do you want me to release 'the king of the Jews'?"—almost as if he were offering to release both, although he never said that. They shouted back, "No, not Jesus! Give us Barabbas!"

Because Pilate wanted to let Jesus go, he asked them what they wanted to happen to Jesus if Barabbas was released. Some of them yelled back, "Crucify Jesus!"

"Why?" Pilate asked. "What crime of his deserves crucifixion? I examined him and found no legal basis for the death penalty. I will punish and release him."

SCOURGING

Scourging was considered the functional equivalent of crucifixion without always leading to death. The prisoner was stripped and shackled to a beating post. Whips were made of leather with strips at the end called thongs to which were tied sharp pieces of stone, metal, and bone. The soldier snapped the whip to imbed the sharp ends into the skin and muscle of the victim's back, arms, and legs. Then he pulled hard to rip across the body, inflicting lines of

> parallel wounds. Ancient records describing scourging are themselves painful to read. Seldom did any prisoner remain fully conscious throughout the beating. Backs were torn to shreds; ribs and other bones were bared and sometimes broken; bodies were mutilated until internal organs could be seen; and veins and arteries were often lacerated, causing severe bleeding. Floggings sometimes resulted in death.

The governor wasn't ready to let a guilty man go free, execute an innocent man, and anger his wife and the gods all in a single decree. He had one last option—to have Jesus beaten. Who knew? Maybe when they saw him after a beating, that would be enough.

Pilate went back inside his palace, where he ordered his soldiers to flog Jesus. Jesus was turned over to the scourging team, and a group of Roman soldiers performed this gruesome task.

What they did to Jesus at that flogging pole fulfilled the prophet Isaiah's description of the Messiah as a suffering servant:

> Look at him if you can—he is so disfigured that he doesn't
> even look human. No one is attracted by his good looks. To
> the contrary, he is despised and repudiated, full of sorrow
> and suffering—the type of person you don't even want to
> look at or respect.

When Jesus reached the point where he could not survive much longer, the soldiers stopped the beating and dressed him up as a mock king. They wove a makeshift crown out of a vine with long sharp thorns and placed it on his head. They put the purple robe that came from the Jerusalem palace of Herod Antipas back on his shoulders and wounded back. They pretended to treat him as if he were royalty, bowing as they approached him but then slapping his face when they came close and jeering, "Hail, king of the Jews!"

Perhaps hoping that this would satisfy the crowd, Pilate ushered Jesus out to where they could see him. Certainly the Sanhedrin could no longer view him as a threat, and maybe the thousands who followed him would abandon him at first glimpse. This could end the whole affair.

Pilate raised his voice to speak. "Look, I present the prisoner to you to confirm that there is no basis for further charges against him." When Jesus came out wearing the crown of thorns and the purple robe and looking so disfigured, it was enough to make some in the crowd cringe at the sight of him. Pilate pointed to Jesus and said, "Here is the man!"

When the chief priests and their officials saw him, they yelled, "Crucify! Crucify!"

Pilate asked the crowd, "What do all of you want me to do with Jesus who is called the Messiah?"

The crowd took their cue from the religious leaders and shouted, "Crucify him!"

Pilate, disgusted, told them, "He's yours. You take him and crucify him. I've told you—there is no basis for crucifixion." It was an impulsive thing to say. He knew it was illegal for Jews to crucify without his approval. He was trying to buy time while he figured out what to do next.

One of the leaders spoke for the Sanhedrin. "We have our law that says he must die because he claimed to be the Son of God."

That statement was enough to frighten the governor even more than his wife's note. At first it had looked like he was simply dealing with one more of a long line of problem people in a place where life was cheap. Keeping the peace and satisfying Rome was far more important than anyone or any issue in Jerusalem. But this Jesus affair was taking on a life of its own. Jesus was so different; his wife had a dream; and now they say he is a god or at least a son of a god. Did he just have a god flogged? What would happen to him if he crucified a god?

Pilate swirled around, his back to the crowd, and went inside. He sat down and ordered Jesus back in front of him. "Where do you come from?" he asked Jesus.

When Jesus stood silent, Pilate said, "You're not going to talk to me? Don't you realize I have power either to release you or to crucify you?"

"You would have no power over me if it were not given to you from heaven. Therefore the one who handed me over to you is guilty of a greater sin."

This was an impressive statement from Jesus. Pilate had already argued to set him free, but there was a crowd outside chanting, "If you let this man go, you are no friend of Caesar. Anyone who claims to be a king opposes Caesar." They knew exactly how to exert enormous political pressure on the governor, because anyone in his position needed to be a friend of Caesar. He certainly didn't want a rumor going back to Rome that he was supporting some renegade king.

A final decision had to be made that morning. If this continued, it would only get worse. Pilate brought Jesus back outside where the crowd could see him and then sat down in his official judgment chair on an outside patio called Gabbatha, which means Stone Pavement.

He ordered a servant to bring a bowl of water and a towel. With the crowd watching, Pilate washed and dried his hands as he announced, "I am innocent of this man's blood. He is your responsibility!"

If the governor thought his drama would change the crowd's mind, he was wrong. They all answered, "Let his blood be on us and on our children!"

The shouting evolved into chants as before: "Take him away! Take him away! Crucify him! Crucify him!"

Pilate didn't even try to quiet them this time. He just shouted back, "Here is your king! Do you really want me to crucify your king?"

The priests up front were the only ones close enough to hear Pilate's question. They answered, "Caesar is our only king!"

Pilate decided to placate the crowd. He ordered soldiers to release Barabbas and have Jesus crucified.

The soldiers grabbed Jesus' arms and pulled him inside the praetorium, where the entire Roman guard had gathered. They were free to play with Jesus in a game they often enjoyed before executing a man. Today it was customized to Jesus' fame and claim. They replaced Herod's robe with a different purple robe, recrowned him with the thorns from earlier that morning, put a staff in his right hand, and knelt in front of him with mock fealty. "Hail, king of the Jews!" they laughed. One after another they took turns spitting on him and taking the staff out of his hand and using it to beat him over the head again and again.

The cross would be next.

CHAPTER NINETEEN

T he crucifixion outside Jerusalem at midday on Friday, April 6, AD 30, was routine as far as Roman crucifixions went. At least at the beginning.

After Pilate ordered Jesus' execution, the soldiers taunted him inside the praetorium and then put his own clothes back on him for the journey to Golgotha, a hill outside the north wall of Jerusalem. § At first Jesus was forced to carry

§ Golgotha was the name of the crucifixion site in Aramaic. The same place was called Calvary in Latin and means "Place of the Skull" in English.

his own cross, but he didn't make it very far. The beating had left him so wounded and weak that he stumbled under the weight and pain. Impatient with the slow progress and concerned that he might die before they could crucify him, or maybe worried about the large crowd that was joining the procession, the soldiers decided to put the cross on a passerby. Roman law allowed soldiers to conscript virtually anyone into their service if needed, so one of them drew his sword and pointed it at Simon of Cyrene. He was a Jewish pilgrim from North Africa who had come to Jerusalem for the Feast and may not have known who Jesus was or what was happening. Suddenly he was forced to carry a heavy cross in a Roman execution entourage.

The sight of any fellow human in such misery would pique the emotions of the most casual observer. Those who actually knew him experienced far stronger passions. Followers who loved and believed in this innocent man so brutally violated were mortified at the awful scene. When a few of Jesus' women disciples came as close as the soldiers would permit, Jesus turned and spoke to them. "Daughters

LEITH ANDERSON

§ To those in later generations and cultures, these sound like strange words from a tortured, dying man, but they must be understood in their context. Jesus was under enormous physical, spiritual, and emotional stress. He warned these women that others were facing horrors ahead—so severe that women will be happy they don't have children going through future cruelties; so severe that people will pray for mountains to crush them and put them out of their misery. Jesus foresaw what the Romans were going to do to everyone in Jerusalem; if they were capable of doing this to him they were capable of doing it to others.

of Jerusalem, don't cry for me; weep for yourselves and your children. There is a time coming when you will say, 'Better off are the barren women whose wombs were never pregnant and breasts that never nursed!' It will get so bad that people will pray for the mountain to fall on them and for the hills to bury them. If evil men will do what they are doing now, what's going to happen when things get worse?" §

The hill of crucifixion wasn't far. With Simon carrying the cross it didn't take long for the tragic parade to stop at Golgotha. Jesus wasn't the only one scheduled for crucifixion that day. Two criminals were also scheduled to die. All three were offered the standard mug of wine mixed with myrrh, which was supposed to dull the senses and take the edge off of the agony. Jesus declined the drink.

Jesus was first. The soldiers laid him on his back on the cross. § The nails were driven through his wrists and feet. The same procedure was done to the two criminals on either side of Jesus' center cross. They also screamed out in anguish and writhed with pain.

§ The Romans developed a standard protocol for crucifixion but may not have always followed the same routine, especially in Judea, which was out on the perimeter of the empire. The basics of crucifixion were awful even if the exact procedures sometimes varied.

CRUCIFIXION

Crucifixion was invented by the Persians some time in the sixth century BC. The Carthaginians borrowed it. The Romans perpetuated and perfected it as an extreme form of capital punishment and a deterrent to crime.

Cicero called it "the most cruel and horrifying death." Although the Romans crucified tens of thousands, they always held crucifixion in contempt. It was against the law to crucify a Roman citizen, and attempts were made to keep crucifixion out of Italy. It was for people in the provinces, for slaves, and for the worst of non-Roman criminals.

"*Ibis ad crucem!*" ("You will go to the cross!") were the sentencing words of a Roman judge at the end of a capital trial. The defendant was then turned over to a quaternion (four) of Roman soldiers, who first flogged him and then tied his arms to the cross for transportation to the crucifixion site. Often it wasn't the whole cross but just the horizontal beam that was later attached to a 9- to 12-foot-high vertical pole that was planted in the ground.

The soldiers prodded the man through the streets of his community to the place of crucifixion—two soldiers at his sides plus one in front and one behind. The front soldier typically carried a placard announcing the crime. This served two purposes: a warning to other would-be criminals and therefore a deterrent to crime, and a last opportunity for witnesses to step forward and give testimony in the condemned man's defense.

Upon arrival at the place of execution, the soldiers would tie or nail the victim to the cross. They held the body to the horizontal bar with one of them kneeling on an arm while another felt for the small soft spot at the base of the hand. Once the spot was found, a square spike was driven through without breaking bones or risking the body tearing free once it was upright. The opposite wrist was similarly nailed, making sure there was adequate bend in the elbow to allow for movement of the arms and body. Often a single spike was used to nail both feet to the vertical timber of the cross, again making sure that the knees were bent to allow for body movement and a slower death.

Sometimes days passed before the crucified person died. During those many hours, the victim suffered from exposure to sun and heat during daylight and cold during the night. Insects and birds were a constant source of irritation. Hunger and thirst compounded the ordeal. Blood loss that began with the flogging continued on the cross. However, few died from any of these aspects of the torture.

Death came from heart failure or, most commonly, from asphyxiation. The victim's arms knotted with pain and strain as his body hung from his hands, and the pectoral muscles of the chest were virtually paralyzed. He could inhale but not exhale. In a desperate attempt to breathe, he would instinctively and violently heave his body upward, pressing all his weight against the nails in his feet. When the pain from so much body weight on his feet became too unbearable, he would fall down again. The repeated thrusting up and down to breathe lasted throughout the crucifixion until he was too weak for another attempt, and then he died from lack of breath. When soldiers wanted to hasten a death, they swung a large board hard against the victim's legs; broken legs made it impossible to straighten up, and the victim quickly suffocated.

The gratuity received by the executioners was the clothing of the condemned. In Jewish culture that usually included shoes, turban, girdle (underwear), and a tunic (outerwear). Many were crucified naked, adding to the humiliation.

With most of the physical work done, the soldiers settled down for the long vigil. Waiting for the end of their duty when the three men were dead, they decided to divide up each of the victim's belongings sooner rather than later. That way they wouldn't need to share with the next shift of guards. When it came to the pile of Jesus' clothes, they rolled their dice to determine who got what. The only piece of much value was Jesus' tunic. It was seamless, woven in one piece from top to bottom, so they didn't want to tear it. They chose a winner-takes-all gamble. What for them was a spur-of-the-moment monetary choice actually fulfilled an Old Testament Scripture written by King David: "They divided my garments among them and cast lots for my clothing."

While their dice were clinking, Jesus spoke for the first time from the cross. It was a prayer to God overheard by at least some of the soldiers. The words must have been incredibly unusual and unsettling, unlike what executioners usually heard. Jesus prayed, "Father, forgive them, for they do not know what they are doing." The dice stopped while the winners took the clothes they wanted.

One remaining chore was the posting of the charge against Jesus. It wasn't ready when they left the praetorium because Jesus was a last-minute addition to the crucifixion list for that day. §

Usually these signs listed murder, robbery, or insurrection. Jesus' sign simply stated:

§ The other two would have had their charges written out the night before to be carried ahead of them in the processional to Golgotha.

This is Jesus of Nazareth
The King of the Jews. §

§ The sign on the cross was written in Aramaic, Latin, and Greek. Passersby literate in any of the major languages could easily read who was being crucified. It was particularly appropriate that these languages be used for Jesus, who was dying as the Savior of the whole world.

The sign displeased the religious leaders, who quickly appealed to Pilate. "Don't write 'The King of the Jews,' but that he *claimed* to be king of the Jews." Pilate rejected their appeal. "I wrote what I wrote," he told them.

Golgotha was along a busy road, and this was a busy time of year, so there were many spectators who passed by. It was customary for some to stop and check out the situation. Since it was a common assumption that anyone who was crucified either deserved this fate or had been cursed by God, many passersby yelled insults at those on the crosses.

They stood watching while Jesus heaved up and down to breathe. Some who had heard Jesus teach or learned about his teachings second hand were cruel in their mockery. At one point Jesus was so exhausted that he fell back down before he could raise himself high enough to exhale. His body shook as he fought to pull himself back up. At this painful and tender moment, they melodramatically shook their heads and called to him, "So! You who are going to destroy the temple and build it back up in three days, get off that cross and save yourself! Come on, you can do it—you're the Son of God, aren't you?"

The proud religious leaders of Israel—chief priests and teachers and elders—were so engrossed in what was happening to Jesus that they came out to Golgotha. They joined in the mockery, only with added theological twists. "He says he saved others," they said, "but he isn't very good at saving himself! Hey, King of Israel! Come on down and then we'll believe in you." They taunted Jesus and played the crowd. "He trusts in God. Why doesn't God come and rescue him if he's so special to God? If he's really God's Son, why isn't God helping him out?"

The cruel mockery was contagious. The soldiers joined in the taunts. When making a routine round, offering wine vinegar to those being crucified, a soldier said to Jesus, "If you are really the king of the Jews, use your power to save your own life!"

Even the criminal on the side cross started making fun of Jesus. He heard what the soldier said and mimicked, "Aren't you the Messiah? Save yourself, and while you're at it, save the two of us as well!"

But the other criminal rebuked his death mate saying, "Aren't you afraid of God? You're being crucified yourself, you know! You and I deserve this, but he's an innocent man!" Then he looked toward Jesus and said, "Jesus, please remember me when you enter your kingdom." It was a short and simple plea from a man gasping for breath.

Jesus saw his faith and answered him, "Good news: today you'll be with me in paradise!" §

§ Here was an interesting choice of words. Paradise was a Persian term referring to a walled garden belonging to a king. Emperors would specially honor individuals by allowing them to walk in paradise with them. It became a synonym for the best and safest of places. It became a synonym for heaven.

None of Jesus' team of male disciples showed up at Golgotha except John. He stood as close to the cross as the soldiers would permit. Next to him were some of Jesus' female disciples.

Mary the mother of Jesus had come to see her son die. She who had given birth, nursed, nurtured, and loved him all his life was now experiencing an enormous suffering of her own. She no doubt remembered that the day had been anticipated more than three decades earlier when Jesus was a baby. Mary and Joseph had taken him to the temple in Jerusalem for consecration. A godly old man named Simeon had taken Mary's baby in his arms and spoken a strange prophecy directly to her: "This child's destiny is to bring failure and success to many people in Israel. Many will criticize him, and the inner thoughts of many people will be revealed by him. And someday he will pierce your own soul too." This Friday was the day for the piercing of her soul.

The other women included Salome, Mary's sister; Mary, the wife of Clopas and mother of James and Joses; Mary Magdalene, from whom Jesus had expelled seven demons; and Mrs. Zebedee, the mother of James and John. In addition there were many other women watching and weeping from a distance who had followed Jesus all the way down from Galilee to care and provide for him.

Jesus wasn't going to be able to fulfill the responsibility of an eldest Jewish son in caring for his widowed mother. He didn't have long to make arrangements for her. When he saw his mother standing near along with his best friend, John, Jesus told his mother, "Mother, this is your son," as he nodded toward John. He told John, "This is your mother," and signaled toward Mary with his eyes. They both knew what he meant and what he wanted—for John to provide for his mother. Later that day, John took Mary back to his home in Jerusalem and cared for her and protected her for the rest of her life.

During Jesus' crucifixion, starting around noon and lasting until about three o'clock, the sky turned so dark that the sun stopped shining. § It seemed like midnight when it was only early afternoon.

§ This midday darkness is reported but not explained by those who were there. Perhaps it was a combination of dense storm clouds and blowing sand.

Around three o'clock Jesus spoke again for the first time in a long time. In a loud, emotional cry, he shouted in his native Aramaic, "*Eli, Eli, lama sabachthani?*" which means, "My God, my God, why have you forsaken me?"

Jesus had said that he had come to bear the sins of the world, like a temple sacrifice. John the Baptizer said that Jesus was "the Lamb of God who takes away the sin of the world." One of the supernatural consequences of Jesus assuming human sin and becoming a sacrifice was that God the Father in some way turned his back on his Son. This was the fulfillment of Jesus' life purpose: to save humanity from sin.

But witnesses nearby hearing Jesus' awful cry missed the super-natural, eternal significance and thought maybe he was delusional and

§ "Eli, Eli" sounded like "Eli-yah, Eli-yah." | calling for the ancient prophet to come and rescue him. §

"Listen, he's calling for Elijah," some said. One of the soldiers got a sponge and filled it with the cheap drink issued to Roman soldiers as part of their rations—a mixture of wine vinegar, egg, and water. He put the dripping sponge on a stick and held it up to Jesus' mouth. Some of the bystanders told him to hold off. "Leave him alone. Let's see if Elijah comes to take him down!" It was probably sarcasm, although there may have been a hint of hope that a last-minute mir-acle would rescue him before he died.

Most victims of crucifixion grew weaker and weaker until they slipped into unconsciousness. Although he had been on the cross only a few hours, Jesus remained awake and alert with full awareness of the physical torment as well as the spiritual agony of God laying all of human sin on him. He knew that the last of the ancient prophe-cies were being fulfilled. His mouth and throat were so parched and swollen that he could hardly swallow or talk. He gasped out, "I'm thirsty!" and the soldier tried again to help Jesus by filling the same sponge and lifting it up to his mouth. This time Jesus sucked in the liquid. He was ready to die and needed strength for his last words.

With a loud voice he prayed, "Father, into your hands I commit my spirit," and then he took a breath and shouted in a strong, pierc-ing voice, "It is finished!" That was his last breath. Jesus had died.

In an apostolic letter to Hebrew Christians later in the century, the death of Jesus was simply and powerfully explained like this: "Jesus Christ was sacrificed once to take away the sins of many people."

When he died, an earthquake rumbled the area, rocks split apart, tombs were torn open. Later, the bodies of holy people who had recently died came back to life and appeared to people in Jerusalem. At the moment Jesus died outside the city, the curtain shielding the holy place in the temple ripped open from top to bottom. Its purpose had been to close off the room entered only once each year by the high priest on Yom Kippur, the Day of Atonement. What was startling and frightening to the ordinary priests on duty that afternoon became an exhilarating symbol to Jesus' followers since then, who believe that his death grants them direct access to God without the intervention of a high priest or animal sacrifice.

When Jesus shouted "It is finished!" and died, the centurion in charge of Golgotha was standing right in front of him. He exclaimed, "This was an innocent, righteous man! Surely he was the Son of God." He and the other soldiers were terrified by the earthquake and everything else that was happening. They echoed the sentiments of the centurion, "Surely he was the Son of God!"

The crowd surrounding the crosses was united in their experience of Jesus' death. Enemies and friends, skeptics and believers, doubters and disciples all beat their chests—a cultural expression of mourning.

"Break their legs and get this over with!" the delegation from the temple encouraged Pilate. The main concern was getting those bodies off the crosses and buried before sunset, which marked the beginning of the Sabbath. And this Sabbath fell during the Feast days, making it extra special and holy. The crucified men would die much more quickly if their legs were broken.

When the soldiers were given the order they swung the boards and heard the shinbones of the criminals on the outer crosses snap with a loud crack, followed by anguished screams from the victims. But when they brought the board to smash Jesus' legs, he was dead already. John stood close enough to witness the scene, and it reminded him of a line from a psalm, "Not one of his bones will be broken." John the Baptizer had called Jesus "the Lamb of God to take away the sin of the world," and the Passover lamb could not have broken bones. Instead of breaking Jesus' legs, one of the soldiers took the sharp point of his spear and pushed it up under his ribs and to his heart. The thrust produced no sign of life or response. A gush of blood and water came out when the spear was pulled back. As the soldier watched for any movement, John recalled the line from Zechariah that says, "They will look on the one they have pierced."

An eyewitness to Jesus' death was a prominent man named Joseph from the Judean town of Arimathea. He was a good and righteous Jew who was waiting for the kingdom of God, and he had become a secret disciple of Jesus. Leaving Golgotha, Joseph walked back into the city and over to the praetorium, where he asked to speak to Pilate. It would take a prominent member of the Sanhedrin to dare request an audience with the governor on short notice. He asked Pilate to grant him custody of Jesus' body so he could bury it.

Pilate was taken by surprise. He had not been informed that Jesus was dead and was amazed that he had died so quickly. To verify the information, Pilate summoned the centurion in command and asked him. Once confirmed, Pilate gave permission for Joseph to take Jesus' body.

Hurrying back to Golgotha to meet the sunset deadline for burial, he was joined by Nicodemus, the man who once met with Jesus secretly at night. Both men were Pharisees and members of the Sanhedrin who did not consent to the council's decisions or actions condemning Jesus to death. To the contrary, both men were seekers after the kingdom of God who increasingly believed in Jesus and became secret disciples. When they met up near Golgotha, Nicodemus and his servants were carrying about seventy-five pounds of embalming materials, a valuable mixture of myrrh and aloes. Joseph had purchased a bolt of clean linen cloth. They didn't have time to properly wash the body as the women usually did before a burial, but they at least wanted to wrap him up as best they could. With the help of the soldiers, they lowered the cross, pulled out the nails, and took possession of his body. Joseph and Nicodemus carried the body while servants carried the embalming mixture and bolt of cloth. Golgotha was right next to a garden that had a cavelike tomb belonging to Joseph that had never been used.

They laid out his body and began to wrap it like a mummy, rolling the embalming mixture into the folds of the cloth. It wasn't ideal, but it was the best they could do with the sun setting behind them. A few minutes before the sun fell below the horizon, they laid Jesus' body on a shelf in the sepulcher and left. The door to seal the tomb was already in place—a heavy rock had been rolled into a groove and then blocked in place. They pulled out the blocks and let the rock neatly roll down the short incline to close off the grave.

Mary Magdalene and Mary the mother of Joses, Clopas's wife, observed all of this from a short distance. They had seen Jesus die on the cross and had followed these two men, strangers to them, to see what they were going to do with Jesus' body. They had followed Jesus all the way from Galilee and were not going to abandon him now. Once they were convinced that the two men were not Jesus' enemies and did not intend to desecrate his body, they went home and prepared more burial spices and perfumes. While they didn't know how they would get permission, they hoped to provide a proper washing, wrapping, and reburial before his body began to decay. Since that was forbidden during the next twenty-four hours of Sabbath, they knew they would have to wait until Sunday morning.

As a precaution and for final closure of the Jesus episode, the chief priests and Pharisees sought another emergency meeting with Pilate the next day. "Sir," they said, "we remembered something you need to know. Before he died, that deceptive Jesus said that he would rise from the dead in three days. We request that you order extra guards and put your seal on the tomb. If you don't do this, some of his disciples might steal his body and say he came back to life. Then we'll have a bigger problem than we had before."

Pilate consented. "Take a guard," he answered. "Go, secure and seal the tomb." They were overly cautious, securing the tomb's stone door with Pilate's Roman seal and posting soldiers to guard the tomb around the clock.

They thought they had won. Jesus of Nazareth was dead and buried, and no one would ever see him again.

CHAPTER TWENTY

A fter days and nights of grief, the women awakened before dawn on Sunday with plans to go back to Jesus' grave. Hearts breaking with sorrow and minds full of questions, Salome and the two women named Mary bought burial spices and went to say their final good-byes.

"Who can we get to roll back that stone and let us into the tomb?" they asked one another as they walked. They were already anxious about moving the stone door, getting past the guards, and dealing with a body that had been dead for three days, but they never antici-pated another earthquake. The ground shook like a stormy sea.

What the women hadn't seen was the angel that came to Jesus' tomb during the earthquake. So brilliantly bright, he looked like a sustained flash of lightning; his clothes were as white as snow. The guards nearly died from fright—shaking at first and then so paralyzed by fear they looked like stone statues. They watched in terrified awe as the angel easily rolled the stone back up its groove and stuck it back where it was positioned before Friday afternoon.

Soon after the earthquake settled, the women arrived at the tomb. Mary Magdalene arrived first. She paused in amazement when she saw that the guards had fled and the tomb was wide open. As soon as the other two women caught up, they all walked past the large stone and into the tomb entrance. They expected to see Jesus' body, but it wasn't there! Instead, the angel was to their right, sitting on the shelf where the body had been. They didn't realize at first that he was an angel. They thought he was just a young man dressed in a white robe.

He stood up, and when he did they saw another man—actually a second angel. They seemed to glow brighter and brighter, like white lightning. The women had already had enough to be startled about that day, but the presence of these celestial beings surely was the most frightening so far. They couldn't look at the brightness of the angels. They bent over and looked down at the ground, shielding their faces.

The first angel said, "Don't be afraid! You are looking for the body of Jesus of Nazareth. Why would you look for the living in a tomb? He has risen! He is not here. Look for yourselves at the shelf where they laid his body. After you've taken a good look, run and tell his disciples and Peter, 'Jesus has risen from the dead and is going to meet you in Galilee. You'll see him there, just as he told you.' "

The women were speechless and trembling with fear and wonder. They turned and ran from the tomb, headed straight to Peter and the other ten disciples. Mary Magdalene told the men, "They have taken the Lord out of the tomb, and we don't know where they have put his body!" As Joanna, the other Mary, and the rest of the women arrived, they all gave the same report. All eleven men listened as they heard news about an earthquake, missing guards, brightly lighted men, an open tomb, and the missing body. The women were excited and searching for words to report these amazing events. None of the men believed much of what they were saying because it sounded like nonsense to them.

Peter eventually determined it was obvious that something amazing had happened, and he wanted to see for himself. "Come on, let's go to Golgotha and see what is going on," Peter told the ten men.

Peter got a head start, but John outran him and arrived first. John stopped at the tomb entrance and looked inside. He saw that the linen burial strips that had been wrapped around Jesus' body on Friday just before sunset were now lying flat on the shelf without being unwound. When Peter arrived, he went past John and walked straight in. Peter examined the linen strips that John had seen from a distance. Then John came inside and suddenly remembered all Jesus' predictions about coming back from the dead. John saw, remembered, and believed. He didn't fully understand all that the Scriptures had said about Jesus' resurrection or how this had happened, but he believed.

They left to report back to the other nine men and somehow missed Mary Magdalene, who was walking back to the tomb while they were leaving. When she arrived, she stood there and started to cry. She couldn't explain her tears or even what she was thinking—it was wonderful and awful and joyful and frightening all at once. After a while, between her sobs, she stepped closer to look into the tomb. The two angels in white were there again. One of them asked, "Why are you crying?"

The last time she had been too scared to speak, but this time she answered, "They took away my Lord, and I don't know where they have put him." And then Jesus himself appeared next to Mary outside the tomb entrance. She turned and saw him but didn't recognize who he was.

"Woman, why are you crying?" Jesus asked the same question that the angel had asked but added another: "Who is it you are looking for?"

He didn't look like the angels inside, so she guessed he must be the gardener. She stopped her weeping and told him, "Sir, if you've moved him somewhere, please tell me where he is. I want to get his body."

Then in a voice she could not mistake and with a smile she had studied a thousand times in the past, Jesus simply said, "Mary!"

She quickly turned and cried out, "Rabboni!" (Aramaic for "Teacher!") Then, throwing decorum to the wind, she reached out to hug him.

Again Jesus smiled and told her not to hold on too long or too tight. "You're going to have to let go of me so I can return to my Father. Here's what I want you to do: Go to my brothers and tell them I am returning to my Father and your Father, to my God and your God."

It's doubtful she had any idea what he meant about returning to the Father, and she certainly didn't want to let go of him easily or quickly. When she finally loosed her embrace, she took off running back to the safe house where she had left the others. Bursting with her incredible news, she went back to those who were still mourning and weeping and told them, "I have seen the Lord! He's alive. I saw him and heard him and touched him! Jesus is alive!" None of them believed her.

When the other women also returned to the Golgotha garden, they suddenly met Jesus just as Mary had. He simply greeted them, and they fell down to the ground, grabbed his feet, and worshipped him. The same array of emotions that Mary had felt only minutes earlier—fear, confusion, and joy all at once—now filled these women's faces. Jesus told them, "Don't be afraid. Go and tell my brothers to meet me in Galilee."

Many events were happening simultaneously. The guards went into the city to report to the chief priests what they had experienced: "We were on guard at the Golgotha garden tomb where Jesus of Nazareth was buried, and there was an earthquake! An angel rolled the stone from the tomb. We were terrified, but we didn't abandon our posts. We looked inside the tomb and it was empty. No one else came. We don't know how he got away, but we know that his body wasn't stolen. It must be true what he said about coming back to life again."

The chief priests and elders quickly convened a private meeting of all who were available. Facing growing evidence that Jesus was alive and the fact that they themselves had actually conspired against and arranged the death of God's Messiah, they now were frantically plotting to conceal the truth. They agreed to pay a large bribe to the guards and told them, "You all need to report the same story. Tell people that his disciples showed up in the middle of the night and stole his body while you were asleep. If the governor hears and wants to bring charges against you for sleeping on guard duty, we'll deal with him and keep you out of trouble."

The guards faced a difficult choice. Falling asleep on duty was a military crime that could have them executed. No amount of hush money was worth dying for. Yet they could be wealthy for life if charges weren't pressed. Maybe Pilate would never find out. Maybe these Jewish leaders could protect them. Maybe it would work. Knowing they were denying a supernatural act, they took the money and hoped to never again be asked about what had happened.

When stories of Jesus' resurrection began spreading through Jerusalem, the religious leaders insisted that his disciples had stolen his body. This explanation satisfied some, but others quickly poked holes in the explanation. "How did the disciples move a rock that weighed more than a ton without awakening the guards? Were they all such sound sleepers? And if the guards were deep in sleep, how do they know who stole the body?" Besides, the number of witnesses who personally had seen Jesus since his crucifixion was rapidly growing.

Two travelers from the village of Emmaus had spent the Sabbath in the overcrowded city of Jerusalem and were headed home, a westward journey of seven miles. The long walk was going quickly as they talked about all the news in Jerusalem. They barely heard the footsteps behind them over their own voices, but when they did, they invited the fellow traveler to walk along with them.

They didn't recognize this person, although they had seen and heard Jesus before. In their minds, Jesus was dead and the possibility of the man on the road being Jesus of Nazareth was beyond their thinking.

The man asked them what they were talking about. The two stopped, surprised that he didn't seem to know. They felt fresh sorrow as they began retelling all the recent events. One of them, a man named Cleopas, said, "You must be the only visitor to Jerusalem who hasn't yet heard the news!" §

§ Only one of the two travelers' names was recorded by historians. It could well be that the other was his wife or perhaps a friend.

"News about what?"

"About Jesus of Nazareth," they answered. "He was a prophet—

not only a great preacher but a miracle worker before God and crowds of people. The chief priests and other leaders had him sentenced to death and crucified. We were grief stricken because we had hoped he was going to save the nation of Israel. This was three days ago, and now some women we know are telling this amazing story. They went to Jesus' tomb early today and couldn't find his body. When they reported to us, they said they saw angels who claimed Jesus is alive again. When some men went to check out their story, they verified what the women said. His body was gone, but they never actually saw him alive."

They still didn't recognize Jesus when he started to give his analysis of the news. "You two are so foolish and your hearts are so slow to believe. Don't you know what the prophets predicted? Didn't you know that the Messiah had to suffer all these atrocities and then enter his glory?" As they walked the rest of the way to Emmaus, he gave them a lesson in Old Testament quotations and stories, beginning with Moses and ending with the latest prophets—all about the Messiah.

Reaching the village that was their destination, the two started into town, and Jesus kept on as if he were going all the way to Joppa. They had been mesmerized by his teaching and wanted to hear more, so they invited him to stay in Emmaus—not the usual courtesy invitation of hospitality but an impassioned plea to join them for dinner and spend the night. "Please stay at our home. It's almost dark," they urged. So Jesus went home with them to Emmaus.

When they washed and settled down for dinner, Jesus conducted himself like he was the host rather than the guest. He took the bread, broke it in pieces for everyone at the meal, and spoke a prayer of thanksgiving. When they heard him pray, they took another look and suddenly recognized that their guest was Jesus. He was indeed alive again! When he finally left and they discussed what had happened along the road, they asked each other, "Wasn't that amazing? The way he opened the Scriptures to us was wonderful. Our hearts nearly exploded with joy."

The more they talked, the more they wanted to tell Jesus' friends that they had been with Jesus and that he was fully alive—talking and walking and eating. They especially wished to tell Jesus' eleven disciples, but it was after dark and they faced a seven-mile walk back to Jerusalem.

The couple from Emmaus agreed that this couldn't wait until morning. They put their sandals back on and returned to Jerusalem in search of the eleven disciples. And they probably weren't all that easy to find. When the two finally found the right house, the eleven were all together. The pair from Emmaus thought they were going to have this wonderful news to report, but when they entered the house they were told, "It's true! The Lord has risen! Peter saw him!" All were trying to be the first to tell their own experiences. When the Emmaus pair got their turn, they gave a detailed account—from the teaching on the road to dinner and their recognition and realization that they were with Jesus.

Secondhand stories now were replaced with a firsthand encounter of their own for eight of the eleven who had not personally seen Jesus alive yet. While they were talking with the Emmaus couple, Jesus suddenly appeared to them in the house, even though the doors had been locked to protect them from the religious authorities. He warmly greeted them as he had so many times in the past: "Peace be with you!"

Even though they had been talking about Jesus being alive, they were still startled and anxious, as if they were seeing a ghost.

"What's your difficulty? Why do you still have doubts? Check out my hands and feet. It's me, all right! Look, touch, whatever it takes. I have skin and bones, and you know that ghosts don't have skin and bones."

He put out his hands, turning them back and forth for them to see. He lifted up his right foot and then his left for them to look at. Then he parted his tunic and exposed the scar on his abdomen. They watched with amazed incredulity. It was obviously Jesus, and they were over the top with joy, but it was still hard to believe.

Jesus offered one more piece of evidence that he truly was alive with a real body. He asked, "Do you have anything here to eat? I'm hungry!" They had already finished dinner, but they handed him some leftover broiled fish that he took in his hand and ate while they talked and laughed together.

It was a joyous reunion. Almost like the old days. Jesus told them, "Peace be with you! Just as the Father sent me, now I'm sending you." He exhaled a long steady breath that settled over them, and then he said, "Receive the Holy Spirit. If you forgive sins, they are forgiven; if you do not forgive them, they are not forgiven."

Jesus said good-night and left them alone to talk over their encounter with the resurrected Messiah. Not much later Thomas the Twin returned to the house. When he rejoined his friends, they said, "You're not going to believe what happened while you were out." They were right. Even though they said, "We've seen the Lord!" and gave detailed reports, Thomas didn't believe them. Not that he was calling them liars, but he told them, "I'm just not going to believe he's really alive until I can see his nail scars and feel his abdomen scar for myself."

For the next seven days, everyone in the circle of about 120 disciples was ecstatic over Jesus' resurrection. Except Thomas. They tried to convince him, but he couldn't get past his inner doubts.

The next Sunday, one week after that first wonderful Easter, they were all locked in their safe house. This time Thomas was with them. Jesus entered the house without opening the doors and stood among them just as he had a week earlier. Again he said, "Peace be with you!" and smiled. Then he turned to Thomas as if he had come just to see him. "Thomas, give me your finger. Examine the nail scars for yourself. Give me your hand. Feel my side. It's time for you to quit doubting and start believing!"

Thomas became an instant open-mouthed believer. He said to Jesus, "My Lord and my God!"

"You believe because you've seen me," Jesus said. "Blessed are those who haven't seen me and believe anyway." Jesus wasn't going to give a private showing to every doubter in first-century Jerusalem or in future generations. This was a special appearance to help Thomas get past his doubts. He would help others with different evidence.

———— ❄ ————

For more than three years, John had witnessed a lot of miracles by Jesus, but this resurrection topped them all. When John wrote an early biography of Jesus toward the end of the first century, he had to decide which miracles to include and which ones to omit. He read other biographies of Jesus and decided to focus on miracles not already published. But he could not leave out the resurrection, even though other biographers had documented it well. He made his selection in order to help people like Thomas who might have doubts. In John's own words, "Jesus did many more miracles witnessed by his disciples that I've not included in this book. I've recorded these so that you may believe that Jesus is the Christ, the Son of God, and that because of your belief you will have eternal life in his name."

Over the next month Jesus appeared to many people in many places. The first appearance outside of Judea was by Galilee Lake. Jesus had told them to meet him up north; besides, it was safer there away from the angry and bewildered religious leaders. The disciples were probably ready to go back home for a while. Seven of them were on the shore—Peter, Thomas, Nathanael, James, John, and two others. "I'm going out to fish," Peter told them. They all decided to go along and ended up staying on the boat all night—without catching one fish.

As they came near shore early the next morning, they saw a man standing on one of the rocks but couldn't see him well enough to recognize him. The man called out to them, "Friends, haven't you caught any fish?" As usual, his voice carried farther on the water than it would have on land. "No fish!" they responded.

"Throw your net on the right side of the boat and you'll find some," he called out to the fishermen. It seemed unlikely, but why not? While they were casting their net off the right side of the boat, John, Jesus' best friend, recognized who was standing on the shore and exclaimed, "It is the Lord!"

When Peter heard that it was Jesus, he grabbed his clothes, quickly wrapped them around him, and jumped overboard. They were only about a hundred yards out, so it wasn't very far or very deep. While Peter made his way to shore, the others realized the net was full of fish. They hauled in the fish and navigated the rest of the way to beach their boat. Everyone jumped out, leaving the fish wiggling in the net that had been pulled into the boat.

Jesus was waiting for them. He already had a fire burning and told them, "Bring some of those fish over to the fire." Peter climbed into the boat and grabbed the end of the net, yanking the net and fish out of the boat and onto the beach. They were businessmen with deeply entrenched habits, so they counted how many fish they had caught. There were so many fish it was cause for laughter and back-slapping congratulations. The grand total set a record. They had just caught 153 fish in a single haul without tearing the net.

Jesus interrupted the inventory with an invitation. "Come and have breakfast!"

Other times they had asked Jesus who he was even after they knew it was Jesus, just to make sure. They had now seen him enough times that they dared not ask one more time. They knew that he was Jesus. They were sure he was their Lord.

That breakfast was his third appearance to them since he rose from the dead. It was a different kind of joyful reunion—both special and common at the same time. Jesus had brought bread for break-fast that he broke and gave to them as he served the cooked fish.

The conversation after breakfast took an interesting turn, address-ing a touchy topic; nothing had been said about Peter's multiple denials of Jesus that night before the crucifixion. Peter hoped for for-giveness and resolution, but there hadn't been a good time to ask.

Jesus said, "Simon son of John, do you truly love me more than these?"

"Yes, Lord," Peter answered, "you know that I love you."

Jesus said, "Feed my lambs."

Again Jesus asked, "Simon son of John, do you truly love me?"

"Yes, Lord, you know that I love you."

Jesus said, "Take care of my sheep."

Remembering how many times he had denied Jesus, it pained Peter when Jesus asked him a third time, "Do you love me?" He said, "Lord, you know everything, so you must know that I love you."

Jesus said, "Feed my sheep. The truth is, Peter, when you were young you dressed yourself and went wherever you pleased; but when you are old you will be forced to stretch out your hands and be dressed by someone else and led where you really don't want to go." Jesus was predicting that Peter was going to die as a martyr to glorify God. Then Jesus said to him, "Follow me!"

Not quite knowing what to say next, Peter pointed to John and asked, "Lord, what about him?"

"If I want John to live until I come back, that's up to me," Jesus said. "It's not your concern. You just follow me!" These words from Jesus about John later produced a rumor among Christians that John would never die. It is true that he outlived all the others before he died a death from natural causes, but John's death wasn't Jesus' point. It was just an illustration to teach Peter that John's time of death wasn't his concern, only God's.

Jesus' appearances over that month after Easter were varied in time and place. The next time after the lakeshore was on a mountain in Galilee district, where Jesus asked them to meet him. This meeting had a different kind of feel to it. No meal. No verbal banter. No laughter. They remembered that time when his glory was exposed to three of them on a similar mountain, and at this meeting they worshipped him in awe. For devout Jews to worship a man meant that they considered the man to be God himself. They had come to this conviction.

Years later when John wrote his biography of Jesus, he began by explaining that Jesus was more than human. He was divine. Before the beginning of time, before the universe was created, Jesus lived and was God. Then he was not yet human; he was only God. Although called the Son of God, he was all that God is—good, great, powerful, knowledgeable, and wise—he was the light. As God, he was the creator of everything in the universe, including earth and humanity.

When he was supernaturally conceived in Mary, there was an unprecedented joining together of deity and humanity. The eternal Son of God became human. He made his home on earth and gave the rest of humanity the opportunity to experience the presence, grace, and truth of God face to face.

In John's opening lines, he wrote that the eternal Son of God "became flesh and made his dwelling among us. We have seen his glory, and it is the glory of the One and Only Son of God who came from God in heaven to us on earth. He is full of grace. He is full of truth. When he came to earth people didn't recognize him for who he was, even though he created the world and humankind. People refused to welcome him. But some did, and when they received him and believed on his name, he gave them the privilege to become eternal children of God."

True, there were still some wonderments and doubts among them with the worship of Jesus on the mountain that day in Galilee, but the longer they knew him, the more they worshipped him as someone far beyond an ordinary friend and teacher. He was their Messiah, Savior, and God.

———— ❋ ————

Jesus had brought them up that mountain to commission them as his ambassadors. He wanted them to tell others about him and persuade them to believe and trust in him. He told the eleven disciples what he wanted them and others after them to do. "I have sovereign authority over heaven and earth. Therefore, I commission you to go and make disciples for me out of people from every nation in the world. Baptize them in the name of the Father and of the Son and of the Holy Spirit. Teach them to obey everything I have commanded you. I promise that I will always be with you—right up to the end of time."

After that commissioning, they increasingly called each other *apostles*, which means "sent ones," since Jesus had sent them to tell the world about him. Others picked up on this and started referring to the apostle Peter, the apostle John, and the apostle James. In one of Jesus' last teaching times with these apostles, he reminded them, "This is what I was talking about back when we were together: Every prediction about me must come true, whether written in the Law of Moses, the Prophets, or the Psalms."

Jesus wanted their teaching to connect everything in the Hebrew Scriptures to him and his coming to bring salvation to humanity. He quoted Old Testament teachings and told them, "This is what was predicted: The Messiah will suffer, die, and rise from the dead on the third day. Repentance and forgiveness of sin will be preached in his name to every nation, starting in Jerusalem. You are witnesses of everything God has done. Now I'm going to send to you the fulfillment of my Father's great promise to you. Just stay put and wait in Jerusalem until you are covered with the power of God from heaven and receive my Father's promised gift to you. You remember the way John baptized with water? In a few days you will be baptized with the Holy Spirit."

During the forty days after Easter he showed himself to more than five hundred different people from Jerusalem to Galilee and from Emmaus to the Mount of Olives. His final appearance was with the eleven disciples at their familiar meeting place on the Mount of Olives between Bethany and Jerusalem. As so often before, his apostles wanted a time line for fulfillment of Jesus' remaining predictions: "Lord, will you restore the kingdom to Israel today?"

Once again Jesus explained, "You're just not going to find out the time or date the Father has set. He has the authority, and he is the only one who knows when. But I can tell you this: You will receive supernatural power when the Holy Spirit comes on you, and then you will be my witnesses in Jerusalem, in all Judea and Samaria and the rest of the world."

With his hands raised up in blessing over them, he rose up in front of their eyes until he was out of their sight in a cloud. As they looked skyward in new astonishment, two men dressed in white appeared next to them—angels. "You men from Galilee," they addressed the group, "why do you keep looking up into the sky? This exact same Jesus will come back down to earth the same way you've seen him go up to heaven."

So much more could be said about Jesus of Nazareth. The apostle John ended his first-century biography of Jesus explaining, "Jesus did many other things as well. If every one of them was written down, I suppose that the whole world would not be big enough to hold all the books that would be written."

Jesus' biography ends like that of no one else who has ever lived. He was dead and became alive. He is gone but promises to return. The best is yet to be.

Resources on the Life and Times of Jesus

Aland, Kurt, ed. 1985. *Synopsis of the Four Gospels*. New York: United Bible Societies.

Barclay, William. 1975. *The Gospel of John*. The Daily Study Bible Series. Louisville, KY: Westminster Press.

————. 1975. *The Gospel of Luke*. The Daily Study Bible Series. Louisville, KY: Westminster Press.

————. 1975. *The Gospel of Mark*. The Daily Study Bible Series. Louisville, KY: Westminster Press.

————. 1975. *The Gospel of Matthew*. The Daily Study Bible Series. Louisville, KY: Westminster Press.

Carson, D.A., R.T. France, J.A. Motyer, and G.J. Wenham, eds. 1994. *New Bible Commentary 21st Century Edition*. Downers Grove, IL: InterVarsity Press.

Evans, Craig A., and Stanley E. Porter, eds. 2000. *Dictionary of New Testament Background*. Downers Grove, IL: InterVarsity Press.

Green, Joel B., and Scot McKnight, eds. 1992. *Dictionary of Jesus and the Gospels*. Downers Grove, IL.: InterVarsity Press.

The Holy Bible: New International Version. 1984. Colorado Springs: International Bible Society.

Peterson, Eugene H. 1993. *The Message: New Testament*. Colorado Springs: Navpress.

Thomas, Robert L. 2000. *Charts of the Gospels and the Life of Christ*. Grand Rapids, MI: Zondervan Publishing House.

Thomas, Robert L., and Stanley N. Gundry, eds. 1988. *The NIV Harmony of the Gospels*. San Francisco: Harper & Row. One of the most influential harmonies grew out of the seminary classes of John A. Broadus from 1859 to 1893. His research and teaching led to a published revision of Broadus' scholarship by renowned New Testament scholar A. T. Robertson in 1922. This modern updating of the scholarship of Broadus and Robertson uses the *New International Version* of the Bible. The overall chronology developed by Broadus, Robertson, Thomas, and Gundry has been followed in *Jesus* with some modifications and reordering.

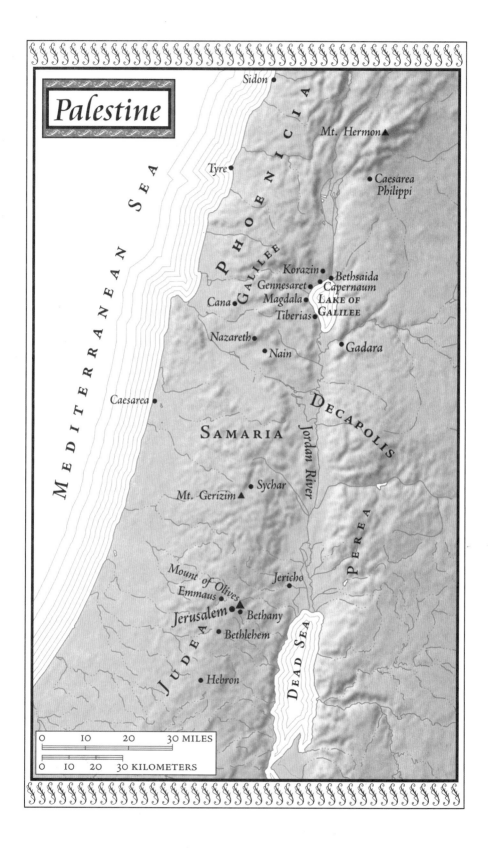

Palestine

Sidon

Mt. Hermon ▲

PHOENICIA

Tyre

• Caesarea
Philippi

MEDITERRANEAN SEA

GALILEE

Korazin • • Bethsaida
Gennesaret • • Capernaum
Cana • Magdala • LAKE OF
• Tiberias GALILEE

Nazareth •
• Nain

• Gadara

DECAPOLIS

Caesarea •

SAMARIA

Jordan River

• Sychar
Mt. Gerizim ▲

PEREA

Mount of Olives
Emmaus • • Jericho
Jerusalem ▲ • Bethany
JUDEA • Bethlehem

DEAD SEA

• Hebron

| 0 | 10 | 20 | 30 MILES |
| 0 | 10 | 20 | 30 KILOMETERS |